Generative AI for Beginners

A Comprehensive Guide to Innovative AI Models, Including LLMs and ChatGPT, To Empower Your AI Journey and Boost Your Professional Growth

Jonathan M. Sterling

Graphic content:
All images in the book are designed by **FREEPIK - www.freepik.com**

INTRODUCTION

Generative AI: Revolutionizing Creativity and Innovation

Generative AI is one of the most groundbreaking technological advancements we have witnessed in recent years. It has already begun to transform a multitude of fields, bringing newfound creativity and innovation to everything from art and design to healthcare and marketing. With its ability to automate creative processes, generative AI holds the promise of revolutionizing the way we conceive, develop, and implement ideas. This book aims to serve as your comprehensive guide to understanding and tapping into the transformative potential of this technology.

For students and aspiring AI practitioners, this book will be an invaluable resource that delves deeply into the world of generative AI. Whether you are a university student, a recent graduate, or someone pursuing online courses or self-study in artificial intelligence and machine learning, this book is designed with you in mind. The zeal to dive into the world of AI is palpable among early career individuals, and this book seeks to satisfy that hunger for knowledge and skill development.

Working professionals seeking to upskill will also find this book immensely beneficial. For those already established in fields like software development, data science, and engineering, expanding your skill set to include generative AI techniques can pave the way for significant career advancements. In a swiftly changing job market, maintaining competitiveness requires gaining relevant skills. By reading this book, you'll gain the practical knowledge needed to transition into AI-focused roles seamlessly.

Tech enthusiasts and hobbyists are another key audience for this book. If you have a passion for technology and enjoy experimenting with the latest advancements, you've come to the right place. This book caters to a broad age range, from teenagers eager to learn more about AI to retirees looking to explore a new interest. With various backgrounds, including graphic designers, digital artists, educators, and tech-savvy professionals in non-tech fields, this group brings a diverse set of perspectives to the table. Curiosity, creativity, and a hobbyist's approach to exploration define this audience, and this book is crafted to nurture these qualities.

Understanding what generative AI is and why it matters forms the cornerstone of this book. Generative AI refers to algorithms capable of generating new content by leveraging the data they've been trained on. Unlike traditional AI, which follows predefined rules, generative AI mimics human-like creativity by generating original content, whether it's an artwork, a piece of music, or even a scientific hypothesis. The importance of generative

1

AI lies in its ability to augment human creativity and productivity, opening up new avenues for innovation.

A brief history of generative AI will give you context on how this fascinating field has evolved over the years. From its humble beginnings in the mid-20th century, when researchers first started exploring the possibilities of machines creating new content, to the sophisticated algorithms of today, generative AI has come a long way. Understanding this evolution will not only provide you with a solid historical background but also help you appreciate the technological leaps that have made current advancements possible.

One of the critical aspects of generative AI is how it stands apart from other forms of AI. Traditional AI systems are predominantly rule-based, relying on extensive data sets and manual feature engineering to make decisions or predictions. In contrast, generative AI models are designed to understand patterns within input data and use this understanding to generate unique output. This capability allows generative AI to excel in applications where creativity, novelty, and complexity are required.

The versatility of generative AI is evident in its wide-ranging applications across various fields. In art and design, it enables the creation of novel artworks and design elements that push the boundaries of creativity. In entertainment, it can generate scripts, music scores, and virtual environments that captivate audiences. In healthcare, generative AI is being used to design new drugs and customize treatment plans. Marketing benefits from personalized content generation that enhances customer engagement. Education sees the creation of interactive learning materials tailored to individual needs. Even scientific research is transformed through the generation of innovative hypotheses and experimental designs.

To recap, the significance of generative AI cannot be overstated. Its ability to automate and elevate creative processes heralds a new era of innovation. This book invites you to explore the vast landscape of generative AI and harness its potential to revolutionize your field of interest, whether you are a student, a professional, a tech enthusiast, or simply curious about the future of AI. Together, let's embark on this journey to discover the limitless possibilities that generative AI offers for creativity and innovation.

CHAPTER 1

Introduction to Generative AI

Generative AI focuses on creating new content rather than just analyzing existing data. Unlike traditional AI, which primarily identifies patterns or makes predictions, generative AI produces original outputs such as text, images, audio, and video. This capability distinguishes it from conventional AI systems and opens up a wide range of possibilities across various industries. The ability to generate new material not only saves time but also democratizes creativity, making it accessible to more individuals and professionals. As technology continues to advance, the applications of generative AI are expanding, influencing numerous fields from art and design to healthcare and education.

This chapter delves into the concept of generative AI, offering an overview of its defining characteristics and historical context. It will explore the practical applications of this technology across diverse sectors, highlighting how it is transforming traditional processes and fostering innovation. Readers will gain insights into the evolution of generative AI, starting from its early theoretical foundations to recent advancements in deep learning and transformer models. The chapter will also discuss the key differences between generative AI and other types of AI, focusing on their distinct objectives and methodologies. By understanding these aspects, readers will appreciate the broad potential and future directions of generative AI.

Definition and Importance

Generative AI is a subset of artificial intelligence focused on the creation of new content rather than merely analyzing or categorizing existing data. At its core, generative AI leverages algorithms and models to produce original outputs in various forms such as text, images, audio, and video. This ability to generate new content sets it apart from more traditional types of AI, which are often designed to recognize patterns, classify data, or make predictions based on historical information.

The importance of generative AI is found in its adaptability and its potential to revolutionize various industries. For instance, in the realm of text generation, models like GPT-3 can write essays, articles, and even code. These abilities not only save time but also create new opportunities for tailored content creation. Similarly, AI tools such as DALL-E are making waves in image generation by creating artworks and designs that were previously unimaginable, effectively democratizing creativity.

Generative AI extends its reach beyond just creativity; it has substantial practical applications. One notable application is in the field of automated creative processes. By streamlining tasks that traditionally required human intervention, such as design prototyping or music composition, generative AI accelerates innovation cycles. Companies can now prototype products more quickly, testing various iterations without the significant time investment usually required, thus speeding up the overall development process.

Another critical aspect of generative AI is its role in human-machine collaboration. Unlike traditional AI systems, which might simply offer data-driven insights, generative AI acts as a co-creator with humans. This augmentation of human creativity means that individuals can push the boundaries of their work further than ever before. Whether it's a writer using AI to brainstorm plot ideas or an artist enhancing their digital artwork with AI-generated elements, the synergy between humans and machines leads to more innovative and high-quality outputs.

When discussing how generative AI differs from traditional AI, it's essential to note that while both fields use complex algorithms, their objectives diverge. Traditional AI primarily focuses on classification, prediction, and optimization. These systems scrutinize existing data to detect patterns and offer well-informed decisions or recommendations. In contrast, generative AI is not concerned with classifying or predicting; its purpose is to generate something entirely new. This difference fundamentally changes how each type of AI is developed and utilized.

Traditional AI relies heavily on supervised learning methods, where models are trained on labeled datasets to perform specific tasks. Generative AI, however, frequently employs unsupervised or semi-supervised learning methods. These methods allow the AI to understand the underlying structure of the data and create new instances that follow similar patterns. This approach makes generative AI particularly suited for tasks requiring creativity and novelty.

Moreover, the applications of generative AI span a wide range of fields, each benefiting uniquely from this advanced technology. In marketing, for instance, AI can generate personalized advertisements and content tailored to individual preferences, significantly improving customer engagement. Similarly, in education, generative AI can create customized learning materials that adapt to the needs of individual students, enhancing their learning experience.

One of the most transformative aspects of generative AI is its ability to automate creative processes. Traditionally, tasks like designing a product prototype or composing a piece of music required significant human effort and expertise. With generative AI, these tasks can be completed more rapidly and efficiently. This automation not only boosts productivity but also allows professionals to focus on higher-level, strategic thinking.

For example, in the automotive industry, generative AI is used to create multiple design prototypes quickly. Designers input specific parameters, and the AI generates numerous variations, each meeting the defined criteria. This rapid prototyping enables designers to explore a broader range of options and refine their ideas faster than ever before. Consequently, businesses can launch groundbreaking products to the market with greater speed and reduced costs.

In addition to automating traditional tasks, generative AI fosters innovation by enabling the creation of entirely new forms of content. A striking example is in the field of art, where AI-generated artworks are now displayed in galleries and sold at auctions. These pieces, created by algorithms, challenge our traditional notions of creativity and authorship, pushing the boundaries of what art can be. Similarly, in music, AI systems can compose original pieces that blend different genres and styles, offering fresh and unique listening experiences.

Beyond automation and innovation, generative AI plays a crucial role in enhancing human creativity. By acting as a collaborative tool, AI augments the creative capacities of individuals and teams. For instance, writers can use AI to generate ideas, plot outlines, or even entire chapters, which they can then refine and develop. This collaboration allows writers to overcome creative blocks and expand their storytelling possibilities.

In the visual arts, AI-powered tools enable artists to experiment with new styles and techniques. Digital painters can use AI to apply different artistic filters or generate novel compositions based on their initial sketches. This interaction between human intuition and machine precision results in artworks that are both deeply personal and technologically advanced. The collaborative nature of generative AI thus fosters a dynamic interplay between human and machine, leading to groundbreaking creative outputs.

Furthermore, the impact of generative AI extends to sectors such as gaming and virtual reality. Game developers use AI to create expansive, immersive worlds with intricate details and dynamic storylines. By generating diverse environments, characters, and narratives, AI enhances the gaming experience, making it more engaging and interactive. In virtual reality, AI-generated content helps create realistic simulations for training and entertainment purposes, blurring the lines between the virtual and real worlds.

Historical Background and Evolution

The journey of generative AI begins with the establishment of foundational AI theories in the 1950s and 1960s. During this period, pioneering work by figures such as Alan Turing laid the groundwork for modern AI. Turing's concept of a machine capable of thinking, known as the Turing Test, sparked initial interest and research into artificial intelligence. Early efforts focused on understanding how machines could perform tasks that typically required human intelligence, leading to experiments in machine learning and neural networks. These early experiments, although rudimentary by today's standards, set the stage for future advancements by demonstrating that machines could be programmed to solve complex problems.

Moving into the 1980s and 1990s, the development of algorithms like genetic algorithms and neural networks marked significant progress in the field. Genetic algorithms, inspired by natural selection, allowed computers to solve optimization problems by simulating the process of evolution. Around the same time, advancements in neural networks revived interest in AI. These networks, designed to mimic the human brain's interconnected neurons, showed promise in recognizing patterns and learning from data. This era saw the emergence of initial generative models, where machines began to create outputs rather than just processing inputs. Despite these advancements, the technology was still in its infancy, and practical applications remained limited.

The breakthrough moment for generative AI came in 2014 when Ian Goodfellow introduced Generative Adversarial Networks (GANs). GANs represented a major leap forward by enabling the creation of highly realistic synthetic data. The architecture of GANs involves two neural networks pitted against each other: one generating data and the other evaluating it. This adversarial setup led to the rapid improvement of generated outputs, making them increasingly indistinguishable from real data. GANs have since become a cornerstone of generative AI, driving innovations in areas such as image synthesis, video generation, and even creating artworks, thereby highlighting the potential for AI to produce creative and original content.

In recent years, significant progress in deep learning and transformer models has further propelled generative AI into mainstream applications. Deep learning, a subset of machine learning, involves training large neural networks on vast amounts of data, allowing models to learn complex patterns and make accurate predictions. Transformer models, introduced in 2017, revolutionized natural language processing by enabling AI to understand and generate human-like text. These models capture contextual relationships within data, making them particularly powerful for tasks such as text generation, translation, and summarization. The introduction of OpenAI's GPT-3 and subsequent models demonstrated the immense capabilities of transformers, with applications ranging from automated content creation to scientific research assistance.

The foundational theories established in the mid-20th century continue to influence current advancements in AI. By understanding the preliminary principles devised by pioneers like Turing, researchers today can build upon these concepts to develop more sophisticated AI systems. The evolution of machine learning techniques during the 1980s and 1990s provided essential building blocks for contemporary AI development. These advancements laid the conceptual framework, which allowed later breakthroughs in generative models and deep learning.

The 1980s and 1990s were periods of exploration and refinement for AI algorithms. During this time, genetic algorithms provided innovative solutions to previously unsolvable optimization challenges, while renewed interest in neural networks paved the way for AI to become more adaptive and intelligent. The incremental advancements in algorithmic efficiency and capability during this period played a crucial role in setting up the technological infrastructure necessary for the development of generative AI in the following decades. This phase also highlighted the cyclical nature of AI research, where periods of rapid growth are often followed by phases of reassessment and consolidation.

Ian Goodfellow's introduction of GANs not only advanced the technical capabilities of AI but also expanded its creative potential. GANs' ability to generate new data that closely resembles real-world data has had profound implications across various fields. From creating lifelike images to generating realistic video game landscapes, GANs have demonstrated the versatility and power of generative AI. Moreover, the concept of adversarial training introduced by GANs has inspired new lines of research focused on improving the robustness and reliability of AI-generated outputs, ensuring that generative models can be deployed safely and effectively in real-world applications.

Recent advancements in deep learning and transformer models have underscored the synergy between data availability and computational power. The success of models like

GPT-3 is largely attributed to their ability to leverage vast datasets and powerful computing resources, resulting in AI systems that can perform a wide range of tasks with impressive accuracy. These models have found applications in numerous domains, including healthcare, where they assist in diagnosing diseases; finance, where they predict market trends; and entertainment, where they enable the creation of personalized content. The continual improvement of these models promises to unlock even more sophisticated applications, cementing generative AI's role as a transformative force in technology and industry.

Key Differences from Other AI Types

Generative AI is distinct from other types of AI in its ability to produce new data instances rather than merely predicting labels or categories. This capacity for generation stems from its fundamental structure, enabling it to create entirely new content that mirrors the patterns and attributes of the original dataset. For instance, generative models can produce realistic images that do not exist in the real world, compose music that resembles a specific style, or generate coherent text that appears as if written by a human. This is in stark contrast to discriminative models, which are designed to classify existing data into predefined categories or predict labels based on input features.

The difference between generative and discriminative models further highlights the uniqueness of generative AI. Discriminative models focus on identifying the boundary between classes within the dataset, meaning they excel at tasks like image recognition or spam detection where the goal is to categorize data points accurately. Conversely, generative models strive to comprehend and mimic the inherent distribution of the data they are trained on. By learning the joint probability distribution of inputs, they can sample from this distribution to generate new, plausible data instances, making them invaluable for creative and exploratory tasks.

Moreover, generative AI commonly relies on unsupervised or semi-supervised learning methods, which stands in contrast to the predominantly supervised learning techniques employed in predictive models. Supervised learning depends on a labeled dataset to train a model to make predictions, while generative AI often learns from an unlabeled dataset, seeking to discover the underlying structure and relationships within the data. This approach allows generative AI to function with less direct human intervention and leverage vast amounts of data that may not be neatly annotated, expanding its utility across a range of fields where labeled data is scarce or costly to obtain.

Traditional AI has historically focused on tasks like classification and regression, which involve predicting outcomes based on input data. Classification tasks, such as determining whether an email is spam or not, and regression tasks, like predicting housing prices based on various features, rely on understanding existing patterns within labeled data to make accurate predictions. While these tasks are crucial for several applications, they are inherently limited to the boundaries set by the available data and the need for explicit labels for training.

In contrast, generative AI thrives in scenarios where creativity and novelty are paramount. For example, in the field of image synthesis, generative models like Generative Adversarial Networks (GANs) have made significant strides by creating realistic images from scratch. This capability is transformative for industries such as graphic design, where designers can use AI-generated images as starting points or inspirations for their work. Similarly, in music composition, generative models can compose entire pieces of music in the style of classical composers or contemporary artists, providing musicians and producers with new material to build upon.

Furthermore, the applications of generative AI extend beyond mere novelty into enhancing human creativity and automating artistic processes. Natural language generation is one such application, where AI systems can draft articles, write stories, or even engage in conversations with users. These systems utilize deep learning models trained on extensive text datasets to produce coherent and contextually relevant text, thereby aiding writers, journalists, and customer service representatives in their work.

Generative AI also plays a pivotal role in augmenting human creativity by serving as a collaborative tool. For instance, digital artists can use generative models to explore new artistic styles or generate various versions of their artwork, providing a broader canvas for experimentation. In architecture and product design, AI can assist in generating innovative designs or optimizing existing ones, thereby accelerating the prototyping phase and reducing time-to-market for new products.

Moreover, the automation of artistic processes through generative AI can lead to significant efficiencies in content production. For example, film studios can use AI to generate special effects or create synthetic characters, reducing reliance on time-consuming manual processes. Marketing agencies can employ generative models to produce personalized advertisements and promotional materials at scale, tailoring content to individual preferences and improving engagement rates.

Overview of Applications in Various Fields

Generative AI has found extensive applications across various sectors, profoundly transforming traditional practices and unlocking new creative possibilities. In the realm of art and design, generative AI is revolutionizing how artists and designers approach their work. Tools like DALL-E and Artbreeder allow artists to produce unique, intricate designs with minimal effort, expediting the creative process by providing an endless array of digital resources from which to draw inspiration. This not only saves time but also enables creators to explore artistic avenues that were previously unimaginable, pushing the boundaries of what is considered possible in visual arts.

Fashion design has similarly benefited from the integration of generative AI. Designers now employ AI algorithms to generate innovative patterns, styles, and even entire clothing lines. This technology facilitates rapid prototyping, allowing designers to experiment with various concepts without the constraints of traditional manual methods. For example, AI can swiftly create multiple variations of a garment design, enabling designers to iterate quickly and select the most compelling options. The efficiency brought about by AI shortens the design cycle and increases productivity within the fashion industry.

In the entertainment industry, generative AI is making significant strides in music composition, special effects, and animation. AI tools like Amper Music and AIVA assist musicians and composers in creating original scores, providing a collaborative partner that can generate melodies based on specified moods or themes. By leveraging these tools, composers can speed up their creative process and explore new musical possibilities they might not have considered independently. This intersection of AI and music not only enhances creativity but also democratizes music production, making it accessible to a broader audience.

Moreover, generative AI is pivotal in producing realistic special effects and animations. Techniques such as deepfake technology and style transfer enable filmmakers to create high-quality visual content with fewer resources. AI-driven models can autonomously generate lifelike animations and special effects that traditionally required extensive manual labor and technical expertise. As a result, small-scale productions can attain professional-level visuals, leveling the playing field in the film and media industries and fostering more diverse content creation.

Healthcare is another sector experiencing transformative benefits from generative AI, particularly in drug discovery and medical imaging. AI models expedite the drug development process by predicting molecular interactions and identifying potential compounds, significantly reducing the time and cost associated with bringing new medications to market. For instance, generative AI can simulate chemical reactions and propose novel compounds likely to have therapeutic properties, streamlining the initial phases of drug research. This accelerates the introduction of life-saving drugs, benefiting both patients and the pharmaceutical industry.

In the field of medical imaging, generative AI improves both diagnostic precision and operational efficiency. AI algorithms can analyze vast datasets of medical images, identifying patterns and anomalies that may be indicative of certain conditions. For example, AI systems can augment MRI or CT scans, highlighting areas of concern that radiologists might overlook. This capability improves early detection rates and allows for more personalized treatment plans, ultimately leading to better patient outcomes. The use of AI in medical imaging represents a significant advancement in the ability to diagnose and treat complex diseases.

Marketing and education are leveraging generative AI for content generation and personalized strategies, enhancing both customer engagement and educational materials In marketing, AI tools create customized content that effectively connects with particular target audiences. By analyzing consumer behavior data, AI can create customized advertisements, social media posts, and even product descriptions that are more likely to engage potential customers. This personalized approach not only increases conversion rates but also builds stronger customer relationships, as consumers feel that brands understand and cater to their individual preferences.

Likewise, in education, generative AI is being utilized to create individualized learning experiences. AI-powered tutoring systems can assess a student's learning style and adapt educational content to meet their needs. For instance, AI can generate practice questions, explanations, and feedback tailored to a student's progress, ensuring a more effective learning process. These systems can deliver critical insights to educators regarding student performance, facilitating data-informed decisions that optimize teaching approaches and elevate educational results.

Generative AI's transformative potential and implications

Throughout this chapter, we have explored the multifaceted realm of generative AI, delving into its definition, historical evolution, and broad spectrum of applications. We began by defining generative AI as a specialized subset of artificial intelligence focused on generating new content, distinguishing it from traditional AI that primarily classifies or predicts based on existing data. This foundational understanding set the stage for examining the transformative potential of generative AI across various fields.

A look back at the history of AI revealed crucial milestones, from early theoretical work in the mid-20th century to significant advancements in neural networks and algorithms in the 1980s and 1990s. Ian Goodfellow's introduction of Generative Adversarial Networks (GANs) in 2014 marked a breakthrough, enabling AI to create highly realistic synthetic data. Recent developments in deep learning and transformer models further propelled generative AI, making it more powerful and versatile than ever.

One of the core distinctions between generative AI and other types of AI lies in their objectives and methodologies. While discriminative models focus on categorizing existing data, generative models aim to replicate and create new data instances, often relying on unsupervised or semi-supervised learning techniques. This distinction underscores the unique capabilities of generative AI in producing novel and creative outputs, which are valuable in fields where innovation and originality are paramount.

Generative AI's practical applications span numerous industries, demonstrating its versatility and impact. In art and design, tools like DALL-E and Artbreeder enable artists to generate intricate designs effortlessly, while in fashion, AI-driven prototypes accelerate the design cycle. The entertainment industry benefits from AI's ability to compose music, create special effects, and animate lifelike characters, democratizing access to high-quality production resources.

Healthcare has also seen significant advancements through generative AI, particularly in drug discovery and medical imaging. AI expedites the development of new medications by predicting molecular interactions and streamlining initial research phases. In medical imaging, AI enhances diagnostic accuracy by identifying patterns and anomalies in vast datasets, leading to better patient outcomes.

Marketing and education sectors leverage generative AI for personalized content generation and adaptive learning experiences. AI-driven marketing strategies improve customer engagement by tailoring content to individual preferences, while educational AI systems adapt to students' learning styles, offering customized practice questions and feedback. These applications not only enhance efficiency but also foster deeper connections with users.

Nevertheless, the broad implementation of generative AI brings up various concerns. Issues related to data privacy, ethical considerations, and the potential misuse of AI-generated content necessitate careful regulation and oversight. As generative models advance in complexity, it becomes increasingly important to maintain transparency, uphold accountability, and ensure fairness in AI operations to preserve public trust and reduce potential risks.

Looking ahead, the implications of generative AI on a broader scale are profound. Its ability to augment human creativity and automate complex tasks will continue to reshape industries and redefine workflows. Professionals and enthusiasts alike must stay informed and adapt to these changes, embracing the opportunities while addressing the challenges posed by this rapidly evolving technology.

In summary, generative AI stands at the forefront of technological innovation, offering unprecedented possibilities for creating new content and solving complex problems. As we move forward, it is essential to navigate this landscape thoughtfully, harnessing the power of generative AI to drive progress while remaining vigilant about the ethical and societal impacts. The journey of generative AI is just beginning, inviting us all to explore and contribute to its unfolding narrative.

References

Bianzino, N., Cremer, D., Falk, B. (2023, April). *How Generative AI Could Disrupt Creative Work. Harvard Business Review.* https://hbr.org/2023/04/how-generative-ai-could-disrupt-creative-work

Bohr, A., Memarzadeh, K. (2020). *The rise of artificial intelligence in healthcare applications. Artificial Intelligence in Healthcare.* https://www.ncbi.nlm.nih.gov/pmc/articles/PMC7325854/

Coursera Staff. (2024, May). *The History of AI: A Timeline of Artificial Intelligence. Coursera.* https://www.coursera.org/articles/history-of-ai

Coursera. (2024, March). *20 Examples of Generative AI Applications Across Industries. Coursera.* https://www.coursera.org/articles/generative-ai-applications

Davenport, T., Mittal, N. (2022, November). *How Generative AI Is Changing Creative Work. Harvard Business Review.* https://hbr.org/2022/11/how-generative-ai-is-changing-creative-work

The Difference Between Discriminative and Generative AI Models - Defense Acquisition University. media.dau.edu. (n.d.). https://media.dau.edu/media/t/1_11mq6tcm

The Difference Between Generative and Discriminative Machine Learning Algorithms. GeeksforGeeks. (2023, July). https://www.geeksforgeeks.org/the-difference-between-generative-and-discriminative-machine-learning-algorithms/

Turner, G. (2023, December). *10 AI milestones of the last 10 years | Royal Institution. www.rigb.org.* https://www.rigb.org/explore-science/explore/blog/10-ai-milestones-last-10-years

CHAPTER 2

Fundamentals of Generative Models

E xploring the fundamentals of generative models is key to understanding the broader field of artificial intelligence. Generative models have transformed how we approach data synthesis, enabling the creation of new data that closely resembles existing datasets. These models are crucial in various domains, from augmenting training data for machine learning algorithms to generating realistic images, text, and audio. By diving into the foundational principles and concepts underlying generative models, readers can gain a comprehensive insight into their potential and applications.

In this chapter, the discussion begins with the basics of probability theory, which forms the cornerstone for understanding randomness and uncertainty within generative models. This includes an exploration of important probability distributions like the Normal and Binomial distributions and how they apply to generative scenarios. The chapter also delves into statistical inference, helping readers comprehend how to generalize findings from sample data to larger populations. Moving forward, it covers random variables and expectation, illuminating how these concepts shape predictive modeling and decision-making processes. Additionally, key probabilistic concepts such as joint, marginal, and conditional probabilities are examined to provide a robust framework for dealing with incomplete or uncertain information. By grasping these fundamental elements, readers will be well-equipped to understand and build effective generative models.

Introduction to Probability

Probability is a cornerstone in understanding randomness and uncertainty, especially within the context of generative models. Probability enables us to quantify the likelihood of various outcomes and make informed predictions about future events. In the realm of artificial intelligence and machine learning, probability provides a structured framework for dealing with incomplete or uncertain information, which is often encountered in real-world scenarios.

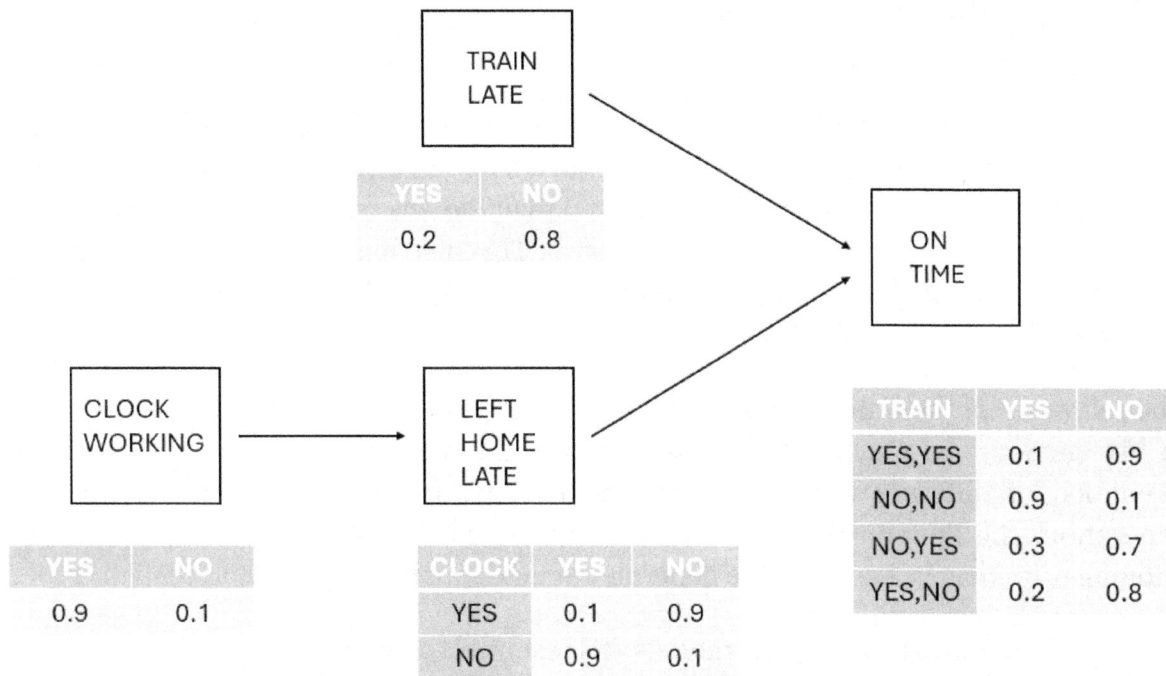

TRAIN LATE	
YES	NO
0.2	0.8

ON TIME

CLOCK WORKING		LEFT HOME LATE		

YES	NO
0.9	0.1

CLOCK	YES	NO
YES	0.1	0.9
NO	0.9	0.1

TRAIN	YES	NO
YES,YES	0.1	0.9
NO,NO	0.9	0.1
NO,YES	0.3	0.7
YES,NO	0.2	0.8

The essence of probability lies in its ability to measure the degree of uncertainty associated with an event. For example, flipping a fair coin yields two possible outcomes: heads or tails, each with a probability of 0.5. This simplistic example demonstrates how probability helps in characterizing the unpredictability of random processes. In generative models, this principle is expanded to more complex scenarios, where the goal is to generate new data points that resemble a given dataset. Without a firm grasp of probability, it would be challenging to build models that accurately capture the nuances of real-world data.

Generative models, by definition, aim to understand and mimic the underlying distribution of data. For instance, in image generation tasks, a generative model might be trained on thousands of images to learn the probability distribution of pixels, colors, shapes, and textures. The effectiveness of these models hinges on their ability to comprehend and manipulate probabilities, allowing them to produce new, realistic images that are indistinguishable from the training data.

Understanding key probability distributions is crucial for anyone working with generative models. The Normal distribution, also known as the Gaussian distribution, is perhaps the most well-known. It is characterized by its bell-shaped curve and is defined by two parameters: mean and standard deviation. This distribution is fundamental because of its widespread occurrence in natural phenomena and its connection to the central limit theorem. The theorem suggests that the sum of a large number of independent variables tends to approximate a normal distribution, irrespective of the original distribution of those variables.

Another important distribution is the Binomial distribution, which describes the number of successes in a fixed number of binary trials, such as flipping a coin multiple times. Conversely, the Poisson distribution is utilized to model the frequency of events occurring within a specified time frame or spatial interval. This distribution is particularly useful in fields like telecommunication, astronomy, and biology, where the occurrence of rare events needs to be quantified.

The relevance of these distributions extends directly to generative models. For example, in text generation, a model might use the multinomial distribution to determine the likelihood of different words following a given word sequence. Similarly, in image generation, the Poisson distribution can help model the occurrence of pixel noise or anomalies in images, ensuring the generated images are both varied and realistic.

To delve deeper into probabilistic models, it's essential to understand joint, marginal, and conditional probabilities. Joint probability refers to the chance of two or more events occurring at the same time. For example, in a dataset containing attributes like age and income, the joint probability could describe the likelihood of encountering individuals who are both young and high-earning. This type of probability is fundamental in modeling the relationships between different variables in a dataset.

Marginal probability is derived from joint probability and represents the probability of a single event occurring, irrespective of other variables. Continuing with the age and income example, the marginal probability would focus purely on the likelihood of encountering individuals of a certain age, without considering their income. This simplifies the analysis and allows for isolated insights into specific variables.

Conditional probability is perhaps the most intuitive yet powerful concept. It represents the probability of an event happening, assuming that another event has already taken place. For instance, knowing that a person is young, we might want to compute the probability that they have a high income. Conditional probability forms the backbone of many machine learning algorithms, including Bayesian networks and Hidden Markov Models, which heavily rely on this concept to make predictions based on observed data.

In generative models, conditional probabilities play a vital role in refining the output. For example, in language models, the probability of the next word in a sentence is highly dependent on the preceding words. By carefully calculating conditional probabilities, these models can produce coherent and contextually relevant text, making applications like chatbots and automated content generation more practical and effective.

Statistical Inference

Descriptive statistics are foundational methods that help summarize and describe the main features of a dataset. Measures of central tendency, including the mean, median, and mode, offer insights into the central value of the data. The mean is calculated by summing all data points and dividing by the number of points, offering an average value. The median, the middle value when data points are ordered, is less influenced by extreme values and provides a robust central location measure. Meanwhile, the mode, the most frequently occurring value, highlights the dataset's most common outcome.

In addition to central tendency, it is essential to understand measures of variability which include variance and standard deviation. Variance quantifies the spread between numbers in a dataset from the mean, providing a sense of how much the values differ from the average. Standard deviation, which is the square root of variance, expresses data dispersion in the same units as the original data, making it easier to interpret. Descriptive statistics also encompass graphical representations such as histograms and box plots, which visually illustrate data distributions and highlight any anomalies or patterns.

Understanding these descriptive measures is fundamental when making inferences about a dataset, as they offer a snapshot of the main characteristics. For instance, in clinical trials, summarized descriptive statistics can reveal the average effect of a treatment and the variability among patients' responses, guiding further investigative steps. These preliminary insights set the stage for deeper analysis through inferential statistics.

Inferential statistics build on descriptive statistics by enabling generalizations from a sample to a broader population. This branch involves techniques like hypothesis testing, confidence intervals, and p-values, each serving a distinct purpose in statistical inference. Hypothesis testing begins with forming a null hypothesis, which posits no effect or relationship exists, and an alternative hypothesis indicating an effect or relationship.

Statistical tests are used to assess whether the observed results significantly differ from what would be expected under the null hypothesis.

Confidence intervals offer a range of values that likely contain the true population parameter. Typically expressed at a 95% confidence level, these intervals offer insights into the precision and reliability of an estimate. A narrow confidence interval signifies high precision, whereas a wider interval indicates more uncertainty. P-values, a key concept, measure the likelihood of obtaining results as extreme as the observed ones, assuming the null hypothesis is true. A low p-value (usually less than 0.05) indicates strong evidence against the null hypothesis, leading researchers to consider the alternative hypothesis.

These inferential tools allow researchers to draw conclusions beyond their immediate data, making informed predictions and decisions. For example, in public health research, inferential statistics can identify significant risk factors for diseases, shaping preventive measures and policies. Understanding and applying these concepts is crucial for valid and reliable data-driven decision-making.

The field of statistical inference splits into two primary approaches: Bayesian and Frequentist. While both aim to make probabilistic statements about populations, they differ fundamentally in philosophy and methodology. Frequentist approaches, based on long-run frequency properties, use fixed parameters and do not incorporate prior knowledge or beliefs. Within this framework, repeated estimations are conducted to gauge the likelihood of various outcomes..

Bayesian approaches, in contrast, incorporate prior information combined with observed data to update the probability of a hypothesis. This method uses Bayes' theorem to revise probabilities continually, making it flexible and dynamic. One key advantage of Bayesian methods is their ability to incorporate existing knowledge, which can be particularly useful in fields with extensive historical data.

However, both approaches have their strengths and limitations. The Frequentist approach is straightforward and widely used due to its simplicity and ease of interpretation. It is highly effective when dealing with large datasets where long-run frequencies approximate probabilities well. On the other hand, Bayesian methods can be computationally intensive and require subjective input for prior distributions, but they offer a coherent way to update beliefs in light of new data, making them powerful in adaptive and iterative study designs.

Choosing the right approach depends on the context, research goals, and available data. In clinical trials, for instance, Bayesian methods might be preferred for their ability to integrate prior knowledge, leading to quicker and potentially more ethical decision-making processes. Conversely, established protocols in large-scale epidemiological studies often leverage Frequentist methods for their robustness and simplicity.

Random Variables and Expectation

Random variables and the concept of expectation are fundamental to understanding generative models. A random variable is a function that assigns a numerical value to each possible outcome in a sample space. Random variables are categorized into two main types: discrete and continuous. Discrete random variables take on countable, distinct values, such as rolling a die or flipping a coin. In contrast, continuous random variables can take on an infinite number of values within a specified range, such as when measuring the height of individuals in a population.

Understanding the difference between these types of random variables is crucial for calculating probabilities and making predictions. For discrete random variables, the probability of each specific value can be directly assessed. In contrast, for continuous random variables, probabilities are evaluated over ranges using probability density functions. These distinctions shape how data and outcomes are interpreted, modeled, and used in various applications across fields like finance, science, and engineering.

The next critical concept in probability theory is the expected value or mean of a random variable. The expected value is a measure of the central tendency of a probability distribution and provides a single summarizing figure around which the values of a random variable tend to cluster. For a discrete random variable, the expected value is calculated by multiplying each possible outcome by its probability and summing these products. Mathematically, it is denoted as $E(X) = \Sigma\,[x * P(x)]$, where x represents possible values, and P(x) their respective probabilities.

For continuous random variables, the expected value is determined using integration. This process involves integrating the product of the variable's value and its probability density function across all possible values. Unlike the summation method used for discrete variables, integration accommodates the continuous nature of the data. The formula for the expected value is given by $\mathbb{E}(X) = \int x \cdot f(x)\,dx$, where $f(x)$ is the probability density function. Grasping the concept of expected value is crucial for predicting long-term averages, making it an essential tool in decision-making under uncertainty.

Variance, another important concept, measures the spread of a distribution around its mean. It quantifies the extent to which the values of a random variable differ from the expected value. For discrete random variables, variance is determined by summing the squared differences between each value and the mean, with each difference weighted by its corresponding probability. The formula for variance is:

$$Var(X) = \Sigma\,[(x - E(X))\wedge 2 * P(x)]\,.$$

A higher variance indicates greater dispersion in the data, signifying more variability in outcomes.

For continuous random variables, variance is calculated through a similar integration process. This involves integrating the squared difference between the variable and its mean, multiplied by the probability density function. The formula for variance in continuous random variables is Var(X)=∫(x−E(X))2f(x) . Calculating variance provides valuable insights into the consistency and reliability of the data, making it a critical factor in risk assessment and statistical inference.

Law of Large Numbers and Central Limit Theorem

The Law of Large Numbers (LLN) is a fundamental theorem in probability that provides the foundation for making reliable inferences from sample data. It states that as the size of a sample drawn from a population increases, the sample mean will converge to the population mean. This is crucial because it assures us that our statistical estimates are meaningful and progressively accurate with larger samples. For instance, if you're assessing the average income of a city by surveying its residents, LLN implies that the more people you survey, the closer your sample's average income will be to the actual average income of the entire city.

One important implication of the LLN is its role in ensuring that long-term averages are stable and predictable. The theorem applies to various real-world situations where repeated measurements are taken over time. For example, casinos rely on LLN to make sure that their games are profitable over the long run, despite short-term fluctuations. Similarly, insurance companies use the law to predict future claims by analyzing historical data, providing them with the ability to set premiums that minimize risk.

Understanding the LLN also helps in grasping the concept of randomness and uncertainty in everyday phenomena. It illuminates why occasional deviations from expected outcomes are normal and to be anticipated. Such insights are essential in fields ranging from finance to engineering, where modeling and simulations frequently involve large datasets. By leveraging the LLN, professionals can develop robust models that reflect reality more accurately and make sound decisions based on empirical data.

The Central Limit Theorem (CLT) is another cornerstone of probability theory that plays a crucial role in understanding sample distributions. It states that as the sample size increases, the distribution of sample means approaches a normal distribution, regardless of the original population's distribution. This result is highly significant because it allows us to make probabilistic statements about sample means using the well-understood properties of the normal distribution.

One major importance of the CLT lies in its ability to simplify complex analyses. Given a sufficiently large sample size, the theorem enables statisticians to apply standard techniques associated with normal distribution, such as confidence intervals and hypothesis tests. This simplifies the analytic process significantly, making it easier to draw inferences from data. For instance, quality control engineers can employ the CLT to determine whether a batch of products meets the required standards without inspecting every single item.

Moreover, the CLT is instrumental in bridging the gap between theoretical models and practical applications. Many statistical methods assume normality due to its mathematical convenience and well-known properties. With the backing of the CLT, these methods remain valid and effective even when dealing with non-normally distributed populations, provided the sample size is adequate. Thus, it equips practitioners across various domains with powerful tools for data analysis and decision-making.

Applications of the Central Limit Theorem extend widely across statistical analysis and real-world scenarios. In educational assessments, for example, the CLT ensures that aggregate test scores approximate a normal distribution, allowing educators to apply standard grading systems. Similarly, financial analysts use the CLT to model asset returns, facilitating the application of portfolio optimization techniques that assume normally distributed returns.

In medical research, the CLT underpins the reliability of clinical trials. Researchers can estimate the efficacy of new treatments by comparing sample means, knowing that these means will approximate a normal distribution with larger sample sizes. This helps in judging the significance of results and making evidence-based conclusions about new drugs or therapies.

Beyond traditional fields, the CLT's implications are also evident in technology-driven areas like machine learning. Algorithms often rely on large datasets to improve accuracy and performance. The CLT supports the assumption that training errors follow a normal distribution, enabling developers to fine-tune models effectively and predict their behavior in real-world applications.

Machine Learning: Definition and Scope

Machine learning is a subset of artificial intelligence (AI) that enables systems to automatically learn and enhance their performance based on experience, without the need for explicit programming. At its essence, machine learning is centered on creating algorithms that can analyze data, recognize patterns, and make decisions with minimal human involvement. Its scope within AI is vast, encompassing various applications from image and speech recognition to predictive analytics and autonomous vehicles.

A key distinction in machine learning lies between supervised and unsupervised learning. In supervised learning, the algorithm is trained on a labeled dataset, where each training example is associated with a corresponding output label. This method enables the model to learn a mapping from inputs to outputs based on the provided examples. For instance, email spam filtering is a classic example of supervised learning; the model learns to classify emails as 'spam' or 'not spam' using previously labeled data.

In contrast, unsupervised learning works with data that has no associated labels. Here, the algorithm tries to learn the patterns and structure from the input data without predefined labels. The objective is typically to uncover hidden patterns or structures within the data. An example of unsupervised learning is customer segmentation in marketing, where the algorithm groups customers based on their purchase behavior without any predefined categories.

Supervised learning can be further categorized into regression and classification tasks. Regression involves predicting a continuous value, such as house prices based on features like size and location. A common approach for this is linear regression, where the goal is to fit a line that best describes the relationship between the input variables and the target variable. On the other hand, classification involves assigning categorical labels to inputs. For example, classifying images of animals into categories like 'cats', 'dogs', or 'horses' is a classification problem often solved using algorithms such as decision trees or support vector machines.

Unsupervised learning includes techniques like clustering and association. Clustering involves grouping similar data points together. For instance, K-means clustering could be used to segment customers into distinct groups based on their purchasing habits. Association rule learning, another aspect of unsupervised learning, discovers relationships between variables within large datasets. Market basket analysis, used by retailers to identify sets of products frequently bought together, is a practical application of association rules.

Comparing the two, supervised learning is akin to learning under a teacher's guidance, where the model learns from labeled examples. Unsupervised learning, however, is more exploratory, searching for unknown patterns in data. While supervised learning is ideal for situations where historical data with labels is available, unsupervised learning is useful for discovering hidden patterns in data without needing explicit instructions on what to look for.

Despite their differences, both types of learning are essential in building intelligent systems. Supervised learning models excel in scenarios where the outcome is known and can be mapped to previous experiences. They are widely used in medical diagnosis, fraud detection, and any application requiring accurate predictions based on past data. Unsupervised learning, by uncovering patterns that were not previously evident, helps in domains like anomaly detection, where it's crucial to identify outliers or unusual occurrences in data.

To illustrate these concepts, consider the task of anomaly detection in network security. Using supervised learning, we might train a model on labeled datasets where intrusions are already identified. The model would then predict future instances of intrusions. Conversely, with unsupervised learning, the model would analyze network activity without prior labels, clustering normal activities together and flagging deviations as potential threats.

Another real-life example is the recommendation system. Supervised learning can be used to predict user preferences based on past behavior, providing personalized recommendations on platforms like Netflix or Amazon. Alternatively, an unsupervised learning approach might cluster users into groups with similar viewing or purchasing habits, recommending items popular within those clusters.

Both supervised and unsupervised learning have unique benefits and limitations. Supervised learning's main advantage is its accuracy and reliability when sufficient labeled data is available. However, obtaining labeled data can be both time-consuming and costly. Unsupervised learning, though more flexible and capable of handling larger, unlabeled datasets, often requires more effort in interpreting the resulting patterns and ensuring they make sense contextually.

Key Concepts in Machine Learning

Understanding the essential concepts in machine learning is pivotal for beginners venturing into this dynamic field. One of the foundational aspects is the use of training and testing data, which involves splitting the dataset into different parts to validate the model's performance. Training data is used to teach the model, while testing data assesses its generalization capability on unseen data. This process helps in gauging how well the model will perform in real-world scenarios. Cross-validation is an essential technique that splits the dataset into multiple folds or subsets, ensuring that each data point is included in the testing set at least once. By doing so, it prevents over-reliance on any particular subset of data and provides a more robust estimate of model performance.

Cross-validation techniques such as k-fold, where the dataset is divided into k equally sized folds, offer a balanced way to utilize the entire dataset. For instance, in a 5-fold cross-validation, the model is trained on four folds and tested on the remaining one, rotating this process until each fold has been used as the testing set. This minimizes variability and ensures a comprehensive evaluation of the model's capabilities. Additionally, stratified cross-validation can be used when dealing with imbalanced datasets to maintain consistent class ratios across folds. Implementing these techniques is essential to avoid misleadingly optimistic predictions that may occur from using just a single train-test split.

Beyond simple splits, nested cross-validation comes into play for hyperparameter tuning and model selection. This method offers an outer loop for measuring the model's performance and an inner loop for parameter tuning, ensuring that the final evaluation remains unbiased by exploratory steps. Proper data splitting and cross-validation are fundamental practices that form the backbone of reliable machine learning experiments. Mastering and properly utilizing these methods can greatly improve the reliability and accuracy of machine learning models.

Overfitting and underfitting are frequent challenges that can negatively impact the effectiveness of machine learning models. Overfitting happens when a model learns the noise in the training data too well, resulting in excellent performance on training data but poor generalization to new, unseen data. Causes of overfitting include overly complex models with too many parameters or insufficient amounts of data relative to model complexity. To address overfitting, methods like regularization (e.g., L1 and L2), dropout in neural networks, or pruning in decision trees can be used. Regularization adds a penalty to the loss function, discouraging overly complex models and promoting simpler, more generalizable solutions.

On the other hand, underfitting happens when a model is too basic to grasp the underlying patterns in the data, resulting in poor performance on both the training and testing sets. Causes include using too few features or an overly simple algorithm that cannot capture the complexities of the data. Mitigation strategies involve increasing model complexity by adding more features, selecting more appropriate algorithms, or gathering additional data. For example, increasing the number of layers and neurons in a neural network or switching from linear regression to polynomial regression can help alleviate underfitting.

Finding the right balance between model complexity and performance, often referred to as the bias-variance tradeoff, is key. High bias (underfitting) leads to systematic errors, while high variance (overfitting) makes the model sensitive to noise. Effective model tuning involves iterative experimentation with different algorithms, feature sets, and hyperparameters. Utilizing techniques like cross-validation during this process helps in maintaining a realistic measure of generalization performance, guiding the choice of models and parameters that strike an optimal balance.

Evaluation metrics are vital tools for measuring the performance of machine learning models. Accuracy, a basic metric, calculates the percentage of correctly classified instances out of the total instances. However, relying solely on accuracy can be misleading, particularly in imbalanced datasets where the majority class overshadows the minority class. In such cases, precision and recall provide deeper insights. Precision quantifies the ratio of true positive predictions among all positive predictions, indicating how many of the identified positives are actually correct. Recall, in contrast, measures the proportion of true positive predictions out of all actual positive cases, indicating the model's effectiveness in identifying all relevant instances.

The F1-score merges precision and recall into a single measure by calculating their harmonic mean. It offers a balanced metric, especially useful in situations where a trade-off between precision and recall is necessary. For instance, in medical diagnostics, where missing a positive case can have severe consequences, a higher recall is critical, whereas in spam detection, precision might be prioritized to avoid misclassifying legitimate emails. The F1-score aids in making informed decisions tailored to the specific needs of the problem at hand.

Common Algorithms in Machine Learning

To understand the fundamentals of generative models, it's essential to first familiarize ourselves with widely-used machine learning algorithms. These foundational algorithms not only help in predictive modeling but also serve as building blocks for more complex applications in artificial intelligence.

Basics of Linear Regression and Its Applications in Predictive Modeling

Linear regression is a fundamental machine learning algorithm used primarily for predictive tasks. It examines the relationship between a dependent variable and one or more independent variables by fitting a linear equation to the observed data. The simplest form is simple linear regression, where we predict a single output variable based on a single input variable. The relationship is described using the equation $Y = b_0 + b_1 X$, where b_0 is the intercept and b_1 is the slope coefficient.

In practical applications, linear regression is often used for tasks such as forecasting sales, predicting housing prices, and even estimating stock market trends. For instance, a company may use historical sales data (independent variable) to forecast future sales (dependent variable). The linear model helps to capture the trend and make informed business decisions.

Multiple linear regression expands on this idea by incorporating several input variables to predict a single output. This can be useful in more complex scenarios, like analyzing the factors affecting house prices, including size, location, and age of the property.

Through these examples, it becomes evident that linear regression is invaluable for making predictions based on historical data, guiding decision-making in various fields.

Structure and Working Principle of Decision Trees, and Their Uses

Decision trees represent another cornerstone in machine learning algorithms, known for their intuitive structure and ease of interpretation. A decision tree algorithm splits data into branches at decision nodes, starting from a root node and progressing through internal nodes until it reaches leaf nodes. Each decision node asks a specific question about the dataset, and the branches represent the possible answers, leading to further nodes or final predictions.

The primary advantage of decision trees lies in their simplicity and transparency. They are especially valuable for classification tasks, like identifying whether an email is spam or not. By asking a series of yes/no questions based on features like keyword presence and sender information, the tree arrives at a final decision. In real-world applications, decision trees play significant roles in sectors such as finance for credit scoring, healthcare for diagnosing diseases, and marketing for customer segmentation.

Moreover, decision trees are versatile as they can process both numerical and categorical data. Despite their many advantages, they can sometimes be prone to overfitting, especially when the tree becomes too complex. Pruning techniques and ensemble methods, like Random Forests, often mitigate this issue, enhancing performance and robustness.

Support Vector Machines, the Kernel Trick, and Their Applications

Support vector machines (SVMs) are robust supervised learning models employed for both classification and regression tasks.

SVMs operate by identifying the optimal hyperplane that best divides the data into distinct classes. The aim is to maximize the margin between support vectors (the data points nearest to the hyperplane) to ensure the model generalizes effectively to new data.

A distinctive aspect of SVMs is the kernel trick, which enables the algorithm to function in a high-dimensional space without the need to explicitly calculate the coordinates. Kernels transform the data into a higher dimension, enabling SVMs to handle complex, non-linear relationships. Common kernels used in SVMs include linear, polynomial, and radial basis function (RBF).

SVMs are particularly effective in high-stakes fields requiring robust accuracy, such as image recognition, bioinformatics, and text categorization. For example, in medical imaging, SVMs can help classify different types of tumors. Similarly, in text categorization, they can distinguish between categories of documents, aiding in tasks like sentiment analysis and spam detection.

Overview of Clustering Algorithms Like K-means and Hierarchical Clustering, and Their Use Cases

Clustering algorithms are essential unsupervised learning techniques used to group similar data points into clusters. K-means clustering is one of the most popular methods, which divides the dataset into k predefined clusters. Each cluster is defined by its centroid, and data points are assigned to clusters based on their proximity to centroids. The algorithm repeatedly updates the centroids to reduce the within-cluster variance.

K-means is widely used in market segmentation, where businesses cluster customers based on purchasing behavior to tailor marketing strategies. In image compression, it reduces the number of colors used in an image while maintaining quality by clustering similar colors. It is also applied in anomaly detection to identify unusual patterns that deviate from norm clusters.

Hierarchical clustering, another prominent method, builds a tree-like structure called a dendrogram to represent nested clusters. It can be either agglomerative (a bottom-up approach) or divisive (a top-down approach). Hierarchical clustering doesn't require specifying the number of clusters in advance, offering flexibility. It's particularly useful in genomic sequencing to cluster genes with similar expression patterns, enhancing our understanding of genetic variations and functions.

Introduction to Neural Networks

Neural networks, pivotal to the realm of artificial intelligence, have a rich history and are biologically inspired by the human brain. The inception of neural network research can be traced back to the 1940s when Warren McCulloch and Walter Pitts modeled the first artificial neuron (McCulloch & Pitts, 1943). Their logical calculus aimed to mimic the way biological neurons function. This breakthrough laid the groundwork for future explorations into creating systems that could simulate human thought processes. In the subsequent decades, researchers like Frank Rosenblatt contributed significantly by developing the perceptron in the late 1950s, a type of neural network capable of pattern recognition (Rosenblatt, 1958).

The biological inspiration behind neural networks is profound. The human brain consists of billions of neurons interconnected by synapses, transmitting signals through electrochemical impulses. Neural networks, specifically artificial neural networks (ANNs), draw from this architecture. Each artificial neuron emulates the function of a biological one, receiving inputs, performing computations, and outputting results. By simulating learning processes observed in the brain, ANNs can adapt, recognize patterns, and make decisions based on input data.

This alignment with biological principles underscores the potential of neural networks to handle complex, nonlinear data with high accuracy. Just as humans learn from experience, neural networks undergo training to enhance their performance incrementally. This cyclic learning process allows neural networks to tackle tasks that traditional algorithms struggle with, such as image and speech recognition. Through this historical and biological lens, the evolution of neural networks becomes a story of relentless pursuit to replicate the intricacies of human cognition within computational frameworks.

Understanding neural networks requires delving into their basic structure, which involves neurons, layers, and activation functions. At the core, a neuron in a neural network is a simple unit that processes input to generate an output. Inputs are typically numerical values representing various features of the data being processed. Each input is assigned a weight to signify its importance. These weighted inputs are then summed up and passed through an activation function, which introduces non-linearity into the system, enabling the network to model complex patterns.

Layers in a neural network are structured hierarchically. The input layer receives the initial data, which is then forwarded to one or more hidden layers where computations take place. Each hidden layer consists of several neurons, and the complexity of the model increases with the number of these layers. Finally, the output layer produces the result, which could be a classification, regression value, or other desired output. The interplay between these layers allows the network to transform and interpret the input data through successive stages of abstraction.

Activation functions are essential in determining a neuron's output. Functions such as the sigmoid, hyperbolic tangent (tanh), and rectified linear unit (ReLU) are commonly employed. Sigmoid and tanh functions bound the output between fixed ranges and are useful for binary classifications. ReLU, introduced later, offers advantages in training deep networks by mitigating the vanishing gradient problem, allowing models to learn faster and perform better. Selecting appropriate activation functions is vital for training effective neural networks.

In contemporary applications, neural networks are ubiquitous due to their versatile architecture tailored to diverse tasks. Feedforward neural networks, the most basic type, illustrate the fundamental structure discussed. Here, information moves unidirectionally from the input layer to the output layer without any loops, making them suitable for simpler tasks. However, as tasks became more complex, advanced architectures like convolutional neural networks (CNNs) and recurrent neural networks (RNNs) emerged, each adding new dimensions to the basic structure to address specific problems in fields like image processing and sequence prediction.

The performance of a neural network largely depends on the quality of its training. During training, the network modifies the weights of the inputs according to the error rate of the output relative to the expected result. This process, known as backpropagation, calculates gradients to optimize the weights iteratively. Optimization techniques such as gradient descent and its variants are employed to minimize the error, improving the network's performance over time. Regularization techniques, such as dropout, are used to prevent overfitting, helping the model generalize effectively to new, unseen data.

Neural networks' ability to learn and generalize makes them indispensable in machine learning. They thrive on large datasets, where they identify intricate patterns that may be invisible to humans. For instance, in natural language processing, neural networks can comprehend and generate human language, powering technologies like chatbots and translation services. Similarly, in healthcare, they assist in diagnosing diseases from medical images, exemplifying their transformative impact across industries.

Despite their capabilities, neural networks are not without challenges. Training deep networks demands considerable computational resources and large quantities of labeled data. Additionally, understanding and interpreting the internal workings of neural networks remains a challenge due to their 'black-box' nature. Research continues to address these issues, striving to create more efficient, interpretable, and accessible AI systems.

Training Neural Networks

The training process of neural networks is central to their ability to learn and make accurate predictions. This process involves several key components, among which the backpropagation algorithm, gradient descent optimization techniques, and common loss functions play pivotal roles.

Backpropagation is a fundamental algorithm used to train artificial neural networks by minimizing the cost function, which measures the difference between the predicted output and the actual output. The algorithm operates in two main phases: forward pass and backward pass. In the forward pass, input data is transmitted through the network layer by layer until the final output is generated. In the backward pass, the error is calculated by comparing the predicted output with the actual output, and this error is then propagated backward through the network. By adjusting the weights and biases using the computed gradients, the model learns to reduce the error gradually. Backpropagation's significance lies in its ability to efficiently compute these gradients, enabling deep neural networks to learn complex patterns from large datasets (Backpropagation in Neural Network. GeeksforGeeks., 2024).

Gradient descent is an optimization technique commonly used during the training of neural networks to minimize the loss function. It operates by iteratively adjusting the model parameters in a way that minimizes the loss. There are several variants of gradient descent, such as stochastic gradient descent (SGD), mini-batch gradient descent, and batch gradient descent.. Stochastic gradient descent updates the model parameters for each training example, leading to faster convergence but higher variance. Mini-batch gradient descent strikes a balance by updating the parameters using small batches of training examples, combining the benefits of both SGD and batch gradient descent. Batch gradient descent, on the other hand, updates the parameters after computing the gradient over the entire dataset, offering more stable convergence but at a higher computational cost. Each variant has its own advantages and is chosen based on the specific requirements of the training process (How Does Gradient Descent and Backpropagation Work Together?. GeeksforGeeks., 2024).

Common loss functions are essential in the neural network training process as they quantify how well the model's predictions match the actual labels. One widely used loss function is the Mean Squared Error (MSE), particularly in regression tasks. MSE calculates the average of the squared differences between the predicted and actual values, providing a sense of how far off the predictions are on average. For classification tasks, Cross-Entropy Loss is frequently employed. This loss function evaluates the performance of a classification model where the output is a probability value ranging from 0 to 1. It increases as the predicted probability diverges from the actual label, thereby penalizing incorrect classifications more severely. Another popular loss function is the Hinge Loss, used mainly for training support vector machines. It focuses on maximizing the margin between classes, contributing to better classification boundaries. The choice of loss function significantly impacts the learning process and ultimately the model's performance.

Types of Neural Networks

Understanding different types of neural networks is crucial for grasping the foundations of generative models. We begin with feedforward neural networks (FNNs), which are one of the simplest forms of artificial neural networks. The basic architecture of an FNN includes an input layer, several hidden layers, and an output layer. Each layer consists of nodes or neurons connected to neurons in subsequent layers by edges. These edges have associated weights that adjust during training to minimize the error between predicted and actual outputs. Activation functions, such as ReLU or sigmoid, introduce non-linearity to the model, enabling it to capture complex patterns in data.

Feedforward neural networks find applications in various fields due to their simplicity and effectiveness. They are often used in tasks like image recognition, where they can classify images into predefined categories. In finance, FNNs help in credit scoring, detecting fraudulent transactions, and predicting stock prices. Additionally, these networks are used in healthcare to diagnose diseases by analyzing medical images and patient records. By adjusting the number of hidden layers and neurons, FNNs can be tailored to solve specific problems, demonstrating their versatility in diverse domains.

When implementing feedforward neural networks, there are guidelines to follow for optimal performance. Firstly, selecting the appropriate number of layers and neurons is vital for balancing model complexity and computational efficiency. Secondly, regularization methods such as dropout help prevent overfitting, ensuring that the network generalizes effectively to new, unseen data. Finally, choosing suitable learning rates and optimization algorithms like Adam or SGD can significantly impact training speed and convergence. By adhering to these guidelines, practitioners can effectively leverage FNNs for various applications, making them a fundamental tool in machine learning.

Convolutional neural networks (CNNs) revolutionize image processing by mimicking the visual perception process of humans. A CNN's structure consists of convolutional layers, pooling layers, and fully connected layers. Convolutional layers apply filters to input images, extracting features like edges or textures, while pooling layers reduce the spatial dimensions, retaining essential information and increasing computational efficiency. The extracted features are subsequently fed into fully connected layers to generate predictions. This hierarchical approach enables CNNs to capture local and global patterns in images, making them highly effective for visual tasks.

The operation of CNNs involves several stages, beginning with the application of convolutional filters to the input image. These filters slide across the image, producing feature maps that highlight regions with high filter response. Pooling layers then downsample these feature maps, typically using max pooling, which retains the most prominent features. After multiple convolutional and pooling layers, the resulting feature maps are flattened and processed by fully connected layers to generate output predictions. This pipeline allows CNNs to learn intricate patterns in images, making them indispensable in computer vision applications.

CNNs have become the benchmark for image processing tasks due to their exceptional performance. In the medical field, CNNs assist radiologists by automatically detecting anomalies in X-rays or MRI scans. In autonomous driving, CNNs enable vehicles to identify pedestrians, traffic signs, and obstacles, thereby enhancing safety. Moreover, facial recognition systems leverage CNNs to identify individuals with high accuracy, finding applications in security and authentication. These practical examples underscore the significance of CNNs in transforming how we interact with and interpret visual data.

Recurrent neural networks (RNNs) excel at handling sequence data, making them ideal for tasks involving temporal dependencies. The working principle of RNNs involves maintaining a hidden state that captures information from previous time steps, allowing the network to model sequential relationships. Unlike feedforward networks, RNNs have loops that enable information to persist, effectively creating short-term memory. This characteristic allows RNNs to understand context and generate coherent sequences in tasks like language modeling and time series prediction.

Applications of RNNs span various domains where sequence data is prevalent. In natural language processing (NLP), RNNs power language translation systems, enabling them to convert text from one language to another while preserving contextual meaning. In speech recognition, RNNs transcribe spoken words into text by considering phoneme sequences. Financial institutions use RNNs for time series forecasting, predicting stock prices based on historical data. By learning the temporal dependencies within sequences, RNNs provide valuable insights and predictions across a range of fields.

To effectively implement RNNs, certain guidelines need to be observed. Managing the vanishing gradient problem is crucial; techniques like Long Short-Term Memory (LSTM) networks and Gated Recurrent Units (GRUs) address this issue by incorporating gating mechanisms that regulate information flow. Regularization methods, such as dropout, help mitigate overfitting, ensuring the model's generalization capability. Furthermore, careful selection of hyperparameters, including learning rate and batch size, impacts training stability and performance. Adhering to these guidelines enhances the efficacy of RNNs, enabling robust modeling of sequential data.

Introduction to Generative Models

Generative models are a class of machine learning models that aim to understand and capture the underlying patterns and distributions in data to generate new, similar data. These models differ fundamentally from discriminative models in their approach and applications. While discriminative models focus on distinguishing between different classes within the given data, generative models are more concerned with modeling the entire data distribution, which allows them to create new data samples that resemble the original dataset.

The importance of generative models in machine learning cannot be overstated. They are essential for tasks where creating new, synthetic data is beneficial. For instance, in scenarios where obtaining large datasets is challenging or expensive, generative models can be employed to augment existing data, thereby improving the performance and robustness of other machine learning models. Moreover, generative models are instrumental in various creative fields such as art, music, and literature, where they can generate new content based on learned patterns.

One of the primary applications of generative models is in the domain of unsupervised learning, where the goal is to detect patterns without labeled inputs. This capability makes generative models invaluable for understanding complex data structures and for applications that require high levels of data augmentation and synthesis. Overall, generative models provide a robust framework for both practical applications and theoretical advancements in machine learning.

To better understand generative models, it is important to contrast them with discriminative models. Generative models learn to model the joint probability distribution of input features (X) and corresponding labels (Y). This means they can create new data instances by sampling from the learned distribution. Examples of generative models include Gaussian Mixture Models (GMMs), Hidden Markov Models (HMMs), as well as more recent advancements like Generative Adversarial Networks (GANs) and Variational Autoencoders (VAEs).

In contrast, discriminative models concentrate on learning the conditional probability of the label given the input features, represented as $P(Y|X)$. Instead of trying to model the entire data distribution, discriminative models aim to find the decision boundary that best separates different classes within the data. Common examples of discriminative models include Logistic Regression, Support Vector Machines (SVMs), and Neural Networks.

This distinction between generative and discriminative models has significant implications for their respective use cases. Generative models excel in tasks that require data generation, such as image synthesis, text generation, and data imputation. For example, GANs have revolutionized the field of image synthesis by generating highly realistic images that are often indistinguishable from real photographs. Conversely, discriminative models are typically used in classification tasks where the goal is to assign an input to one of several predefined categories. They outperform generative models in scenarios where the decision boundary needs to be accurately learned and applied, such as in object recognition and spam detection.

Another noteworthy aspect of generative models is their flexibility and adaptability across different domains. For instance, in natural language processing (NLP), recurrent neural networks (RNNs) and transformers can be used as generative models to produce coherent and contextually relevant text. These models learn the statistical properties of text data and can generate new sentences that fit the learned patterns. Similarly, in the domain of music, generative models can compose new pieces by learning from existing compositions, allowing for novel creations that follow the stylistic nuances of the training data.

Moreover, generative models are pivotal in handling incomplete data scenarios. Since they model the entire data distribution, they can infer missing values based on observed patterns, making them suitable for applications like medical diagnosis, where some clinical data may be missing or incomplete. By predicting and filling in these gaps, generative models enable more accurate and reliable analyses, leading to better-informed decisions.

The use of generative models also extends to the entertainment industry. In video game development, for instance, procedural generation techniques rely on generative models to create expansive and unique worlds without the need for extensive manual design. This not only reduces development time and costs but also enhances the gaming experience by providing players with ever-changing environments and scenarios.

Understanding the technical foundations of generative models further underscores their versatility. At a mathematical level, generative models aim to estimate the joint probability distribution $P(X, Y)$. This involves learning the prior distribution of the classes ($P(Y)$) and the class-conditional distribution of the input features ($P(X|Y)$). Techniques like maximum likelihood estimation (MLE) and Bayesian inference are often employed to derive these probabilities, enabling the models to generate new data points by sampling from the learned distributions.

Discriminative models, on the other hand, simplify the problem by directly learning the conditional probability $P(Y|X)$. They employ optimization techniques like gradient descent to minimize error rates and improve the accuracy of their predictions. By focusing solely on the decision boundary, discriminative models can efficiently handle large-scale classification tasks, provided ample labeled data is available for training.

The interplay between generative and discriminative models offers a comprehensive toolkit for tackling diverse machine learning challenges. While generative models provide the creative and inferential capabilities necessary for data generation and synthesis, discriminative models deliver the precision required for classification and decision-making tasks. Understanding and leveraging the strengths of each can lead to more effective and innovative solutions in various fields.

Probabilistic Generative Models

Probabilistic generative models are a cornerstone in the field of artificial intelligence, particularly useful for tasks that require understanding and simulating complex data distributions. These models aim to capture the underlying structure and dependencies within the data, enabling the generation of new, similar data samples. Unlike discriminative models that focus on predicting labels from input features, generative models learn the joint distribution of inputs and outputs, which allows them to create new data points that are representative of the observed dataset.

One of the most well-known probabilistic generative models is the Bayesian Network. Bayesian Networks are graphical models that depict the conditional dependencies among random variables through directed acyclic graphs. In the graph, the nodes represent the variables, and the edges illustrate the probabilistic dependencies between them. This structure allows for efficient computation of the joint probability distribution by factoring it into simpler conditional probabilities. Bayesian Networks are particularly valuable when dealing with incomplete data or when trying to model causal relationships because they inherently encode the directions of influence among variables.

The inference mechanism in Bayesian Networks is based on the principles of Bayesian updating. When new evidence is introduced, the network updates the probabilities of various hypotheses in a consistent manner, leveraging Bayes' Theorem. This updating process allows for dynamic adjustment of the model as more data becomes available, making Bayesian Networks highly flexible and adaptive. They are often used in fields like healthcare for diagnostic systems, where modeling uncertainty and making decisions under uncertainty are critical.

To implement a Bayesian Network, one starts by defining the structure of the network and then estimating the parameters from data. The structure can be learned from data using algorithms like the K2 algorithm, or it can be specified based on expert knowledge. Once the structure is defined, parameter estimation involves calculating the conditional probability tables (CPTs) for each node given its parents. For practical applications, software tools like Netica and BayesiaLab facilitate the creation and manipulation of Bayesian Networks, streamlining both the learning and inference processes.

Another fundamental probabilistic generative model is the Hidden Markov Model (HMM), which is widely used in time series analysis. HMMs are statistical models that describe a sequence of observed events generated by an underlying process that transitions between hidden states. Each state has a probability distribution governing the possible observations, and the system moves from one state to another according to a transition probability matrix. This dual-layered probabilistic framework makes HMMs particularly suited for sequential data where temporal dependencies are significant.

The applications of HMMs are diverse, ranging from speech recognition to finance. In speech recognition, HMMs are employed to model phonemes, where each phoneme corresponds to a hidden state, and the observed acoustic signal is the emission from these states. This allows the model to capture the temporal variability and coarticulation effects in speech, leading to more accurate recognition performance. Similarly, in finance, HMMs can be used to model market regimes, where each hidden state represents a different market condition (e.g., bull or bear markets), thereby facilitating better forecasting and risk management.

Training an HMM involves estimating the parameters that maximize the likelihood of the observed data. This usually encompasses the initial state distribution, the transition probabilities between states, and the emission probabilities. The Baum-Welch algorithm, an expectation-maximization technique, is commonly used for this purpose. Once trained, the Viterbi algorithm allows for efficient determination of the most likely sequence of hidden states given a sequence of observations, enabling practical applications such as decoding and prediction.

In time series analysis, HMMs provide a powerful tool for tasks such as anomaly detection and pattern recognition. By modeling the normal behavior of a system through the sequences of observations, any deviation from the expected pattern can be flagged as an anomaly. This capability is invaluable in domains like network security, where detecting unusual activity is crucial for preventing cyber-attacks. Additionally, HMMs can be extended to accommodate more complex structures, such as hierarchical HMMs, which provide even richer modeling capabilities for intricate sequential data.

Combining Bayesian Networks and Hidden Markov Models highlights the versatility and robustness of probabilistic generative models. Bayesian Networks excel in capturing static dependencies and making decisions under uncertainty, while HMMs are adept at modeling dynamic processes with temporal dependencies. Together, they offer comprehensive solutions for a wide range of applications, from healthcare diagnostics to financial modeling and natural language processing.

Generative Adversarial Networks (GANs)

Generative Adversarial Networks (GANs) have transformed the field of artificial intelligence by presenting a robust approach for data generation. At their core, GANs comprise two neural networks: the generator and the discriminator. The generator strives to produce data that closely resembles real data, whereas the discriminator's task is to distinguish between real and generated data. This dual structure leads to a fascinating adversarial process where both networks improve over time, making the generated data increasingly realistic.

The architecture of GANs begins with defining the roles of the generator and discriminator. The generator creates data samples from random noise, essentially learning how to map simple inputs to complex outputs. On the other hand, the discriminator evaluates these samples alongside real data, assigning probabilities to classify them correctly. Over multiple iterations, or epochs, the generator becomes adept at producing data that can deceive the discriminator. This constant back-and-forth improves the performance of both components, leading to high-quality data generation.

Understanding GANs also involves grasping their training methodology. Training GANs is an intricate process that requires balancing the improvements of both the generator and discriminator without one overpowering the other. The standard approach includes using loss functions like binary cross-entropy to measure the success of the discriminator in distinguishing real from fake data. The generator's objective is to maximize the discriminator's mistakes, effectively "tricking" it into misclassifying generated data as real. This adversarial training is computationally intensive and often requires sophisticated techniques to stabilize and enhance the training process.

Training GANs presents several challenges, primarily due to the adversarial nature of the setup. One major problem is mode collapse, where the generator produces a limited range of data, failing to capture the full diversity of the target distribution. Another challenge is ensuring convergence; both networks must reach an optimal state simultaneously, which is difficult to achieve. Researchers employ various strategies like Wasserstein loss and feature matching to address these challenges, aiming for more stable and effective training outcomes (Andreini et al., 2020).

Additionally, tuning hyperparameters such as learning rates and batch sizes plays a crucial role in training GANs. Hyperparameters need to be carefully adjusted to ensure that the learning progresses smoothly and efficiently. Additionally, employing regularization techniques can help reduce overfitting and improve the model's generalizability. Properly managing these aspects contributes significantly to the successful deployment of GANs in practical applications.

The applications of GANs are vast and varied, finding utility across numerous domains. In image generation, GANs have demonstrated remarkable capabilities by creating highly realistic images from scratch. These methods are particularly valuable in fields that require large datasets for training but suffer from limited availability of real-world data. Generating synthetic images helps in augmenting datasets, thereby improving the performance of machine learning models in tasks like object detection and classification.

Beyond image generation, GANs excel in style transfer, allowing users to apply specific artistic styles to images seamlessly. By learning the textures and patterns associated with different art styles, GANs can reimagine existing images in entirely new ways. This application has gained popularity among digital artists and content creators, who leverage GANs to explore creative possibilities effortlessly (Murali et al., n.d.).

Moreover, GANs are employed in areas such as medical imaging, where they assist in enhancing image quality and generating plausible medical scans. This is particularly useful for training purposes, enabling practitioners to gain expertise with diverse case scenarios. Furthermore, GANs contribute to advancements in video game development, music composition, and even pharmaceutical research, showcasing their versatility and transformative potential across various sectors.

Variational Autoencoders (VAEs)

Variational Autoencoders (VAEs) are a class of generative models that aim to learn a probabilistic mapping from an input space to a latent space and back to the input space. Unlike traditional autoencoders, VAEs introduce stochasticity in the encoding process, allowing for the generation of new data points that are similar to the training data. The core idea behind VAEs is to encode the input data into a continuous latent space, from which new samples can be generated by decoding this latent representation back to the original data space. This makes VAEs particularly useful for tasks such as generating images, creating new music, or synthesizing text.

The architecture of Variational Autoencoders consists of two main components: the encoder and the decoder. The encoder transforms the input data into a latent space, representing it as a probability distribution rather than a single point. Specifically, the encoder outputs the parameters of a Gaussian distribution, namely the mean and variance, which define the latent variables. The decoder then takes these latent variables and attempts to reconstruct the original input data. The key innovation here is the reparameterization trick, which allows gradients to flow through the stochastic sampling process, enabling efficient training of the model using gradient descent techniques.

Training a VAE involves optimizing an objective function that balances two goals: accurately reconstructing the input data and ensuring the latent space follows a predefined prior distribution, typically a standard Gaussian distribution. This is accomplished by minimizing a loss function that includes two components: the reconstruction loss and the Kullback-Leibler (KL) divergence. The reconstruction loss measures how well the decoded output matches the original input, while the KL divergence quantifies how closely the learned latent distribution matches the prior distribution. By optimizing both terms simultaneously, the VAE learns a meaningful latent representation that facilitates seamless data generation.

One crucial aspect of VAE training is the use of the encoder and decoder networks. The encoder network is tasked with learning the parameters of the latent distribution from the input data. This involves passing the input through several layers of neural networks to generate the mean and variance parameters. Once these parameters are obtained, the reparameterization trick is employed to sample latent variables from the distribution.

These latent variables are then fed into the decoder network, which aims to reconstruct the original data by passing the latent variables through multiple layers and producing an output that resembles the input data. The effectiveness of this training process hinges on the careful design of the encoder and decoder networks, as well as the choice of hyperparameters like learning rate and batch size.

Moreover, training VAEs requires balancing the trade-off between reconstruction quality and latent space regularization. Overemphasizing reconstruction loss might lead to overfitting, where the model learns to memorize the training data without capturing the underlying data distribution. Conversely, focusing too much on KL divergence may result in poor reconstruction performance. To address this, researchers often employ techniques like annealing, where the weight of the KL divergence term is gradually increased during training, allowing the model to first focus on learning good reconstructions before enforcing the prior distribution.

The applications of VAEs are vast and varied, making them a versatile tool in the realm of generative models. One prominent application is data generation, where VAEs can produce new data samples that resemble the training data. For instance, in the domain of image generation, VAEs can create realistic images by sampling from the latent space and decoding the latent variables into images. This capability has been leveraged in fields like art generation, where artists and designers use VAEs to generate novel artistic creations based on existing styles.

Another important application of VAEs is in anomaly detection. By learning the underlying distribution of normal data, VAEs can detect anomalies or outliers that deviate from this learned distribution. This is particularly useful in scenarios like fraud detection, where identifying unusual patterns in transaction data can help flag potentially fraudulent activities. Similarly, in industrial settings, VAEs can monitor sensor data to detect equipment failures or malfunctions, improving maintenance and operational efficiency.

Additionally, VAEs have found applications in the realm of personalized medicine and healthcare. By analyzing patient data, VAEs can generate synthetic patient profiles that preserve privacy while enabling the study of rare diseases or treatment outcomes. This synthetic data can be used to train machine learning models without compromising patient confidentiality. Furthermore, VAEs have been employed in drug discovery, where they help generate novel molecular structures with desirable properties, accelerating the development of new pharmaceuticals.

Autoregressive Models

Autoregressive models are a fundamental type of generative model used extensively in various machine learning tasks. These models predict subsequent data points by conditioning on previous ones, making them highly effective for sequential data. Notable examples of autoregressive models include PixelCNN and PixelRNN, both of which have demonstrated substantial success in generating high-quality images. PixelCNN employs convolutional layers to capture spatial dependencies, while PixelRNN uses recurrent layers to model temporal dependencies effectively. These models highlight the core principle of autoregression—leveraging past information to predict future outcomes.

PixelCNN generates images pixel by pixel, where each pixel is conditioned on the previously generated pixels. This conditioning allows PixelCNN to produce coherent and visually appealing images. The model's architecture involves stacking multiple convolutional layers, enabling it to capture complex patterns within the image. On the other hand, PixelRNN extends this approach by utilizing recurrent neural networks (RNNs) to handle pixel dependencies. The use of RNNs makes PixelRNN particularly adept at capturing long-range dependencies, offering improvements over traditional convolutional methods. Both models underscore the versatility and efficiency of autoregressive techniques in handling image data.

The mechanics of autoregressive models revolve around sequence generation and likelihood estimation. In these models, the goal is to generate sequences where each element depends on its predecessors. For instance, in text generation, an autoregressive model predicts the next word based on the previous ones. This process continues iteratively until the desired sequence length is achieved. Likelihood estimation plays a crucial role here, as the model must assign probabilities to each predicted element. By maximizing the likelihood of observed data, the model fine-tunes its parameters to improve prediction accuracy over time.

Sequence generation in autoregressive models involves step-by-step sampling from the learned distribution. During each step, the model uses previously sampled elements to guide the next prediction. This iterative process ensures that the generated sequence adheres to the patterns found in the training data. Additionally, likelihood estimation aids in evaluating the quality of these predictions. High likelihood values indicate that the model is confident in its predictions, while low values suggest uncertainty. Balancing these aspects enables autoregressive models to produce sequences that are both plausible and contextually relevant.

Applications of autoregressive models span across various domains, with remarkable impact in text and image generation. In text generation, models like GPT-3 exemplify the power of autoregression, producing coherent and context-aware paragraphs based on initial prompts. These models facilitate a wide range of applications, including automated content creation, chatbots, and language translation. By predicting each word progressively, they maintain grammatical accuracy and semantic consistency, providing valuable tools for natural language processing tasks.

In image generation, autoregressive models like PixelCNN and PixelRNN have set new benchmarks for visual creativity. These models enable the creation of photorealistic images, artistic renditions, and even novel visual styles. Their ability to generate images pixel by pixel ensures high fidelity and coherence. Moreover, autoregressive image models find applications in fields such as art, design, and entertainment, where generating high-quality visuals is paramount. Whether creating new artwork or enhancing existing images, these models offer powerful capabilities for visual exploration and innovation.

Other Generative Models

Normalizing flows are an advanced type of generative model that seeks to transform simple distributions, such as a Gaussian distribution, into more complex ones through a series of invertible and smooth transformations. The underlying concept revolves around the chain rule for calculating the probability density function of transformed variables. Flow-based models utilize these principles to provide exact likelihoods for data generation and reconstruction tasks, making them a powerful tool in scenarios requiring precise probabilistic outputs.

The working principle of normalizing flows begins with selecting a simple initial distribution from which samples are drawn. This distribution is then passed through a sequence of invertible transformations, each designed to progressively increase the complexity of the data representation while maintaining the ability to calculate the exact probability density using the change-of-variable formula. This process allows normalizing flows to learn intricate data patterns and relationships in a highly interpretable and mathematically tractable manner.

One notable use case for normalizing flows is in generating high-resolution images where exact likelihood evaluation is crucial, such as medical imaging or satellite image processing. They are also employed in anomaly detection within large datasets due to their capacity for precise density estimation. Moreover, normalizing flows have found applications in reinforcement learning as they enable efficient sampling from complex action spaces, thus enhancing the decision-making processes in dynamic environments (Unifying Simulation and Inference with Normalizing Flows. arxiv.org., n.d.).

Energy-based models (EBMs) offer another approach to generative modeling by leveraging the concept of energy functions to capture data dependencies. Unlike other models that directly parameterize probability distributions, EBMs compute an energy score for each possible state of the data, where lower energy corresponds to higher probability. This technique stems from statistical physics and helps model the potential and constraints inherent in complex systems.

Training EBMs involves minimizing the energy values assigned to observed data points while ensuring higher energy for improbable configurations. This process typically employs gradient-based optimization techniques, facilitated by modern advancements in deep learning frameworks. One challenge in training EBMs is estimating the partition function, a normalizing constant needed to convert energy scores into valid probabilities. Despite this, strategies like contrastive divergence and score matching have been developed to alleviate computational costs, making EBM training more feasible.

Applications of EBMs span various domains, including image and speech synthesis, where they excel in generating realistic and high-fidelity outputs. Additionally, EBMs are used in natural language processing tasks for text generation and sentiment analysis, benefiting from their robust capacity to handle high-dimensional data and capture contextual nuances. Furthermore, EBMs play a vital role in scientific computing, particularly in simulating physical phenomena and understanding the behavior of complex systems in fields like biology and chemistry (F. Necati Çatbaş et al., 2023).

Summary of Fundamental Principles in Generative Models

This chapter has delved into the foundational principles and concepts underlying generative models, emphasizing the critical role of probability in modeling randomness and uncertainty. We began by exploring probability distributions like the Normal, Binomial, and Poisson distributions, which are essential for understanding data patterns and making predictions. These distributions are pivotal in various applications within artificial intelligence and machine learning, particularly when dealing with incomplete or uncertain information.

We then examined statistical inference, highlighting the importance of descriptive statistics in summarizing datasets and inferential statistics in making generalizations about populations. Descriptive measures like mean, median, mode, variance, and standard deviation offer insights into data characteristics, while inferential techniques such as hypothesis testing and confidence intervals help draw conclusions from sample data. The frequentist and Bayesian approaches were compared, each with its strengths and limitations, underscoring the importance of context in choosing the right method.

The discussion on random variables and expectation provided a deeper understanding of how these concepts are used to model real-world phenomena. Discrete and continuous random variables were differentiated, and the significance of expected value and variance in predicting long-term averages was explained. These concepts form the backbone of risk assessment and statistical inference, crucial for decision-making under uncertainty.

The Law of Large Numbers and the Central Limit Theorem are fundamental theorems in probability theory. They assure that with larger samples, our estimates become more accurate and stable. Understanding these theorems is vital for anyone working with large datasets, as they underpin many statistical methods and real-world applications, from quality control to clinical trials.

We also touched upon the definition and scope of machine learning, differentiating between supervised and unsupervised learning, and introducing various algorithms. Machine learning techniques like regression, classification, clustering, and association were covered, alongside models such as linear regression, decision trees, and support vector machines. Key concepts such as training and testing data, cross-validation, overfitting, underfitting, and evaluation metrics were discussed, providing a robust framework for building effective machine learning models.

Neural networks, such as feedforward neural networks, convolutional neural networks, and recurrent neural networks, were examined in depth. Each type's structure, operation, and applications were highlighted, emphasizing their versatility and effectiveness in handling complex tasks like image recognition, time series prediction, and language processing. The training process involving backpropagation, gradient descent, and loss functions was explained, along with guidelines for implementing these networks effectively.

Understanding the intricacies of generative models, including probabilistic generative models, GANs, VAEs, autoregressive models, normalizing flows, and energy-based models, allows us to appreciate their diverse applications and potential. From generating realistic images and text to anomaly detection and personalized medicine, these models open new avenues for innovation and practical solutions across various fields.

As we move forward, it is essential to consider the ethical implications and potential societal impact of these advanced technologies. While generative models offer remarkable capabilities, they also raise concerns about data privacy, security, and misuse. It is crucial for practitioners to navigate these challenges responsibly, ensuring that the benefits of generative AI are harnessed while mitigating risks.

In conclusion, the foundational principles and concepts discussed in this chapter provide a comprehensive understanding of generative models and their significance in artificial intelligence. As you continue your exploration, consider how these models can be applied to solve real-world problems and contribute to advancements in technology and society.

The journey into the world of generative AI is just beginning, with endless possibilities waiting to be discovered.

References

7 Machine Learning Algorithms to Know: A Beginner's Guide. Coursera. (n.d.). https://www.coursera.org/articles/machine-learning-algorithms

Andreini, P., Bianchini, M., Bonechi, S., Mecocci, A., Scarselli, F. (2020, February). *Image generation by GAN and style transfer for agar plate image segmentation.* Computer Methods and Programs in Biomedicine. https://pubmed.ncbi.nlm.nih.gov/31891902/

Backpropagation in Neural Network. GeeksforGeeks. (2024, March). https://www.geeksforgeeks.org/backpropagation-in-neural-network/

Bansal, S. (2019, April). *Supervised and Unsupervised learning.* GeeksforGeeks. https://www.geeksforgeeks.org/supervised-unsupervised-learning/

Bradley University. (2020, February). *DNP-level nurses will encounter both descriptive and inferential statistics.* Bradley University Online. https://onlinedegrees.bradley.edu/blog/whats-the-difference-between-descriptive-and-inferential-statistics/

Cavey, P. (n.d.). *Chapter 7 Central Limit Theorem and law of large numbers | Foundations of Statistics.* bookdown.org. https://bookdown.org/peter_neal/math4081_notes/Sec_CLT.html

Crossa, D., López, A., López, O. (2022, January). *Overfitting, Model Tuning, and Evaluation of Prediction Performance.* www.ncbi.nlm.nih.gov. https://www.ncbi.nlm.nih.gov/books/NBK583970/

Exploring Generative Models: Applications, Examples, and Key Concepts. GeeksforGeeks. (2024, May). https://www.geeksforgeeks.org/exploring-generative-models-applications-examples-and-key-concepts/

GeeksforGeeks. (2023, August). *Machine Learning Algorithms.* GeeksforGeeks. https://www.geeksforgeeks.org/machine-learning-algorithms/

Geeksforgeeks. (2019, January). *Neural Networks | A beginners guide.* GeeksforGeeks. https://www.geeksforgeeks.org/neural-networks-a-beginners-guide/

Guetterman, T. (2019, March). *Basics of Statistics for Primary Care Research.* Family Medicine and Community Health. https://www.ncbi.nlm.nih.gov/pmc/articles/PMC6583801/

How Does Gradient Descent and Backpropagation Work Together?. GeeksforGeeks. (2024, February). https://www.geeksforgeeks.org/how-does-gradient-descent-and-backpropagation-work-together/

Modern Statistics for Modern Biology - 1 Generative Models for Discrete Data. web.stanford.edu. (n.d.). https://web.stanford.edu/class/bios221/book/01-chap.html

Probabilistic Models in Machine Learning. GeeksforGeeks. (2023, May). https://www.geeksforgeeks.org/probabilistic-models-in-machine-learning/

Real-Life Examples of Supervised Learning and Unsupervised Learning. GeeksforGeeks. (2024, March). https://www.geeksforgeeks.org/real-life-examples-of-supervised-learning-and-unsupervised-learning/

Reid, E. (n.d.). *Library Guides: ChatGPT, AI, and Implications for Higher Education: History of AI and Neural Networks. libguides.aurora.edu.* https://libguides.aurora.edu/ChatGPT/History-of-AI-and-Neural-Networks

Research Portal. iro.uiowa.edu. (n.d.). https://iro.uiowa.edu/esploro/outputs/conferenceProceeding/An-Evolutionary-Approach-to-Variational-Autoencoders/9984259431602771

Robinson (https://ts-robinson.com),,) T. (n.d.). *Chapter 4 Weak Law of Large Numbers and Central Limit Theorem | 10 Fundamental Theorems for Econometrics. bookdown.org.* https://bookdown.org/ts_robinson1994/10EconometricTheorems/wlln.html

The Difference Between Generative and Discriminative Machine Learning Algorithms. GeeksforGeeks. (2023, July). https://www.geeksforgeeks.org/the-difference-between-generative-and-discriminative-machine-learning-algorithms/

Unifying Simulation and Inference with Normalizing Flows. arxiv.org. (n.d.). https://arxiv.org/html/2404.18992v1

ved from https://ieeexplore.ieee.org/document/8999068/

CHAPTER 3

Generative Adversarial Networks (GANs)

Generative Adversarial Networks (GANs) represent a transformative approach within the realm of deep learning. Ever since their inception by Ian Goodfellow and his colleagues in 2014, GANs have significantly altered how synthetic data is generated and utilized across various fields. By setting up an adversarial dynamic between two neural networks—the generator and the discriminator—GANs have carved out a unique niche in machine learning, particularly by advancing the capabilities for generating realistic images, enhancing data quality, and innovating new applications.

This chapter delves into the core principles and architectural components that make GANs a pivotal technology. Readers will gain insights into the foundational structure consisting of the generator and discriminator, understanding their interplay and individual roles in the adversarial setup. The challenges encountered during training, such as mode collapse and stability issues, are examined alongside practical solutions to mitigate these problems. Furthermore, the chapter explores various GAN variants like DCGAN, WGAN, CycleGAN, and StyleGAN, highlighting their distinctions and specific use cases. Finally, real-world applications in diverse domains such as image generation, data augmentation, super-resolution, and medical imaging underscore the practical utility and ongoing innovations enabled by GANs.

Concept and Architecture

Generative Adversarial Networks (GANs) have emerged as a groundbreaking approach in the field of deep learning. Introduced by Ian Goodfellow and his colleagues in 2014, GANs have since revolutionized generative modeling, an unsupervised learning technique that automatically discovers and learns patterns in input data. The primary significance of GANs lies in their ability to generate new, realistic data that mirrors the original dataset, making them highly useful across various domains such as image synthesis, super-resolution, and data augmentation.

At its core, a GAN's architecture comprises two primary components: the generator and the discriminator. The generator's role is to produce synthetic data that closely resembles the real data it has been trained on. It starts with a random noise vector, which it transforms through multiple layers to produce an output that imitates real data. Conversely, the discriminator functions as a classifier, distinguishing between real data samples and those produced by the generator. This adversarial setup creates a dynamic where the generator continuously strives to improve its outputs to fool the discriminator, while the discriminator simultaneously gets better at detecting fake data.

The interplay between the generator and discriminator forms the essence of the adversarial nature of GANs. In this game-theoretic framework, both models are engaged in a zero-sum game: the generator attempts to generate data so realistic that it can deceive the discriminator, and the discriminator endeavors to correctly identify whether the data is real or fake. This continuous back-and-forth pushes both models to enhance their capabilities, resulting in highly realistic synthetic data over time. The adversarial training process involves alternately updating the weights of the generator and discriminator based on a predefined loss function, ensuring that both networks continue to evolve and improve.

Central to the training of GANs is the min-max optimization problem, which defines how the generator and discriminator are trained. The objective for the generator is to maximize the probability of the discriminator misclassifying generated data as real, while the discriminator aims to minimize this probability. This is formalized mathematically as a min-max game where the generator tries to minimize the maximum loss inflicted by the discriminator. Specifically, the generator seeks to minimize the log probability of the discriminator being correct, and the discriminator aims to maximize this value. This dual objective ensures that both networks are constantly pushed to refine their outputs and predictions.

Understanding the origins and foundational architecture of GANs is crucial for grasping their transformative impact on deep learning. By framing the problem of generative modeling as a supervised learning task with two competing neural networks, GANs have introduced a novel way to train models capable of creating highly realistic synthetic data. This innovation has paved the way for numerous applications and advancements in artificial intelligence, making GANs one of the most influential developments in recent years.

GENERATIVE ADVERSIAL NETWORK DIAGRAM:

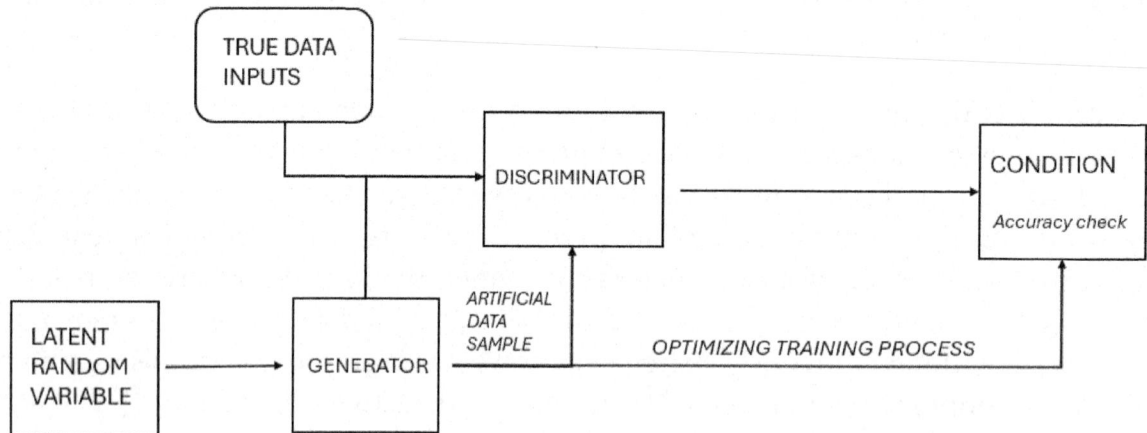

Detailed Explanation of Generator and Discriminator

In the context of Generative Adversarial Networks (GANs), the generator and discriminator serve as two foundational components that work together to create synthetic data that mimics real-world data. The primary function of the generator is to create synthetic data samples that are indistinguishable from real data to an observer or another model, such as the discriminator. This process begins with the generator receiving a random input, commonly referred to as "noise." By processing this noise through its neural network layers, the generator produces a data sample that aims to mimic the properties and characteristics of real data.

The effectiveness of the generator lies in its ability to learn and adapt. At the start, the generated samples may be far off from real data. However, through continuous training and adjustments based on feedback from the discriminator, the generator improves its output. The ultimate goal is for the generator to produce samples so realistic that even the discriminator, a sophisticated binary classifier, cannot reliably distinguish them from actual data. This creates a self-improving loop where the generator continually refines its techniques to achieve high-quality synthetic data generation.

There are several common architectures deployed for designing generators, with fully connected networks and Convolutional Neural Networks (CNNs) being the most prevalent. In simpler tasks, fully connected networks may suffice, but for more complex and high-dimensional data such as images, CNNs are often preferred due to their ability to capture spatial hierarchies efficiently. CNN-based generators typically consist of several layers, including convolutional layers, upsampling layers, and activation functions like ReLU or Tanh. These layers work together to transform the initial noise into a coherent and realistic data sample, using learned patterns and features from the training set.

The transformation of random noise into realistic data occurs through an abstract representation known as latent space. Latent space allows the generator to map high-dimensional noise vectors to meaningful data distributions. To achieve this, the generator employs various layers including linear transformations, reshaping mechanisms, and non-linear activations. During training, these parameters are adjusted to optimize the mapping, ensuring that the generated outputs become increasingly realistic over time. Essentially, latent space acts as an intermediary representation that captures the essence and structure of the real data, enabling the generator to create convincing synthetic samples.

Understanding how latent space operates provides insight into the versatility and power of GANs. For instance, by manipulating points within the latent space, one can generate diverse outputs, highlighting the flexibility and creativity embedded in the generator's architecture. Whether it's altering a few dimensions to change specific features of the data (like rotation or color in images) or exploring entirely different regions of the latent space to produce novel examples, this mechanism underscores the adaptability of GANs in generating varied and realistic data samples.

The discriminator also plays a critical role by assessing the authenticity of the data samples. Its primary objective is to distinguish between real data obtained from the training set and synthetic data produced by the generator. Acting as a binary classifier, the discriminator assigns probability scores indicating whether a given data sample is real (closer to 1) or fake (closer to 0). Through this evaluation process, the discriminator provides essential feedback to the generator, guiding it on how to improve its outputs.

The architectural choices for discriminators often mirror those of generators, particularly when dealing with image data. Convolutional Neural Networks (CNNs) are also commonly used in discriminators due to their proficiency in extracting hierarchical features and patterns from images. A typical discriminator network might include convolutional layers, pooling layers, and fully connected layers, all working together to scrutinize the input data rigorously. The application of activation functions like LeakyReLU further enhances the model's ability to make nuanced decisions about the authenticity of the data.

One of the core elements of the discriminator's operation is its loss function, which quantifies its performance. The most commonly used loss functions are the Binary Cross-Entropy Loss or variations involving the Wasserstein distance in more advanced GAN versions like Wasserstein GANs (WGANs). The discriminator seeks to maximize its accuracy in identifying real versus fake samples, while the generator simultaneously works to minimize the discriminator's success in this task. This adversarial setup creates a dynamic training environment where both models progressively enhance their capabilities.

Training Techniques and Challenges

Training Generative Adversarial Networks (GANs) involves a meticulous process that demands careful attention and strategy. The training procedure typically follows a step-by-step approach where the generator and discriminator are alternately updated to improve their respective functionalities. Initially, the generator produces synthetic data from random noise. This synthetic data is then fed into the discriminator alongside real data. The discriminator's role is to distinguish between the real data and the synthetic data. During each iteration, the parameters of the generator are adjusted to minimize the discrepancy between its synthetic data and the real data, while the discriminator's parameters are tuned to maximize its ability to distinguish the two.

The alternating updates ensure that both networks improve simultaneously. For instance, one common practice is to update the discriminator several times for every update of the generator. This ensures that the discriminator is well-trained to find flaws in the generator's output, thereby pushing the generator to create more accurate and realistic data. Different learning rates can also be employed for the generator and discriminator to balance their training progress, as suggested by Wenzel (2023). This nuanced approach helps maintain equilibrium and prevents either network from overpowering the other too quickly.

Moreover, another critical aspect of the training procedure involves hyperparameter tuning. Parameters like batch size, learning rate, and epochs play significant roles in determining the success of the GAN model. Properly setting these values can avoid pitfalls and enhance the performance of the networks. Using techniques like batch normalization and regularization can further stabilize training by reducing variance and overfitting. By meticulously following these steps, the training of GANs becomes more robust and effective, yielding high-quality synthetic data.

One of the most prominent challenges faced during GAN training is mode collapse. Mode collapse happens when the generator produces a narrow range of outputs, failing to capture the full diversity of the training data's distribution. This problem manifests when the generator finds an easy solution that the discriminator cannot easily detect, leading to repetitive and similar synthetic outputs. To tackle this issue, it is essential to employ strategies that promote diversity in the generated data.

Various techniques have been devised to address mode collapse. One effective method is minibatch discrimination, which involves calculating the similarity between generated samples within a mini-batch. If the samples are too similar, a penalty is applied to the generator. This incentivizes the generator to produce a more diverse range of outputs. Another commonly used method is feature matching, which uses the average features of real and fake examples as a new objective. Instead of just minimizing the discrepancy between individual samples, the generator aims to match the statistical properties of the real data, thus promoting variety.

Additionally, adjusting the learning rate can mitigate mode collapse, as highlighted by the NCBI Bookshelf (Wenzel, 2023). A lower learning rate provides more stability and allows for finer adjustments, which can prevent the generator from converging on a single mode prematurely. Combining these strategies effectively reduces the chances of mode collapse and enhances the diversity and realism of the outputs produced by GANs.

Stability issues often arise during GAN training, posing another significant challenge. Non-convergence is a common problem where neither the generator nor the discriminator reaches an optimal state. This instability stems from the adversarial nature of GANs, where the generator and discriminator are continuously trying to outsmart each other. If one network gets too far ahead of the other, it can lead to oscillations or divergence in the training process.

To ensure convergence and stability, various methods can be employed. One approach is to use different architectures for the generator and discriminator. For example, using convolutional layers in both networks, as seen in Deep Convolutional GANs (DCGANs), has been shown to improve training stability. Another technique is one-sided label smoothing, where instead of using a hard label of 1 for real images, a slightly lower value is used. This prevents the discriminator from becoming overconfident and helps maintain a balanced training dynamic.

Furthermore, cost function selection plays a vital role in maintaining stability. Traditional loss functions like binary cross-entropy can lead to unstable training if not properly tuned. Alternative loss functions such as the Wasserstein distance, used in Wasserstein GANs (WGANs), offer a more stable gradient signal and can significantly improve convergence properties. By adopting these methods, the stability of GAN training can be enhanced, leading to more reliable and consistent results.

Another formidable obstacle in GAN training is the problem of vanishing gradients. Vanishing gradients occur when the gradient signals become too small during backpropagation, hindering the learning process. This issue is particularly prevalent when using certain activation functions or initializing weights poorly. In the context of GANs, vanishing gradients can severely slow down the training progress and impede the development of both the generator and discriminator.

To counteract vanishing gradients, one common strategy is to employ advanced initialization techniques such as Xavier or He initialization. These methods help set appropriate initial weight values, ensuring that gradients remain at a manageable scale during the early stages of training. Another effective approach is to utilize alternative activation functions like Leaky ReLU, which allows a small, non-zero gradient when the unit is not active. This helps maintain a positive flow of gradients throughout the network.

Variants of GANs

To address the growing demands for more efficient and effective GAN models, various variants have been developed. A notable variant is the Deep Convolutional GAN (DCGAN). DCGAN leverages convolutional layers in both the generator and discriminator components of the GAN architecture. This adaptation significantly enhances image generation tasks by improving the model's ability to capture and replicate intricate details present in training data. The convolutional layers help to preserve spatial hierarchies and structures within images, leading to higher-quality synthetic outputs.

DCGAN DIAGRAM:

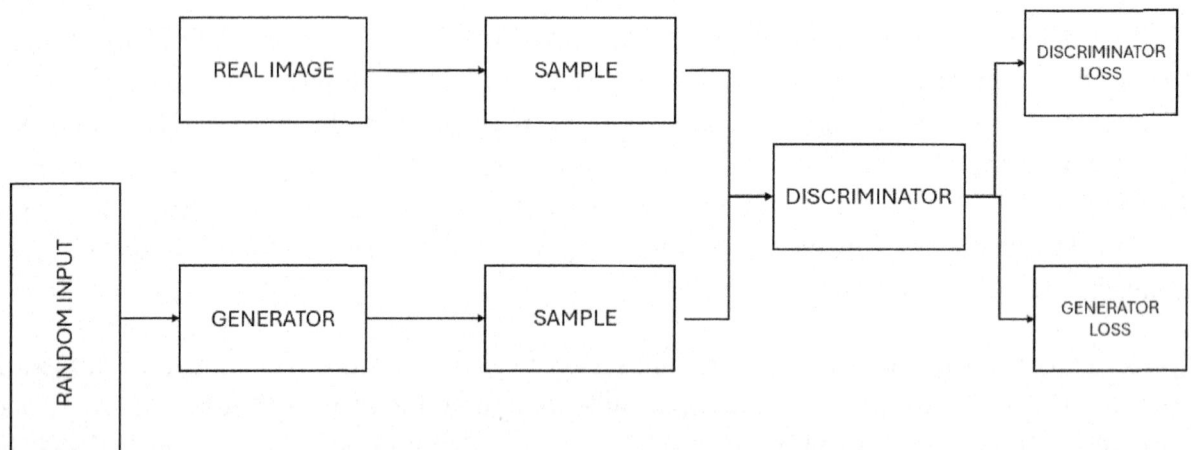

The implementation of convolutional layers in DCGANs not only boosts the quality of generated images but also stabilizes the training process. Unlike traditional fully connected networks, convolutional layers apply filters that traverse over the input data, allowing the network to learn important features at different scales. This hierarchical feature extraction is crucial for generating realistic images, as it mimics the way human visual systems process visual information. As a result, DCGANs are better equipped to produce visually coherent and detailed images compared to their predecessors.

Moreover, the stability offered by DCGANs contributes to their widespread adoption in various applications. The improved performance and reliability make DCGAN an attractive choice for tasks such as image synthesis, super-resolution, and style transfer. By addressing some of the limitations of earlier GAN models, DCGAN has paved the way for further exploration and innovation in the field of generative adversarial networks.

Another significant variant is the Wasserstein GAN (WGAN), which introduces the concept of Wasserstein distance, also known as Earth Mover's Distance. Unlike traditional GANs that use binary cross-entropy loss, WGAN employs the Wasserstein distance to measure the difference between the generated and real data distributions. This approach addresses the issue of vanishing gradients prevalent in standard GANs, ensuring more stable and efficient training. The use of Wasserstein distance provides a smoother and more informative gradient signal, leading to improved convergence properties.

WGANs differ from conventional GANs in both architecture and training procedures. Instead of using sigmoid activation functions, WGANs utilize linear output layers and remove the need for logarithmic transformations in the loss calculation. Additionally, WGANs enforce a Lipschitz constraint on the critic (the new name for the discriminator), often achieved through weight clipping or gradient penalty techniques. These modifications result in a more robust and reliable training process, mitigating common issues like mode collapse, where the generator produces limited variations of outputs.

The advantages of WGANs extend beyond their theoretical improvements. In practice, WGANs have demonstrated superior performance in generating high-quality images, especially in scenarios where standard GANs struggle. By providing a more consistent gradient flow and better handling of the underlying data distribution, WGANs enable the creation of more diverse and realistic outputs. This makes WGANs a valuable tool for applications requiring precise and reliable synthetic data generation.

CycleGAN is another notable variant designed for image-to-image translation without paired examples. Traditional methods for this task often require a set of matching image pairs to train the model. CycleGAN eliminates this requirement by introducing cycle consistency loss, a key innovation that ensures the translated image can be converted back to its original form. This bidirectional mapping allows CycleGAN to learn from unpaired datasets, making it highly versatile and applicable to a wide range of domains, such as artistic style transfer, photo enhancement, and domain adaptation.

The CycleGAN architecture features two pairs of generators and discriminators, with each pair responsible for converting images between different domains. The cycle consistency loss ensures that an image translated from domain A to domain B and then back to domain A should closely resemble the original image. This constraint encourages the generators to produce realistic and accurate translations while preserving essential features and details. Consequently, CycleGAN can achieve impressive results even in challenging tasks where acquiring paired training data is impractical or impossible.

The impact of CycleGAN extends to numerous real-world applications. For instance, in medical imaging, CycleGAN can be used to enhance or transform images from different imaging modalities, aiding in better diagnosis and analysis. In the field of computer graphics, CycleGAN enables seamless conversion between different artistic styles or enhancing low-quality photos. By overcoming the limitations of paired data requirements, CycleGAN has unlocked new possibilities for image-to-image translation, broadening the scope of what can be achieved with GAN-based models.

Lastly, StyleGAN represents a breakthrough in high-quality image synthesis and style mixing. What sets StyleGAN apart is its unique architecture, specifically designed to enable fine-grained control over the generated images' style and content. At the core of StyleGAN's architecture are style blocks that modulate intermediate feature maps at different layers of the generator. This allows for the separation of high-level attributes, such as pose and identity, from low-level details, like texture and color, facilitating targeted adjustments and manipulations.

StyleGAN's innovative design leads to remarkably diverse and realistic image outputs. The style mixing capability allows users to blend features from different source images, creating entirely new and unique visuals. For example, by combining the facial attributes of two individuals, StyleGAN can generate a novel face that inherits traits from both sources. This level of control and flexibility is particularly valuable in creative industries, such as digital art, advertising, and entertainment, where tailored and distinctive visuals are highly sought after.

Furthermore, StyleGAN has set new benchmarks in terms of image fidelity and variety. The combination of style blocks and progressive growing of the generator network enables StyleGAN to produce images with unprecedented levels of detail and realism. This has positioned StyleGAN as a leading tool for generative tasks, from creating photorealistic portraits to designing virtual avatars. The versatility and power of StyleGAN continue to inspire new research and applications, pushing the boundaries of what generative models can achieve.

Real-World Applications of GANs

Generative Adversarial Networks (GANs) have made remarkable strides in image generation and editing, especially within fields like art, fashion, and entertainment. In the art world, GANs are used to create new artistic styles or replicate existing ones with a level of detail and creativity previously unattainable by traditional methods. Artists can input sketches or abstract designs, and GANs can transform these into lifelike images or imaginative artworks. This capability allows artists to explore new creative avenues without being limited by manual skill constraints.

In the fashion industry, GANs assist designers in conceptualizing clothing designs from rough sketches or patterns. By generating photorealistic images of potential apparel, designers can visualize their ideas in full color and texture before moving on to the physical production stage. This reduces the time and cost associated with prototyping and enhances the designer's ability to experiment with various designs more freely. Entertainment industries, including film and video games, also see substantial benefits. GANs can produce high-resolution, realistic characters and environments from low-quality drafts, thereby expediting the visual development process and permitting creative teams to focus more on storytelling and gameplay elements.

In machine learning, large volumes of heterogeneous data are needed. GANs can help increase training datasets. Synthetic yet realistic data from GANs can be contributed to training sets to increase machine learning model performance and durability. Synthetic data from GANs can be useful when real-world data is scarce or expensive. Autonomous driving, where different environmental variables and uncommon events must be represented, benefits from this.

Moreover, GAN-generated data helps address biases present in initial datasets. By creating a wide variety of synthetic instances, GANs contribute to a more balanced dataset that better represents the real-world scenario. This not only enhances the model's accuracy but also ensures fairness and reduces the likelihood of biased outcomes. Various industries, including finance and healthcare, utilize this approach to train models more effectively, leading to improved predictive capabilities and more reliable decision-making processes.

Enhancing the resolution of images and videos through super-resolution techniques is another compelling application of GANs. Traditional methods often fall short in upgrading low-resolution content to high-definition levels without losing significant details. GANs, however, excel in this area by learning the intricate patterns and textures present in high-resolution images. This capability has profound implications in several sectors, including media, security, and mobile technologies.

For instance, film restoration can upgrade ancient, low-quality footage to new standards, safeguarding cultural heritage and making it accessible to modern audiences. Enhancing surveillance film visual quality can improve identification and investigation in security applications. In smartphones, GAN-driven super-resolution improves photo and video quality, giving users professional-grade imaging capabilities.

Applications of GANs in generating and improving medical images for diagnostics represent one of the most impactful uses in healthcare. High-quality medical images are essential for precise diagnosis and effective treatment planning. However, obtaining high-resolution images can be challenging due to limitations in current imaging technology and other practical constraints like patient movement. GANs bridge this gap by enhancing the resolution and clarity of medical images, making it easier for healthcare professionals to identify and analyze critical features.

Furthermore, GANs can generate synthetic medical images that mimic real patient data, providing an abundant source of training material for developing better diagnostic models. This is particularly important in fields like radiology and pathology, where detailed image analysis is essential. By augmenting the training datasets with high-quality synthetic images, GANs help improve the accuracy and reliability of AI-driven diagnostic tools. This leads to better patient outcomes through more precise and timely diagnoses.

Comprehensive Insights into GANs

We covered Generative Adversarial Networks' foundations, components, problems, varieties, and real-world applications in this chapter. We started by exploring GAN architecture and the generator-discriminator dynamic. GANs provide realistic synthetic data thanks to this adversarial framework's constant improvement.

The detailed explanation of the generator and discriminator revealed how these two neural networks collaborate to create and evaluate synthetic data. The generator transforms random noise into coherent data samples, while the discriminator strives to distinguish between real and fake data. This intricate process, involving latent space manipulation and sophisticated network architectures like Convolutional Neural Networks (CNNs), underscores the powerful complexity of GANs in generative modeling.

Training GANs presents unique challenges, such as mode collapse, stability issues, and vanishing gradients. To mitigate these problems, various techniques, including minibatch discrimination, feature matching, and advanced initialization methods, are employed. These strategies ensure that both the generator and discriminator evolve effectively, leading to robust and high-quality synthetic data generation.

We also explored several notable GAN variants, each tailored to address particular limitations and improve performance. Deep Convolutional GANs (DCGANs) leverage convolutional layers for better image generation, while Wasserstein GANs (WGANs) introduce the Wasserstein distance to stabilize training and improve gradient flow. CycleGANs enable unpaired image-to-image translation through cycle consistency loss, expanding the range of applications. StyleGANs offer fine-grained control over generated images, allowing users to manipulate styles and features with remarkable precision.

Real-world applications of GANs demonstrate their versatility and transformative impact across various domains. In art, fashion, and entertainment, GANs facilitate the creation of innovative designs and realistic visuals, enhancing creative processes. By augmenting training datasets, GANs address data scarcity and bias, improving the performance of machine learning models. Super-resolution techniques powered by GANs enhance image and video quality, benefiting fields such as media, security, and mobile technology. In healthcare, GANs generate and improve medical images, aiding in accurate diagnostics and better patient outcomes.

Understanding the capabilities and challenges associated with GANs provides valuable insights for aspiring AI practitioners, professionals looking to upskill, and tech enthusiasts. While the potential of GANs is immense, it is important to remain mindful of the ethical considerations and limitations inherent in using synthetic data. As GAN technology continues to advance, it will undoubtedly shape the future of artificial intelligence, driving innovation and opening new avenues for research and application.

Looking ahead, the development of more sophisticated GAN models and training techniques promises even greater advancements in generative modeling. By addressing current limitations and exploring new possibilities, GANs can further revolutionize industries and contribute to solving complex real-world problems. Exploring the ongoing evolution of GANs offers exciting opportunities for those keen on pushing the boundaries of artificial intelligence.

References

Agrawal, R., Sharma, K., Gonge, S., Joshi, R., & Singh, D.K. (Year of Publication). *Towards the Applications of Generative Adversarial Networks Beyond Images. IEEE Conference Publication.* https://doi.org/10.1109/XXXXX

Basics of Generative Adversarial Networks (GANs). GeeksforGeeks. (2020, July). https://www.geeksforgeeks.org/basics-of-generative-adversarial-networks-gans/

Chatterjee, S. (2024, May). *Generative Adversarial Networks: Everything You Need to Know. Emeritus Online Courses.* https://emeritus.org/blog/generative-adversarial-networks/

Jabbar, A., Li, X., Omar, B. (2020, June). *A Survey on Generative Adversarial Networks: Variants, Applications, and Training.* *arXiv:2006.05132 [cs, eess].* https://arxiv.org/abs/2006.05132

Roy, R. (2019, January). *Generative Adversarial Network (GAN).* *GeeksforGeeks.* https://www.geeksforgeeks.org/generative-adversarial-network-gan/

Wenzel, M. (2023, July). *[Box], Box 4: Best Practices for Stable GAN Training.* *www.ncbi.nlm.nih.gov.* https://www.ncbi.nlm.nih.gov/books/NBK597493/box/ch5.FPar103/?report=objectonly

CHAPTER 4

Variational Autoencoders (VAEs)

Variational Autoencoders (VAEs) are central to the evolving landscape of generative models, empowering practitioners to create meaningful and flexible data representations. VAEs stand out from traditional autoencoders by incorporating a probabilistic framework, which allows them to handle data uncertainty and generate diverse outputs. This paradigm shift not only enhances data reconstruction and generation capabilities but also provides a robust tool for exploring complex data distributions.

In this chapter, we will delve into the architecture and components that make VAEs unique, starting with an in-depth look at the encoder and decoder mechanisms. We will then explore the mathematical foundations underpinning VAEs, such as the Evidence Lower Bound (ELBO) and Kullback-Leibler (KL) divergence, which are crucial for understanding how these models learn and generalize. Additionally, we'll cover key training techniques, including balancing reconstruction and regularization losses, and address common challenges like mode and posterior collapse. By the end of this chapter, readers will have a comprehensive understanding of VAEs' structure, functionality, and their applications in various fields.

Concept and Architecture

Variational Autoencoders (VAEs) are generative models designed to learn a meaningful representation of data within a latent space. Unlike traditional autoencoders that aim for simple data compression and reconstruction, VAEs introduce a probabilistic approach that captures the inherent uncertainty in data generation. This unique characteristic allows VAEs to generate diverse outputs by sampling different points in the latent space, providing greater flexibility and robustness in data representation.

The core principle of VAEs lies in learning an effective encoding and decoding process through a neural network architecture. The encoder transforms input data into a probability distribution, which is then sampled to obtain a latent code. This latent code serves as a compressed representation of the data. The decoder uses this latent representation to reconstruct the original data with high accuracy. By incorporating probabilistic elements, VAEs can model complex data structures more accurately than deterministic models.

One key advantage of VAEs over traditional autoencoders is their ability to generate new data samples that resemble the training data. While traditional autoencoders typically output a single deterministic value for each encoded feature, VAEs output a distribution, allowing for multiple possible reconstructions. This probabilistic nature helps in better extrapolating and interpolating between data points within the latent space, enhancing the model's generative capabilities.

VAEs differentiate themselves from traditional autoencoders through their unique probabilistic framework. In a traditional autoencoder, the encoder compresses the input data into a fixed-size latent representation, and the decoder reconstructs the data from this representation. However, in a VAE, the encoder produces two vectors: the mean and the variance, defining a Gaussian distribution for each latent variable. This results in a more informative and flexible latent space representation compared to the single-point encoding in traditional autoencoders.

Moreover, traditional autoencoders lack the regularization mechanism present in VAEs. The KL divergence term in the VAE loss function ensures that the learned latent distribution aligns closely with a prior distribution. This regularization prevents overfitting and encourages smoother latent spaces, resulting in better generalization and more coherent sample generation. Consequently, VAEs provide a structured way to infer and generate data, making them suitable for various applications like image synthesis, anomaly detection, and data augmentation.

Incorporating probabilistic elements into the latent representation significantly enhances the robustness and flexibility of VAEs. Instead of treating latent variables as fixed points,

VAEs consider them as random variables drawn from a learned probability distribution. This approach mitigates overfitting by introducing stochasticity, ensuring that the latent space covers diverse data characteristics and variations. Such flexibility is crucial for handling real-world data's variability and noise.

The probabilistic nature of VAEs also facilitates more effective exploration of the latent space. By sampling from the learned distributions, VAEs can generate novel and realistic data instances not seen during training. This capability is particularly useful in creative tasks such as artwork generation or designing new molecules in drug discovery. Moreover, by tweaking the parameters of the learned distributions, one can control the diversity and specific features of the generated data, providing valuable insights and utility in various domains.

Ultimately, the integration of probabilistic elements makes VAEs powerful tools for data representation and generation. Their ability to model complex data distributions and generate varied outputs sets them apart from simpler autoencoder architectures and many other generative models. This holds promise for advancing AI applications that demand sophisticated data handling and innovative generation capabilities.

Differentiating VAEs from traditional autoencoders hinges on understanding their unique characteristics. Traditional autoencoders operate deterministically, focusing on direct data compression and reconstruction. They encode input data into a fixed-size latent vector and decode it back to the original data form. While effective for noise reduction and feature extraction, traditional autoencoders fall short in generating new, realistic data samples due to their limited representation capacity and deterministic nature.

Conversely, VAEs offer a more nuanced approach by incorporating probabilistic principles. By encoding data into a distribution rather than a single point, VAEs capture the underlying data variability more effectively. This not only improves data reconstruction but also enables the generation of diverse and plausible data samples. The KL divergence component in the VAE loss function further differentiates VAEs by ensuring that the latent space conforms to a predefined distribution, enhancing model robustness and generalization.

Additionally, VAEs excel in balancing reconstruction accuracy with latent space regularization. The interplay between the reconstruction loss and KL divergence ensures that the encoded representations are both faithful to the input data and organized within a meaningful latent space. This balance is crucial for achieving high-quality data generation and robust performance across various tasks, highlighting the superiority of VAEs over their traditional counterparts.

Highlighting the advantages of VAEs over other generative models underscores their significance in the field of AI. One major advantage is their structured latent space, which allows for controlled and interpretable data generation. By manipulating the latent variables, users can explore different aspects of the data manifold, leading to insightful discoveries and practical applications in fields like image editing and synthetic data creation.

Another notable benefit of VAEs is their capacity for semi-supervised learning. By leveraging part of the labeled data and a larger set of unlabeled data, VAEs can improve classification performance and reduce the need for extensive labeled datasets. This makes them especially valuable in scenarios where labeling data is expensive or impractical, such as medical imaging or rare event detection.

Understanding the Encoder, Decoder, and Latent Space

In the realm of Variational Autoencoders (VAEs), understanding the roles and functionalities of the encoder, decoder, and latent space is essential for grasping how these models achieve efficient data representation and generation. This section delves into each component, elucidating their functions, interactions, and benefits within the VAE framework.

VARIATIONAL AUTOENCODER DIAGRAM:

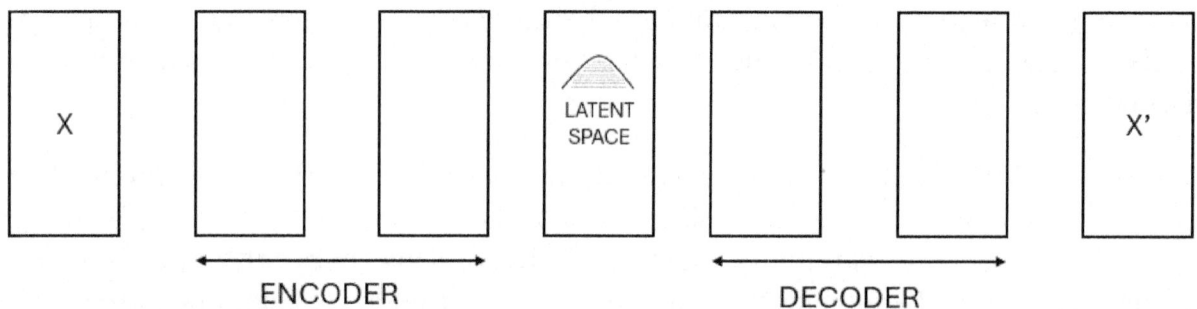

The encoder in a VAE plays the critical role of compressing input data into the latent space. This compression process involves transforming high-dimensional input data into a lower-dimensional representation by generating mean and variance vectors. These vectors define a distribution from which latent variables are sampled. The encoder essentially maps the input data to parameters of this distribution rather than specific points, ensuring that the encoded representation captures the inherent variability and uncertainty of the data. By leveraging neural networks, the encoder learns to identify and encode salient features of the input data, facilitating more meaningful representations even with complex datasets.

For example, when dealing with image data, the encoder extracts significant visual features such as shapes and textures, encoding them into a probabilistic latent representation. This probabilistic nature allows VAEs to handle variations and generate new data samples that are not mere replicas but variations guided by the learned distributions. This probabilistic encoding significantly enhances the model's ability to generalize from the training data, making it effective in various applications such as image generation and anomaly detection.

Moving on to the decoder, its primary function is to reconstruct data from the latent space, emphasizing the reconstruction process. Once the latent variables are sampled from the distribution defined by the encoder, the decoder transforms these variables back into the original data space. This transformation is akin to unraveling the compressed representation to retrieve the initial data or its close approximation. The decoder's neural network is trained to learn this reverse mapping accurately, ensuring that the reconstructed data retains the quality and fidelity of the input data to the highest possible degree.

In practical terms, if the VAE has been trained on images of handwritten digits, the decoder will use the latent variables to recreate digit images. Even when the latent samples are interpolated between known digits, the decoder can generate plausible new images, demonstrating the VAE's capacity for creativity and innovation. The success of the decoder in producing coherent outputs directly hinges on the optimization of the model, where reconstruction loss is minimized, reinforcing the decoder's ability to approximate the input data closely.

The latent space representation itself is a crucial aspect of VAEs, as it defines the structure and properties of the space where compressed data resides. Unlike traditional autoencoders that map inputs to fixed points, VAEs use a latent space characterized by continuous probability distributions. This latent space is often regularized to follow a specific prior distribution, commonly a standard normal distribution. By imposing such a constraint, the latent space becomes smooth and continuous, allowing for seamless interpolation between different data points and enabling the generation of novel samples by sampling from this space.

A well-structured latent space implies that similar inputs are mapped to nearby points in the space, preserving the intrinsic relationships among the data. For instance, different handwritings of the same digit would cluster around a specific region, while distinct digits occupy separate regions. This organization facilitates tasks like data interpolation and morphing, where smooth transitions between different samples can be achieved naturally, showcasing the generative power of VAEs.

One of the significant benefits of the probabilistic nature of the latent space in data generation is its ability to introduce stochasticity and diversity in the generated outputs. By sampling from the learned distribution during the generation phase, VAEs can produce a wide range of plausible data points rather than deterministic outputs. This capability is particularly beneficial in creative domains where generating diverse and original content is valuable, such as in art and music generation.

Furthermore, the probabilistic framework aids in handling uncertainties and variations in the data. In applications such as anomaly detection, the VAE learns the normal distribution of input data, enabling it to effectively identify outliers that deviate significantly from this learned distribution. This attribute makes VAEs robust tools in security and monitoring systems, where detecting anomalies swiftly and accurately is paramount.

Mathematical Foundations (ELBO, KL Divergence)

To optimize a Variational Autoencoder (VAE), understanding the mathematical underpinnings is crucial. A key concept is the Evidence Lower Bound, often abbreviated as ELBO. ELBO serves as the primary optimization objective for training VAEs. The essence of ELBO lies in its ability to balance the trade-off between reconstructing input data accurately and ensuring that the latent space representation closely follows a desired distribution.

The significance of ELBO becomes apparent when considering how it integrates both the reconstruction loss and the difference between the posterior and prior distributions. By maximizing the ELBO, a VAE effectively learns to generate new data samples that are similar to the input data while maintaining a continuous and smooth latent space. This capability is especially vital for generating diverse and realistic data samples, making VAEs valuable in various applications such as image generation and anomaly detection.

In practical terms, ELBO ensures that during training, the model not only focuses on minimizing the error in reconstructing the original data but also aligns the learned latent representations with a predefined prior distribution. This dual objective helps the model generalize better to new, unseen data, which is a hallmark feature of generative models like VAEs.

Next, we delve into KL Divergence, an important measure in the context of VAEs. KL Divergence quantifies the difference between two probability distributions—in this case, the approximate posterior distribution and the true prior distribution. In simpler terms, it quantifies the extent to which one probability distribution deviates from another.

For VAEs, minimizing KL Divergence ensures that the learned latent representations are close to the chosen prior, typically a standard normal distribution. This alignment is important for maintaining the continuity and smoothness of the latent space, enabling the generation of coherent new data points. Without this regularization, the latent space could become disjointed, leading to poor-quality generated samples.

KL Divergence serves as a regularizer in the VAE loss function, penalizing deviations of the approximate posterior from the prior. This penalty encourages the model to produce latent representations that are not only useful for reconstruction but also adhere to the desired statistical properties of the prior distribution. Consequently, KL Divergence plays a critical role in shaping the latent space in a way that facilitates effective generative modeling.

Understanding the loss function in VAEs involves breaking it down into two main components: the reconstruction loss and the KL Divergence term. The reconstruction loss measures how well the VAE can reproduce the input data from its latent representation. Typically, this is calculated using metrics such as mean squared error or binary cross-entropy, depending on the nature of the input data.

The second component of the VAE loss function is the KL Divergence, which, as discussed earlier, ensures the latent space remains aligned with the chosen prior distribution. By balancing these two terms, the VAE loss function achieves a harmony between accurate data reconstruction and a structured latent space. This balance is critical for the model's ability to generalize and produce high-quality generative outputs.

During training, the overall objective is to minimize the combined loss function, which includes both the reconstruction loss and the KL Divergence term. This approach allows the VAE to learn meaningful latent representations that retain essential features of the input data while adhering to the probabilistic constraints imposed by the prior. As a result, the VAE can generate new data that is not only similar to the input data but also statistically coherent.

These components guide the VAE training process by providing clear objectives for optimization. The reconstruction loss drives the model to accurately capture and reproduce the input data, ensuring that the generated samples stay true to the source data. Meanwhile, the KL Divergence term keeps the latent space organized and consistent with the prior distribution, facilitating smooth interpolation and variation within the generated data.

Effective training of VAEs requires careful balancing of these objectives to prevent either term from dominating the learning process. For instance, if the reconstruction loss is overly prioritized, the model might neglect the latent space structure, leading to overfitting. Conversely, if KL Divergence is too heavily weighted, the model might struggle to reconstruct data accurately. Achieving this balance often involves tuning hyperparameters and adopting strategies such as annealing the weight of the KL term during training.

Training Techniques and Challenges

Training Variational Autoencoders (VAEs) presents unique challenges and requires a deep understanding of various optimization strategies to achieve effective and efficient models. One common approach is the use of stochastic gradient descent (SGD) and its variants like Adam and RMSprop. These optimization techniques are crucial for minimizing the loss function, which in the case of VAEs includes both reconstruction loss and the Kullback-Leibler (KL) divergence. SGD works by iteratively adjusting the model's parameters to minimize the overall loss, making it essential for fine-tuning the VAE's performance.

Adam, an adaptive learning rate optimization algorithm, merges the advantages of the AdaGrad and RMSProp algorithms to effectively manage sparse gradients in noisy problems. It adjusts the learning rate for each parameter dynamically, which can be particularly beneficial in training complex VAE architectures. RMSprop, another popular variant, keeps a moving average of the squared gradients to normalize the gradient, helping in smoothing out large fluctuations and ensuring steady convergence. Employing these optimization strategies can significantly affect the training outcome, leading to faster convergence and more accurate models.

In addition to selecting a suitable optimizer, it's essential to monitor and adjust the learning rate throughout the training process. A well-tuned learning rate can prevent overshooting the minimum loss while ensuring that the model converges in a reasonable time. Learning rate schedulers, such as reducing the learning rate on a plateau or employing cyclical learning rates, can further enhance the training efficiency. Balancing these aspects effectively can lead to robust VAEs capable of generating high-quality data representations.

Balancing reconstruction loss and KL divergence during training is critical for the success of VAEs. Reconstruction loss measures how well the VAE reconstructs input data from the latent space, while KL divergence ensures that the latent variables follow the desired prior distribution. Striking the right balance between these two loss components is essential for generating meaningful latent representations without overfitting to the training data.

A useful technique for managing this balance is the beta-VAE, where a hyperparameter beta scales the KL divergence term. By adjusting beta, one can control the trade-off between regularization and reconstruction accuracy. Higher values of beta encourage disentangled and interpretable latent representations but may cause poorer reconstructions. Conversely, lower values focus on reconstruction quality at the expense of latent space regularity. Finding the optimal beta value is key, often requiring experimentation and careful evaluation of model performance on validation data.

Another strategy involves annealing the KL divergence term during training. Starting with a small weight for KL divergence and gradually increasing it can help the model first focus on reconstructing data accurately before enforcing strong regularization. This staged approach often results in better overall performance and a smoother training process. Understanding and applying these balancing techniques can greatly enhance the effectiveness of VAEs in capturing intricate data distributions.

Common challenges in training VAEs include mode collapse and posterior collapse, which can hinder the generation of diverse and distinct data representations. Mode collapse occurs when the generator produces limited variations, concentrating on a few modes of the data distribution. Posterior collapse, on the other hand, happens when the approximate posterior distribution reduces to the prior, leading to a loss of meaningful latent variable information.

To address mode collapse, one effective method is using a modified ELBO that incorporates additional constraints encouraging diversity in the generated samples. Techniques like adding noise to the input data during training or employing a discriminator network, similar to Generative Adversarial Networks (GANs), can also promote diversity and reduce mode collapse. Ensuring a rich and varied dataset and employing data augmentation techniques can further mitigate this issue by providing the model with a broader range of examples.

Posterior collapse often stems from an overly powerful decoder overshadowing the encoder's learning process. One solution is to limit the decoder's capacity, thus forcing the encoder to learn richer latent representations. Another approach is to use a hierarchical VAE structure, where multiple layers of latent variables can capture more complex dependencies in the data. Adjusting the annealing schedule of the KL divergence term, as previously mentioned, can also alleviate posterior collapse by initially allowing the encoder to focus more on reconstruction tasks before imposing stricter regularization.

Hyperparameter tuning is a pivotal aspect of optimizing VAE performance, requiring careful consideration of various model parameters. Key hyperparameters include the learning rate, batch size, latent space dimensions, and the weights of different loss components. Properly tuning these parameters can significantly influence the training dynamics and the quality of the learned representations.

Steps for effective hyperparameter tuning start with a thorough grid or random search for the initial parameter ranges. Once a promising set of hyperparameters is identified, finer adjustments can be made using techniques like Bayesian optimization or Hyperband. Monitoring metrics such as validation loss, reconstruction quality, and latent space interpretability is essential for evaluating the impact of different hyperparameter configurations.

Applications of VAEs in Various Fields

Variational Autoencoders (VAEs) have brought a transformative approach to multiple applications across diverse fields. One of the most prominent applications is in the realm of image generation and reconstruction, which has significantly advanced computer vision. VAEs enable the creation of realistic images from noise by learning a compressed representation of the data in a latent space. This capability is valuable for tasks such as image denoising, super-resolution, and even creative endeavors like generating art. For instance, in medical imaging, VAEs can reconstruct high-quality images from noisy or incomplete scans, enhancing diagnostics and treatment planning.

VAEs are also instrumental in generating synthetic data for training other machine learning models, thus overcoming the limitations of small datasets. Additionally, VAEs have been employed in style transfer and image inpainting, where missing parts of an image are filled in plausibly based on learned patterns. These applications not only enrich the user experience but also aid in preserving privacy when creating datasets. By generating new data points that maintain the statistical properties of original datasets, VAEs help expand the scope and quality of available data without direct exposure of sensitive information.

Moreover, VAEs facilitate enhanced anomaly detection in images by identifying and reconstructing deviations from expected patterns. This application is critical in quality control processes, such as detecting defects in manufacturing or identifying anomalies in surveillance footage. By reconstructing images and comparing them with the input, VAEs can highlight discrepancies indicative of faults or irregularities, thus ensuring higher standards and greater reliability in various industries.

In natural language processing (NLP), VAEs play a pivotal role in text generation and sentiment analysis. They allow for the modeling of complex textual data by learning the distribution of words and phrases in a latent space. This enables the generation of coherent and contextually relevant text, which improves chatbot interactions, automated content creation, and language translation services. For example, VAEs can generate human-like responses in chatbots, making them more interactive and engaging in customer service applications.

Sentiment analysis benefits from VAEs by utilizing the latent space to capture the underlying emotional tone in text data. This helps businesses understand customer feedback, reviews, and social media sentiments more accurately. By analyzing these sentiments, companies can make informed decisions about product improvements, marketing strategies, and customer engagement. Furthermore, VAEs assist in summarizing large documents or articles by extracting key themes and presenting concise summaries, saving time and effort for users.

Recent advancements have seen VAEs being integrated into tasks like text classification and topic modeling. Here, VAEs help discern the hidden structure of a corpus, allowing for efficient categorization and retrieval of information. This enhances search engine capabilities and recommendation systems, making them more intuitive and responsive to user needs. By leveraging the probabilistic nature of VAEs, these systems become more adept at handling ambiguous or uncertain inputs, leading to better performance and user satisfaction.

Anomaly detection using VAEs is another significant area of application, with use cases spanning across domains such as fraud detection and industrial monitoring. In fraud detection, VAEs analyze transaction data to learn normal behavior patterns and identify deviations that may indicate fraudulent activity. By reconstructing transactions and assessing the reconstruction error, VAEs can flag potentially fraudulent actions for further investigation. This proactive approach is crucial for financial institutions aiming to mitigate losses and enhance security measures.

In industrial monitoring, VAEs contribute to predictive maintenance by detecting machinery anomalies before they lead to failures. By continuously analyzing sensor data, VAEs can predict equipment breakdowns and schedule maintenance activities, thereby reducing downtime and operational costs. This application extends to energy management, where VAEs help identify inefficiencies and optimize resource usage within industrial plants. The ability to predict and prevent issues ensures smoother operations and promotes sustainability.

Apart from fraud and industrial applications, VAEs are also utilized in cybersecurity for identifying network intrusions. By modeling normal network traffic and detecting deviations, VAEs help secure systems against potential cyber-attacks. This ability is particularly crucial for safeguarding sensitive data and preserving the integrity of digital infrastructures. The integration of VAEs in these processes underscores their versatility and effectiveness in safeguarding assets in various sectors.

Biomedical research has greatly benefited from the contributions of VAEs, particularly in drug discovery and medical image analysis. VAEs accelerate drug discovery by generating novel molecular structures that conform to desired properties, thereby expanding the pool of potential candidates for testing. This computational approach reduces the time and cost involved in traditional drug development processes. Additionally, VAEs help identify relationships between molecular features and biological activity, leading to more targeted and effective treatments.

In medical image analysis, VAEs assist in the segmentation and classification of images, facilitating accurate diagnosis and treatment planning. For example, VAEs can assist radiologists in identifying tumors by highlighting abnormal regions in scans. This aids early detection and intervention, improving patient outcomes. Moreover, VAEs help in the analysis of histopathological images, providing insights into disease progression and aiding in research for better therapeutic strategies.

The processing capability of VAEs also extends to single-cell analysis and spectrographic data. By clustering and analyzing cellular behaviors, VAEs contribute to understanding complex biological phenomena and improving biomedical research methodologies. This application is particularly relevant in genomics and proteomics, where VAEs facilitate the integration and interpretation of multi-omics data, leading to groundbreaking discoveries in personalized medicine and genetic research.

Summary of the key points discussed in Chapter 4.

Throughout this chapter, we delved deeply into the architecture, components, mathematical foundations, training techniques, and applications of Variational Autoencoders (VAEs). We explored how VAEs differ from traditional autoencoders by incorporating probabilistic elements that enhance data generation capabilities. The introduction of a probabilistic framework in VAEs enables rich latent space representations, fostering better data generalization and new data synthesis.

Revisiting the concept, VAEs transform input data into probability distributions rather than fixed points, allowing them to capture inherent data variability more effectively. This process is governed by key mathematical principles such as the Evidence Lower Bound (ELBO) and KL Divergence. ELBO balances reconstruction accuracy with latent space regularization, while KL Divergence ensures that the learned latent space aligns with a prior distribution, imposing a discipline on the representation. These foundations are crucial for achieving a smooth and continuous latent space conducive to generating diverse outputs.

An essential aspect that readers should be mindful of is the balance between reconstruction loss and KL divergence during training. Striking this balance is pivotal for optimal VAE performance, as an imbalance can lead to either overfitting or underfitting. Techniques like beta-VAE and annealing the KL term are useful strategies to manage this trade-off, ensuring that the model remains both effective and efficient.

On a broader scale, VAEs hold substantial potential across various fields. Their ability to generate realistic and high-quality data representations opens up numerous applications. From enhancing image processing tasks in computer vision to improving text generation and sentiment analysis in natural language processing, VAEs demonstrate versatility and robustness. Additionally, their role in anomaly detection across different sectors, such as fraud detection and industrial monitoring, underscores their practical significance.

As we continue to advance in AI, understanding and leveraging VAEs will remain a crucial endeavor. The integration of probabilistic elements in neural networks not only pushes the boundaries of what generative models can achieve but also provides novel ways to interact with and interpret complex data structures. This journey into the world of VAEs highlights their importance and sets the stage for further exploration and innovation in generative modeling.

References

Bonassar, L., Cohen, I., Delco, M., Teoh, H., Zheng, J. (2024, May). *Application of a variational autoencoder for clustering and analyzing in situ articular cartilage cellular response to mechanical stimuli.* *PLOS ONE.* https://www.ncbi.nlm.nih.gov/pmc/articles/PMC11104615/

How to train your VAE. arxiv.org. (n.d.). https://arxiv.org/html/2309.13160v3

Variational AutoEncoders. GeeksforGeeks. (2020, July). https://www.geeksforgeeks.org/variational-autoencoders/

Variational Autoencoders for Anomaly Detection in Respiratory Sounds. arxiv.org. (n.d.). https://arxiv.org/html/2208.03326v2

Notebook. Umich.edu. (2023). https://socr.umich.edu/HTML5/ABIDE_Autoencoder/

CHAPTER 5

Autoregressive Models

Autoregressive models are fundamental in the realm of statistical analysis and prediction, focusing on predicting future data points by utilizing the information from previous values. This approach is particularly valuable for time-series data and sequence modeling where the current output is influenced by its historical data. Autoregressive models assume that past values hold essential insights into future data points, enabling accurate predictions based on previously observed patterns.

In this chapter, we will delve into several core aspects of autoregressive models. We will begin by exploring their basic concepts and architectures, followed by a detailed examination of their mathematical underpinnings. The chapter will also cover various training techniques used to optimize these models and discuss their applications across different fields such as economics, finance, and natural language processing. By understanding these areas, readers will gain a comprehensive view of how autoregressive models function and their significance in predictive analytics.

Introduction to Autoregressive Models

Autoregressive models are a cornerstone in the field of statistical analysis and prediction. These models primarily focus on predicting future data points by regressing a variable against its own previous values. This technique is advantageous in scenarios where the current output is heavily dependent on its past outputs, making it particularly useful for time-series data and sequence modeling. The fundamental principle behind autoregressive models is the assumption that information from prior values holds crucial insights into upcoming data points.

In an autoregressive model, the value at any given time step depends linearly on its preceding values. Mathematically, this can be represented as:

$$y_t = c + \phi_1 y_{t-1} + \phi_2 y_{t-2} + \cdots + \phi_p y_{t-p} + \varepsilon_t$$

where:

- y_t represents the current value,
- ccc is a constant term,
- $\phi_1, \phi_2, \ldots, \phi_p$ are coefficients corresponding to prior values,
- ε_t is the error term.

The degree of regression, denoted as p, determines how many previous time steps influence the current value. By adjusting these parameters, the model can effectively capture different patterns and complexities inherent in the data.

The autoregressive approach assumes that the current output is closely related to prior outputs, which is instrumental in handling time-series data and sequence modeling. This characteristic is evident in applications involving temporal dependencies, such as economic forecasting or natural language processing. For example, in financial markets, stock prices often show a clear trend based on past performance. Therefore, using autoregression, one could predict future prices with greater accuracy by considering historical price movements (What Are Autoregressive Models?. Coursera., 2024).

The ability of autoregressive models to capture temporal dependencies and relationships within data makes them exceptionally effective for various real-world applications. In economics, they are used to forecast variables like GDP growth rates or inflation by leveraging past economic indicators. In finance, traders use these models to predict stock prices and market trends, enabling more informed investment decisions. In natural language processing, autoregressive models are employed to generate text by predicting the next word based on previously generated words, thus creating coherent and contextually relevant sentences. This versatility demonstrates the broad applicability and significance of autoregressive models across different domains.

One of the most notable aspects of autoregressive models is their effectiveness in capturing the underlying structure of time-related data. Through careful parameter estimation and model fitting, they can identify patterns and trends that may not be immediately apparent. This capacity for detailed analysis is particularly beneficial in fields like economics, where understanding long-term trends is crucial for policy-making and strategic planning. By examining historical data, these models provide valuable insights into potential future developments, aiding economists in formulating accurate predictions and recommendations.

Furthermore, autoregressive models have been widely applied in finance to model and predict time series data related to stock prices, interest rates, and other economic indicators. They allow financial analysts to anticipate market movements and develop strategies to maximize returns while minimizing risks. For instance, an autoregressive model can help in predicting the future volatility of a stock by analyzing past price fluctuations, providing investors with critical information for decision-making.

In natural language processing, autoregressive models play a vital role in tasks such as text generation, machine translation, and speech recognition. By analyzing previously generated words or phrases, these models can accurately predict the next element in a sequence, resulting in coherent and contextually appropriate outputs. For example, in text generation, an autoregressive model might generate a sentence word by word, each time considering all the previously generated words to ensure grammatical and logical consistency.

Another major advantage of autoregressive models lies in their flexibility and adaptability. They can be tailored to suit a wide range of data types and structures, making them suitable for various applications beyond just economics, finance, and natural language processing. This adaptability is due to the models' inherent design, which allows for easy modification and extension to accommodate different levels of complexity and data characteristics.

Despite their numerous advantages, it is important to consider the limitations of autoregressive models. One significant challenge is the need for stationary data, meaning the properties of the time series should not change over time. Non-stationary data can lead to inaccurate predictions and necessitates additional preprocessing steps, such as differencing or detrending, to achieve stationarity. Additionally, determining the appropriate lag length (p) for the model can be complex and requires thorough analysis and testing.

Moreover, autoregressive models assume a linear relationship between past and present values, which may not always be the case in real-world scenarios. In situations where non-linear relationships exist, alternative modeling techniques, such as neural networks or support vector machines, might be more effective. Nonetheless, with proper adjustments and enhancements, autoregressive models remain a powerful tool for predictive analysis in many applications.

BASIC AUTOREGRESSIVE MODEL ARCHITECTURE:

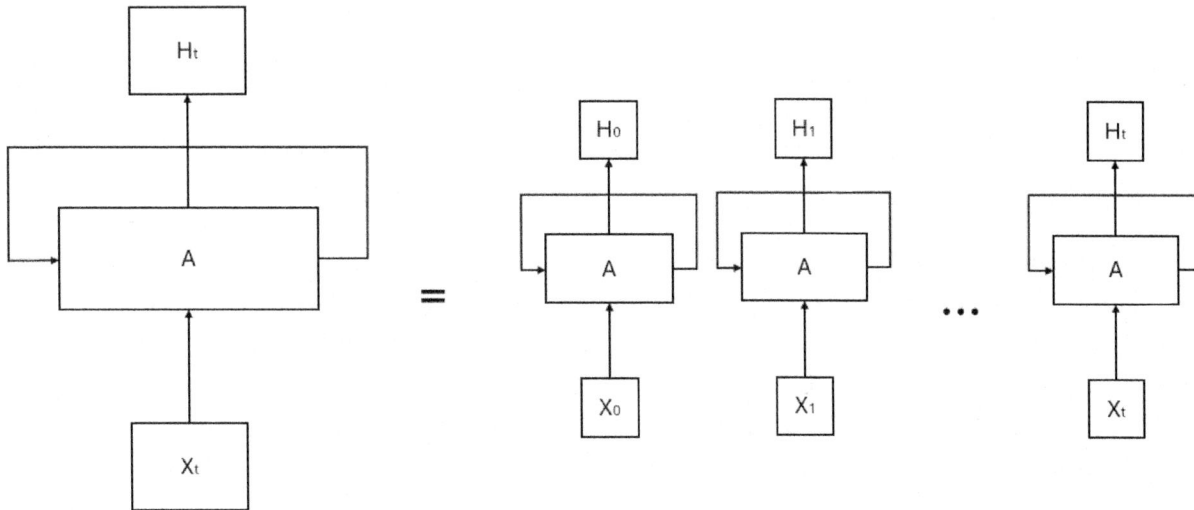

PixelRNN

PixelRNN, a model designed for image generation, follows an autoregressive approach to synthesize high-quality images. The core idea is that PixelRNN processes images pixel by pixel, predicting each pixel's value sequentially based on previously generated pixels. This means that the network starts from the top-left corner of an image and moves across each row to the bottom-right corner, making predictions one pixel at a time. Each prediction incorporates information about all previously generated pixels, capturing the intricate dependencies within the image.

The sequential nature of PixelRNN leverages Recurrent Neural Network (RNN) layers to model spatial dependencies. These dependencies are crucial for creating coherent and high-fidelity images, as each pixel value relies on its surrounding context. RNNs are adept at handling such sequences due to their ability to maintain a memory state, which allows them to learn the complex relationships between adjacent pixels. This process differs notably from feedforward networks that consider pixels independently, enabling PixelRNN to achieve more realistic and contextually accurate image generation.

To optimize the modeling of pixel dependencies, several variants of PixelRNN have been developed, including Row LSTM and Diagonal BiLSTM. The Row LSTM variant processes pixels in a row-wise manner, capturing horizontal dependencies more effectively. In contrast, the Diagonal BiLSTM enhances this by also considering diagonal dependencies, allowing the model to integrate both horizontal and vertical information simultaneously. These variations help in refining the quality of the generated images by better addressing the positional relationships within the image.

However, while PixelRNN excels in producing high-quality images, it comes with significant computational demands. The inherent nature of processing each pixel sequentially means that the model cannot leverage parallel computations effectively. This sequential processing leads to slower training and inference times compared to other architectures that can process multiple parts of an image concurrently. As a result, PixelRNN is often considered computationally intensive and slow, making it less practical for applications requiring rapid image generation or real-time performance.

Another critical aspect of using RNN layers in PixelRNN is their capacity to capture long-range dependencies within the image. This ability ensures that even distant pixels can influence each other, contributing to the coherence of larger structures within the generated image. For instance, when generating an image of a face, the position and color of eye pixels can influence the subsequent predictions for neighboring pixels, resulting in a more realistic and consistent facial structure.

Despite these advantages, the heavy computational load remains a primary challenge in deploying PixelRNN at scale. The need for sequential processing limits its scalability, especially for large image datasets or high-resolution images. Researchers continue to explore ways to mitigate these limitations, such as developing more efficient variants or combining PixelRNN with other techniques like convolutional neural networks (CNNs) to balance accuracy and speed.

PixelCNN

PixelCNN is an advancement in autoregressive models for image generation. Unlike its predecessor, PixelRNN, which uses recurrent layers to process images, PixelCNN leverages convolutional layers. This architectural choice allows PixelCNN to perform parallel processing of pixels within a row, significantly enhancing efficiency. Convolutional layers can handle multiple pixels simultaneously, reducing the computational time required compared to the sequential processing in PixelRNN. This results in faster image generation while maintaining high-quality outputs.

Masked convolutions are a crucial component of the PixelCNN architecture. These convolutions ensure that predictions for each pixel are made based only on previously generated pixels, adhering to the autoregressive nature of the model. By masking certain parts of the convolutional filters, PixelCNN guarantees that the dependency structure adheres to the natural ordering of pixels in an image. This ensures that the model does not cheat by looking at future pixels, thereby maintaining the integrity of the generation process.

Several variants of PixelCNN have been developed to address specific limitations and enhance performance. Gated PixelCNN introduces gating mechanisms similar to those in

LSTM networks, improving the model's ability to handle complex dependencies between pixels. This variant has shown notable improvements in generating more realistic images. Conditional PixelCNN further extends the architecture by incorporating additional context or conditions, such as class labels or other side information. This makes the model versatile, allowing it to generate images conditioned on specific attributes, which is valuable in applications requiring controlled generation.

One of the primary advantages of PixelCNN over PixelRNN is its speed. The parallel processing capability of convolutional layers makes PixelCNN much faster than the sequential nature of PixelRNN. This speed advantage is significant, especially when generating high-resolution images where computational efficiency becomes critical. Despite being faster, PixelCNN manages to maintain a high level of image quality, often producing results comparable to PixelRNN.

However, PixelCNN is not without its challenges. One of the main issues is handling long-range dependencies within images. While convolutional layers are efficient for local dependencies, capturing global structures that span large portions of an image can be difficult. This limitation can affect the overall coherence of the generated images, particularly in scenarios requiring a deep understanding of the entire image context. Researchers continue to explore methods to mitigate this issue, including combining PixelCNN with other models or architectural modifications.

Generative Pre-trained Transformer (GPT)

The GPT architecture is a predominant model in the field of natural language processing (NLP). It leverages the Transformer architecture, which has revolutionized how dependencies between tokens are modeled. The core innovation within Transformers is the self-attention mechanism. This mechanism allows the model to weigh the importance of each token with respect to others in a sequence, understanding context dynamically. Unlike traditional RNNs that process sequences linearly, the self-attention mechanism enables parallel processing of tokens, significantly improving efficiency and performance.

Transformers are composed of multiple layers called transformer blocks, each consisting of multi-head self-attention and feed-forward layers. Multi-head self-attention splits input into several smaller attention mechanisms, allowing the model to simultaneously focus on different parts of a sentence or paragraph. This layered approach ensures that the model captures various levels of abstraction and patterns within the data. Feed-forward layers then process this information, combining insights from different heads and refining the representations to make meaningful predictions or generate coherent text.

One of the key strengths of the GPT model lies in its pre-training on vast amounts of text data followed by fine-tuning for specific tasks. During pre-training, the model learns general linguistic structures and patterns by predicting the next word in sentences from a massive text corpus. This extensive training imbues the model with a broad understanding of language. Fine-tuning involves adapting the pre-trained model to particular NLP tasks such as question-answering, translation, or sentiment analysis by training it further on task-specific datasets. This two-stage training process significantly enhances the model's ability to perform diverse NLP tasks effectively.

The scalability of the GPT model is another crucial aspect of its design. Built to handle large-scale data, GPT can be scaled up by increasing the number of layers, the size of the embeddings, and the amount of training data. Such scaling improves the model's performance and enables it to tackle complex NLP challenges. However, this scalability comes with a cost—GPT models demand substantial computational resources and vast datasets to train effectively. Training these models requires powerful hardware, such as GPUs or TPUs, and considerable time, making it resource-intensive.

Despite its demanding nature, the effectiveness of GPT in various applications cannot be understated. By fine-tuning, it can excel in generating human-like text, creating chatbots that hold more natural and engaging conversations, drafting coherent articles, and even aiding in creative writing. The capability to generate contextually relevant text makes GPT an invaluable tool in fields like automated content creation and customer support.

Summary of the exploration of autoregressive models

In this chapter, we have delved into the core concepts of autoregressive models, their mathematical foundations, and various applications across fields like economics, finance, and natural language processing. We began by establishing that autoregressive models predict future data points based on previous values, making them invaluable for time-series analysis and sequence modeling.

Emphasizing the linear dependency on past values, we explored how these models capture temporal relationships. Economists use them to forecast important variables, while financial analysts leverage them to predict stock prices and market trends. In natural language processing, they assist in generating coherent text by predicting subsequent words based on prior ones.

We also highlighted specific models like PixelRNN and PixelCNN, which apply autoregressive principles to image generation. PixelRNN processes images sequentially, pixel by pixel, using RNN layers to maintain spatial dependencies. Its variants, such as Row LSTM and Diagonal BiLSTM, further enhance its ability to capture horizontal and vertical dependencies. However, its computational demands limit its practicality for large-scale or real-time applications.

PixelCNN, an advancement over PixelRNN, uses convolutional layers to parallelize pixel processing within rows, improving efficiency without compromising quality. Masked convolutions ensure that predictions adhere to autoregressive principles, maintaining the integrity of the generation process. Despite challenges in capturing long-range dependencies, PixelCNN's speed advantage makes it a preferred choice for high-resolution image generation.

The chapter also touched upon the Generative Pre-trained Transformer (GPT) architecture, which revolutionizes natural language processing through self-attention mechanisms. These mechanisms enable the model to understand token dependencies dynamically, allowing parallel processing and improving efficiency. GPT's effectiveness is amplified by pre-training on vast text corpora, followed by fine-tuning for specific tasks, making it versatile and powerful for various NLP applications. Its scalability, although demanding significant computational resources, enables it to tackle complex challenges and generate human-like text.

While autoregressive models offer numerous benefits, they are not without limitations. The necessity for stationary data can complicate their application, requiring additional preprocessing steps for non-stationary data. Moreover, the assumption of linear relationships between past and present values may not always hold true, potentially limiting their accuracy in certain scenarios. Alternative techniques, such as neural networks or support vector machines, might be more effective for handling non-linear relationships.

As we move forward, it is essential to recognize both the strengths and constraints of autoregressive models. Their ability to capture temporal dependencies and their adaptability to different data types make them powerful tools for predictive analysis. However, addressing their computational demands and ensuring accurate lag length determination remain critical for maximizing their potential.

The exploration of autoregressive models demonstrates their significance in various domains, from economic forecasting to image and text generation. By understanding their underlying principles and applications, readers can appreciate their impact on modern predictive analysis. As advancements continue, these models will likely evolve, offering even greater precision and efficiency in handling complex data patterns.

References

8.3 Autoregressive models | Forecasting: Principles and Practice (2nd ed). otexts.com. (n.d.). https://www.otexts.org/fpp/8/3

EITCA Academy. (2024). *What are the primary advantages and limitations of using Generative Adversarial Networks (GANs) compared to other generative models?.* EITCA Academy. https://eitca.org/artificial-intelligence/eitc-ai-adl-advanced-deep-learning/advanced-generative-models/modern-latent-variable-models/examination-review-modern-latent-variable-models/what-are-the-primary-advantages-and-limitations-of-using-generative-adversarial-networks-gans-compared-to-other-generative-models/

Kalchbrenner, N., Kavukcuoglu, K., Oord, A. (2016, January). *Pixel Recurrent Neural Networks.* Semantic Scholar. https://www.semanticscholar.org/paper/Pixel-Recurrent-Neural-Networks-Oord-Kalchbrenner/41f1d50c85d3180476c4c7b3eea121278b0d8474

What Are Autoregressive Models?. Coursera. (2024, March). https://www.coursera.org/articles/autoregressive-models

CHAPTER 6

Building and Training Generative Models

Building and training generative models is a fundamental task in artificial intelligence. These models have the capability to create new, original data that resembles a given dataset, making them invaluable for a variety of applications such as image generation, text creation, and music composition. The task involves not just algorithm development but also a comprehensive understanding of the entire lifecycle from data collection to model evaluation. This chapter is designed to serve as a detailed guide to navigate through these essential steps.

The chapter will start with an exploration of the importance of high-quality data, emphasizing how it is foundational for accurate model training. It will then delve into various sources of data, including online datasets, APIs, and web scraping, which are crucial in accumulating the required training data. Following this, you'll engage with data preprocessing techniques that clean, normalize, and augment the data to enhance model performance. The discussion will continue with strategies to handle imbalanced datasets, ensuring fair and unbiased training across all classes. Lastly, the chapter will introduce you to popular frameworks like TensorFlow and PyTorch, each offering unique advantages for building and training generative models. By the end of this chapter, you'll gain practical insights and tools necessary for effectively developing and deploying your own generative models.

Importance of High-Quality Data

Data plays an indispensable role in the performance of generative models. High-quality data is fundamental for accurate model training. Without a rich, diverse, and representative dataset, even the most sophisticated models can fall short of their potential. To illustrate this, consider a scenario where a model is being trained to generate human faces. If the training dataset only includes images of adults but lacks images of children or older adults, the model will struggle to accurately generate faces representing these age groups. This highlights the need for datasets that encompass a broad spectrum of examples to ensure the model can learn and generalize effectively.

Poor quality data can lead to models that perform inadequately and generalize poorly. Data that has noise, missing values, or biases introduces inaccuracies into the learning process. These inaccuracies propagate through the model, leading it to produce unreliable or even nonsensical outputs. For instance, if a dataset used for training a chatbot contains numerous typographical errors or incomplete sentences, the resulting chatbot might generate responses that reflect these flaws. This not only diminishes the user experience but also undermines the credibility of the model. Therefore, ensuring the quality of data used for training is paramount.

Moreover, the quality of data directly impacts the ability of models to generate plausible new samples. For generative models, the goal is often to create new instances that are indistinguishable from real-world data. This requires the training data to be both comprehensive and clean. Consider a generative model designed to create new pieces of music. If the training data consists of melodies that lack variety or are of low audio quality, the generated music will likely sound monotonous or distorted. A high-quality dataset, on the other hand, would enable the model to capture the nuances and richness found in authentic music, thereby producing more credible and appealing compositions.

Ensuring consistency in data collection methods further enhances model reliability. Consistency involves using standardized protocols for gathering data, which helps in minimizing variations and anomalies that could compromise the training process. For example, when building a model to generate realistic textual content, it's crucial that all text samples in the dataset adhere to similar linguistic norms and formatting. This prevents the model from learning inconsistencies that could result in awkward or jarring outputs. Hence, consistent data collection practices contribute significantly to the robustness and dependability of generative models.

Sources of Data

In building and training generative models, a crucial first step is gathering ample data for model training. Understanding various sources for collecting data is essential. These sources vary in ease of use, completeness, and suitability depending on project needs. Three primary methods offer reliable ways to obtain vast datasets: online datasets, APIs, and web scraping.

Online datasets such as MNIST and CIFAR-10 are popular among practitioners because they provide well-curated, ready-to-use data for training and validating machine learning models. MNIST, for example, includes a large set of handwritten digits commonly used for training image processing systems. Similarly, CIFAR-10 offers a collection of 60,000 32x32 color images in ten different classes. These datasets are valuable not only for their size but also for the quality and consistency of the data they contain, making them ideal for experimenting with new algorithms or benchmarking existing ones.

However, reliance solely on these datasets might not always suffice, especially when specific data characteristics are required that these standard datasets do not cover. For instance, if one needs data on financial transactions or social media interactions, turning to publicly available repositories may prove necessary. Often, specialized datasets from various domains can be found through governmental databases, university research projects, and repositories like Kaggle. Such resources expand the scope of data available for experimentation and application-specific training.

APIs (Application Programming Interfaces) offer another powerful means of accessing large amounts of data. They allow developers to connect directly to services and extract the data needed in a more structured and automated manner. Many organizations and platforms, including Twitter, Google, and Facebook, provide APIs that enable access to user data, public posts, and even metrics. Using APIs, one can collect real-time information efficiently without manual intervention, which is particularly beneficial for applications requiring up-to-date data.

The programmatic nature of APIs ensures repeatability and scalability, crucial features when working on large-scale AI projects. APIs typically come with documentation detailing how to authenticate requests, define parameters, and handle responses, which simplifies the integration process. Additionally, since APIs often impose rate limits on the number of requests over a specified period, they foster responsible data usage policies and help prevent server overloads. However, implementing API calls requires familiarity with programming principles and handling JSON or XML data formats.

When APIs do not exist, web scraping presents an alternative method for data collection. Web scraping involves extracting data from websites using automated scripts that parse HTML content. This technique becomes particularly useful for sourcing data from smaller websites, blogs, or pages without a dedicated API. Tools like BeautifulSoup and Scrapy in Python make web scraping accessible even to those with limited programming experience by providing libraries designed to simplify the extraction process.

Web scraping enables access to a broad spectrum of data types, from textual content to images and files, across diverse internet sources. Its flexibility allows users to gather niche data sets tailored to specific research needs. However, web scraping comes with challenges and legal considerations. Websites regularly change their structure, which can break previously functional scrapers. Ethical concerns and terms of service violations also need to be managed carefully to avoid potential legal repercussions.

Data Preprocessing Techniques

Effective data preprocessing is paramount in building and training generative models. The first crucial step is data cleaning, which involves removing duplicates and correcting errors. Duplicates in the dataset can lead to skewed model training, where the model might overfit certain patterns that are not representative of the real-world distribution. For instance, if duplicate images are present in a dataset used for training a generative adversarial network (GAN), the generator might learn to produce those specific images rather than discovering generalizable patterns. Similarly, errors such as misspellings in text data or noise in audio recordings need to be corrected to ensure the integrity of the training data.

Cleaning also encompasses handling missing values, which can occur due to various reasons such as sensor malfunctions or human error during data collection. Methods like imputation can be employed to estimate missing values based on other available data points. Another approach is to remove instances with missing values if they constitute a small portion of the dataset. Proper cleaning processes ensure that the dataset is representative and free from anomalies that could detrimentally affect the model's learning process.

Moreover, outlier detection is a critical aspect of data cleaning. Outliers are data points significantly different from others and can lead to misleading trends and poor model performance. Techniques such as statistical methods, clustering-based approaches, or even simple visualization can help identify and remove these outliers. By ensuring the dataset is clean and accurate, we lay a strong foundation for effective model training.

Normalization is the subsequent step, essential for scaling data values to a common range. This process helps in reducing biases towards features with larger magnitudes. For example, in image data, pixel values range from 0 to 255, and normalizing these values to a range of 0 to 1 ensures uniformity, making it easier for the model to process and learn from the data. Techniques such as min-max normalization, z-score normalization, and decimal scaling are commonly used.

Min-max normalization scales the data to a fixed range, usually between 0 and 1, enhancing comparability across different features. On the other hand, z-score normalization standardizes the data by scaling it around the mean with a unit variance, which is particularly useful when the features exhibit normal distribution. Decimal scaling involves shifting the decimal point of data values, often used when data ranges have various units of measurement.

Proper normalization is vital because machine learning algorithms, especially generative models, often assume that the input data follows a particular distribution. If the data is not normalized, the model might converge slowly or fail to achieve optimal performance. It leads to better gradient descent convergence and more efficient computation, ultimately boosting the model's ability to generate high-quality outputs.

Data augmentation is another critical technique that enriches training datasets, significantly impacting model robustness. Augmentation methods such as cropping, rotation, flipping, and color adjustments artificially increase the diversity of the training data. By creating multiple variations of existing data, models become more resilient to variations and can generalize better to new, unseen data. For example, rotating images at random angles helps the model learn to recognize objects from different perspectives, thereby improving its overall accuracy and flexibility.

Cropping is particularly useful in scenarios where the focus is on specific regions within an image. By randomly cropping different parts of an image, the model learns to detect relevant features irrespective of their position. Similarly, applying random flips horizontally or vertically introduces positional variance, enabling the model to understand symmetry and asymmetry in objects, thus enhancing its interpretative capabilities. Color adjustments such as changing brightness, contrast, or saturation can mimic varying lighting conditions, making the model robust to environmental changes.

Furthermore, advanced augmentation techniques include adversarial training, where augmented samples are created by adding perturbations to the original data. These perturbations are designed to fool the model, pushing it to improve its decision boundaries. Another method is mixup, which generates new samples by combining features of two existing samples. Such techniques create challenging scenarios for the model, ensuring it learns more comprehensive feature representations.

Proper preprocessing, encompassing cleaning, normalization, and augmentation, significantly improves model performance and robustness. When data is meticulously cleaned, normalized, and augmented, the generative model can effectively learn underlying patterns, leading to higher quality and more realistic generated outputs. Cleaning removes inconsistencies, normalization standardizes data ranges, and augmentation increases data variability, all contributing synergistically to the model's efficacy.

Handling Imbalanced Data

Handling imbalanced datasets is a crucial aspect of building and training generative models, as it ensures that the model performs well across all classes within the dataset. One common method to address this issue is oversampling, which involves increasing the number of instances in the minority class to match those in the majority class. Oversampling can be as simple as duplicating existing instances or applying more sophisticated techniques like Synthetic Minority Over-sampling Technique (SMOTE). SMOTE generates new synthetic samples by interpolating between existing minority class examples. This helps in creating a more balanced dataset, allowing the model to better learn and generalize from the underrepresented class.

Oversampling can significantly enhance the performance of generative models when dealing with imbalanced data. By augmenting the minority class, the model has more opportunities to understand the characteristics of this class, leading to a more equitable learning process. However, care must be taken to avoid overfitting, as merely duplicating samples might cause the model to memorize rather than generalize. To mitigate this risk, combining oversampling with other techniques such as data augmentation, which introduces slight variations in the duplicated samples, can be beneficial.

While oversampling is advantageous, it is also essential to monitor the computational cost and time associated with generating synthetic data. The added instances increase the dataset size, potentially demanding more processing power and longer training times. Despite these challenges, the benefits of achieving a balanced representation in the dataset often outweigh the drawbacks, as it directly translates to improved model accuracy and robustness.

Undersampling is another effective technique for handling imbalanced datasets, where the focus is on reducing the number of instances in the majority class. This approach aims to create a balance by selectively removing some majority class instances, thereby aligning its size closer to that of the minority class. Random undersampling is a straightforward method that randomly picks instances to discard. However, more advanced methods consider the informational value of each instance, retaining those that are most representative of the majority class's diversity.

Reducing the number of majority class instances through undersampling can help prevent the model from becoming biased towards the more prevalent class. When the dataset is less skewed, the model has an equal chance of learning the characteristics of both minority and majority classes. This balance enhances the model's ability to make accurate predictions across all classes. However, the downside of undersampling is the potential loss of valuable information from the discarded majority class instances, which could impact the model's overall performance.

To counteract the possible negative effects of undersampling, it is often used in conjunction with other balancing techniques. For example, combining undersampling with oversampling can optimize the balance without excessively reducing the majority class size or overly increasing the minority class size. Such hybrid approaches strive to maintain a comprehensive representation while addressing the imbalance effectively.

One innovative solution for imbalanced datasets is synthetic data generation, which involves creating entirely new samples for the underrepresented classes. Unlike oversampling, which relies on existing data points, synthetic generation uses algorithms to produce new, plausible instances that capture the minority class's intrinsic characteristics. Techniques such as GAN-based augmentation leverage the generative capabilities of GANs to synthesize realistic samples, enhancing the diversity and richness of the minority class.

Synthetic data generation provides a powerful means to tackle severe class imbalances without the risk of overfitting associated with plain duplication in oversampling. By producing novel samples instead of replicating existing ones, models gain exposure to a broader range of scenarios and variations within the minority class. This leads to a more robust learning experience, fostering better generalization and predictive performance.

However, generating high-quality synthetic data requires a deep understanding of the underlying data distribution and modeling techniques. It is essential to ensure that the synthetic samples are representative and add genuine value to the training process. This method often demands substantial computational resources and careful tuning to achieve the desired outcomes. Nevertheless, the investment in synthetic data generation can pay off, particularly in domains where data collection is challenging or costly.

Balancing techniques are pivotal for ensuring fair training and optimal performance in generative models. Implementing strategies like cross-validation and monitoring class-wise performance metrics enables continuous assessment of the model's behavior across different classes. Measures like precision, recall, and F1-score for each class provide insights into how well the model handles imbalance during training and testing phases.

Effective balancing not only improves model accuracy but also enhances its reliability when deployed in real-world applications. Ensuring fairness in training implies that the model does not favor any specific class, resulting in more dependable and credible outputs. Balancing techniques foster resilience against biases and disparities, which is particularly critical in sensitive fields such as healthcare, finance, and autonomous systems.

Ultimately, adopting a combination of oversampling, undersampling, and synthetic data generation can lead to the best results in managing imbalanced datasets. Integrating these methods aligns with the goal of creating a balanced dataset that fosters unbiased learning and robust model performance. Practitioners should evaluate the trade-offs and synergize these techniques to tailor them according to the specific needs and constraints of their projects.

Introduction to TensorFlow and PyTorch

TensorFlow and PyTorch are two of the most prominent frameworks used in the field of deep learning. TensorFlow, developed by Google, offers extensive tools and libraries designed to cater to various aspects of deep learning. One of its standout features is the comprehensive ecosystem that includes tools like TensorBoard for visualization, TensorFlow Hub for reusable modules, and TensorFlow Lite for deploying models on mobile and edge devices. These tools streamline the development process, making it easier to build, train, and deploy models efficiently. Additionally, TensorFlow provides high-level APIs such as Keras, which simplify model building for beginners and experts alike.

Another strength of TensorFlow is its graph-based computation, where operations are represented as nodes in a data flow graph. This approach allows for significant optimization opportunities, particularly in large-scale distributed environments. The static computational graph enables efficient use of resources, making TensorFlow a robust choice for production-level applications. Its scalability is well-recognized, with the framework being capable of running across various hardware configurations, from personal computers to large server clusters.

Community support for TensorFlow is extensive, benefiting developers through an abundance of tutorials, documentation, and community-contributed resources. Google's backing has ensured continuous updates and a strong community presence, making it accessible to both industry professionals and academic researchers. This broad adoption means that newcomers can find ample learning materials, easing the onboarding process into deep learning projects.

On the other hand, PyTorch, developed by Meta AI (formerly Facebook AI Research Lab), has gained popularity due to its flexibility and ease of use, particularly in research settings. PyTorch's dynamic computation graph, known as Autograd, allows users to modify the architecture of neural networks on-the-fly, which is invaluable for experimentation and iterative development. This feature makes PyTorch highly suitable for tasks requiring frequent model adjustments, such as research and prototyping.

PyTorch is also characterized by its intuitive, Pythonic interface, which integrates seamlessly with Python programming conventions. This integration ensures that developers who are familiar with Python find PyTorch straightforward to learn and use.

The ease of debugging and the interactive nature of its API enable developers to quickly identify and fix issues, promoting a smooth development experience.

The PyTorch ecosystem includes powerful libraries like TorchVision for computer vision tasks, TorchText for natural language processing, and more, providing a versatile toolkit for different types of deep learning projects. Furthermore, PyTorch's support for GPU acceleration ensures that large models can be trained efficiently, leveraging modern hardware capabilities to reduce training times significantly.

Both TensorFlow and PyTorch are suited for generative modeling but differ significantly in their syntax and features. While TensorFlow's static graph structure can offer performance optimizations, PyTorch's dynamic graph provides greater flexibility during model development. For example, PyTorch's ability to construct graphs dynamically allows for seamless incorporation of control flow statements within the neural network, facilitating complex architectures that might be cumbersome to implement in TensorFlow.

Moreover, the choice of framework often depends on specific project needs and personal preference. TensorFlow may be preferable for projects requiring deployment at scale, due to its optimization capabilities and extensive tools for production environments. Its structured approach benefits scenarios where models need to be scalable and highly optimized, such as enterprise applications with significant computational demands.

Conversely, PyTorch is frequently favored in academic and research contexts, where flexibility and rapid prototyping are paramount. Researchers value the ability to alter model structures dynamically, test hypotheses quickly, and iterate based on experimental results. PyTorch's design philosophy emphasizes user-friendliness and adaptability, making it an ideal choice for exploratory research and development.

Summary of building and training generative models

Throughout this chapter, we have explored the comprehensive process of building and training generative models, starting from data collection to meticulous evaluation. The importance of high-quality data cannot be overstated, as it forms the backbone for accurate and effective model training. Ensuring that datasets are rich, diverse, and representative is crucial in enabling models to generalize well and produce reliable outputs.

We discussed various sources to gather data, highlighting the significance of online datasets, APIs, and web scraping techniques. Each method presents unique advantages and challenges, depending on the specific needs of the project. For instance, while online datasets provide well-curated options, APIs and web scraping offer more customized and real-time data collection possibilities. Effective data collection strategies lay a solid foundation for subsequent preprocessing steps.

Data preprocessing plays a pivotal role in refining datasets before they are fed into generative models. Techniques like data cleaning, normalization, and augmentation help in enhancing the quality and variability of the data. These processes ensure that the model learns efficiently from the data, thereby improving its performance and robustness. Addressing issues such as duplicates, errors, missing values, and normalization biases helps build a dataset that supports optimal learning.

Handling imbalanced data is another critical aspect covered in this chapter. Methods like oversampling, undersampling, and synthetic data generation are essential for creating balanced datasets. These techniques ensure that the model does not become biased towards any particular class, leading to fair and accurate predictions across all classes. Balancing the dataset contributes significantly to the model's reliability and generalization capabilities.

The introduction to TensorFlow and PyTorch provided insights into two prominent frameworks widely used for deep learning projects. Understanding the strengths and distinctive features of each framework allows practitioners to make informed decisions based on their specific requirements and preferences. While TensorFlow's graph-based computation offers optimization benefits, PyTorch's dynamic graph provides flexibility for experimentation and rapid prototyping.

In conclusion, this chapter has equipped you with a thorough understanding of the essential stages involved in building and training generative models. High-quality data collection, effective preprocessing, and addressing imbalanced datasets form the core practices that drive successful model training. Choosing the right tools, such as TensorFlow or PyTorch, depends on your project needs and development preferences. As you move forward, consider how these elements intertwine to impact the overall efficacy of your generative models. By focusing on these fundamental aspects, you can enhance the performance and credibility of your models, ensuring they meet both practical and innovative goals.

References

Alvi, F. (2024, January). *PyTorch vs TensorFlow in 2024: A Comparative Guide of AI Frameworks.* OpenCV. https://opencv.org/blog/pytorch-vs-tensorflow/

GeeksForGeeks. (2020, June). *What is Web Scraping and How to Use It?. GeeksforGeeks.* https://www.geeksforgeeks.org/what-is-web-scraping-and-how-to-use-it/

Keras vs Tensorflow vs Pytorch. GeeksforGeeks. (2024, February). https://www.geeksforgeeks.org/keras-vs-tensorflow-vs-pytorch/

Kesari, G. (2024, January). *The Enduring Power of Data Storytelling in the Generative AI Era. MIT Sloan Management Review.* https://sloanreview.mit.edu/article/the-enduring-power-of-data-storytelling-in-the-generative-ai-era/

Lane, I. (n.d.). *Chapter 2 Working with Web Data and APIs | Big Data and Social Science. textbook.coleridgeinitiative.org.* https://textbook.coleridgeinitiative.org/chap-web.html

Maharana, K., Mondal, S., Nemade, B. (2022, April). *A Review: Data Pre-Processing and Data Augmentation Techniques. Global Transitions Proceedings.* https://www.sciencedirect.com/science/article/pii/S2666285X22000565

School, S. (2023, March). *AI Data Stewardship Framework. Stanford Law School.* https://law.stanford.edu/2023/03/09/a-data-stewardship-framework-for-generative-ai/

Shelke, M. (2017, January). *A Review on Imbalanced Data Handling Using Undersampling and Oversampling Technique. www.academia.edu.* https://www.academia.edu/71149653/A_Review_on_Imbalanced_Data_Handling_Using_Undersampling_and_Oversampling_Technique?hb-g-sw=75293686

CHAPTER 7

Text Generation with Generative AI

Text generation with generative AI explores the intricate world of creating coherent and natural-sounding text using artificial intelligence. This chapter delves into a variety of models that serve as the backbone of this technology, each contributing uniquely to the landscape of text generation. By understanding these models, readers can appreciate how they enable machines to produce anything from simple sentences to complex narratives.

The chapter will guide you through three main types of text generation models: rule-based models, statistical models, and neural network models. You'll explore foundational techniques like template-based systems and N-gram models, learning about their strengths and limitations. The discussion advances to more sophisticated methods like Recurrent Neural Networks (RNNs), Long Short-Term Memory networks (LSTMs), and the cutting-edge Transformer models. Each section not only clarifies the mechanics behind these models but also examines their practical applications, offering a comprehensive overview of how generative AI is revolutionizing text creation across various domains.

Overview of Text Generation Models

Understanding the various models used for text generation in AI is crucial for anyone entering the field. Among these, rule-based models, statistical models, and neural network models are foundational. Each offers unique advantages and use cases that contribute to the evolving landscape of AI-driven text generation.

Rule-based models were some of the earliest techniques used in text generation. These models operate on predefined rules and structures. Template-based systems, for instance, generate text by filling in pre-made templates with variable data. This approach ensures high control over the output, making it reliable for specific tasks like generating form letters or standardized reports. However, the rigidity of templates limits their flexibility and scalability.

Grammar-based systems, another type of rule-based model, utilize a set of grammatical rules to generate text. These systems can produce more varied and human-like sentences than template-based ones but still fall short in handling complex language structures. While rule-based models offer simplicity and reliability, they cannot adapt well to the dynamic nature of human language, which limits their effectiveness in more nuanced applications.

Transitioning to statistical models, we encounter N-gram models, which predict the next word in a sequence based on the previous N words. These models are straightforward and computationally efficient, making them suitable for basic text generation tasks. They rely heavily on probability distributions derived from large corpora of text. Despite their simplicity, N-gram models struggle with capturing long-range dependencies in language, leading to repetitive or nonsensical outputs in longer texts.

The limitations of N-gram models stem from their dependency on fixed-size contexts, which prevents them from understanding broader linguistic patterns. As the value of N increases, the model's complexity and the required training data grow exponentially. This inefficiency makes N-gram models less practical for more sophisticated text generation tasks, paving the way for more advanced approaches.

Neural network models have significantly advanced the field of text generation. Recurrent Neural Networks (RNNs) are among the early neural architectures designed for sequential data like text. RNNs process input sequences one element at a time, maintaining a hidden state that captures information from previous elements. This design enables RNNs to learn patterns over longer contexts compared to N-gram models. However, traditional RNNs suffer from issues like vanishing gradients, hindering their ability to retain information over very long sequences.

To address these issues, Long Short-Term Memory (LSTM) networks were developed as an improvement over RNNs. LSTMs include mechanisms called gates that regulate the flow of information, allowing them to capture long-range dependencies more effectively. This capability makes LSTMs particularly useful in applications requiring extended context, such as language translation and speech recognition. Nevertheless, LSTMs still face challenges in parallelization due to their sequential nature, which can limit their efficiency in training and inference.

Transformers represent the latest advancement in neural network models for text generation. Unlike RNNs and LSTMs, Transformers do not process data sequentially; instead, they employ a mechanism called self-attention to weigh the importance of different words in a sentence, regardless of their position. This allows Transformers to capture both local and global dependencies in text, enabling them to generate coherent and contextually rich paragraphs. The architecture's parallelizability also speeds up training and inference processes, making Transformers highly efficient.

The advantages of each type of text generation model highlight their respective use cases. Rule-based models excel in scenarios where precision and predictability are paramount, such as generating legal documents or technical manuals. Their structured nature ensures consistency and adherence to predefined standards, albeit at the cost of flexibility.

Statistical models, like N-grams, find their niche in simpler applications where computational efficiency is crucial. They can be effective in autocomplete systems or basic chatbots that do not require deep language understanding. However, their inability to grasp long-range dependencies makes them unsuitable for more complex text generation tasks.

Neural network models bring versatility and depth to AI-driven text generation. RNNs and LSTMs, with their capacity to handle sequential data, are well-suited for tasks like machine translation and sentiment analysis. Meanwhile, Transformers' robust performance across various language tasks, from summarization to creative writing, underscores their dominance in current AI research and applications.

Applications in Content Creation and Chatbots

Generative AI, particularly text generation models, are transforming industries by automating tasks and enhancing creative processes. One notable application is in automated news writing, where generative AI can swiftly generate content. News organizations are leveraging AI to produce articles on sports events, financial reports, and breaking news with remarkable speed. Automation allows for real-time updates and ensures that news outlets can keep up with the rapid pace of information dissemination.

Additionally, AI-generated news articles can cover a wide range of topics, providing more comprehensive coverage than would be possible with human writers alone.

Moreover, generative AI models contribute to reducing operational costs for news organizations. By automating routine reporting tasks, human journalists can focus on investigative journalism and in-depth analysis, thereby increasing the overall quality of news content. The Associated Press, for example, uses AI to automate the production of quarterly earnings reports, freeing up reporters to engage in more creative and impactful work. These advancements illustrate how generative AI is becoming an indispensable tool in the newsroom.

However, the use of AI in news writing also poses challenges. Ensuring accuracy and avoiding biases in AI-generated content is critical. Developers must continually refine algorithms to improve the reliability of the information produced. Ethical considerations, such as transparency about AI involvement in content creation, are also crucial to maintain reader trust. Despite these challenges, the benefits of generative AI in automated news writing are readily evident, offering both efficiency and enhanced journalistic capabilities.

In addition to news writing, generative AI is making significant strides in creative writing. Authors utilize AI to assist in crafting stories, poems, and scripts, opening new avenues for creativity. AI tools like OpenAI's GPT-3 can generate text based on prompts, providing writers with inspiration and overcoming writer's block. This technology allows authors to experiment with new styles and ideas, enriching the creative process.

Furthermore, AI-driven creative writing tools can analyze vast amounts of literary data, identifying patterns and trends that can help writers improve their craft. For instance, AI can suggest plot developments, character traits, and stylistic nuances based on successful literary works. This assists not only seasoned authors but also emerging writers who may lack extensive experience. By augmenting human creativity with AI's analytical power, the boundaries of storytelling are expanded.

Nonetheless, the integration of AI in creative writing generates debates about authenticity and originality. Critics argue that AI-generated content lacks the human touch and emotional depth inherent in traditional literature. To address this, many writers use AI tools as collaborators rather than replacements, incorporating AI-generated suggestions while preserving their unique voice and vision. This symbiotic relationship between humans and AI highlights the potential for technology to enhance, rather than detract from, creative endeavors.

Marketing and advertising represent another area where AI-generated content plays a pivotal role. Businesses employ generative AI to create engaging copy for advertisements, social media posts, and email campaigns. AI can analyze consumer data to tailor messages that resonate with specific audiences, resulting in more effective marketing strategies. Personalization at this scale was previously unattainable, but generative AI makes it possible to deliver highly targeted content efficiently.

The ability of AI to generate diverse content quickly is invaluable in maintaining a consistent online presence. Brands can ensure that their messaging remains fresh and relevant, adapting to changing market trends and consumer preferences. For example, AI can create variants of an advertisement to test which version performs best, optimizing marketing efforts in real time. This dynamic approach enhances brand visibility and engagement across digital channels.

Despite its advantages, reliance on AI in marketing raises concerns regarding authenticity and consumer trust. It's essential for businesses to balance automation with genuine human interaction. Consumers value authentic connections with brands, and overly automated interactions can feel impersonal. Therefore, integrating AI-generated content with personalized customer experiences is crucial for building and maintaining trust. When used thoughtfully, AI can amplify marketing efforts without compromising authenticity.

Lastly, the implementation of chatbots and virtual assistants showcases the versatility of AI in customer service, personal assistance, and mental health support. In customer service, AI-powered chatbots provide instant responses to queries, improving customer satisfaction and reducing wait times. Companies like Amazon and Microsoft use chatbots to handle routine inquiries, allowing human agents to address more complex issues. This combination enhances overall service efficiency.

For personal assistance, AI virtual assistants like Siri and Google Assistant manage tasks such as scheduling, reminders, and information retrieval. These tools offer convenience and accessibility, particularly beneficial for individuals with busy lifestyles. Moreover, AI virtual assistants continuously learn from user interactions, progressively improving their functionality and personalization over time.

In the realm of mental health support, AI offers innovative solutions through virtual therapists and self-help apps. AI-driven platforms provide cognitive-behavioral therapy techniques, mood tracking, and mindfulness exercises. These tools make mental health resources more accessible, especially for those reluctant to seek face-to-face therapy. While AI cannot replace professional mental health care, it serves as a valuable supplementary resource, offering support and interventions when needed.

Step-by-Step Guide to Building a Text Generator

Building a text generator using generative AI involves several critical steps, starting with data gathering. This foundational phase requires collecting a large and diverse dataset representative of the type of text you intend to generate. For instance, if your goal is to produce Shakespearean-style prose, you would need an extensive collection of works by Shakespeare. The data should be varied enough to capture different writing styles, vocabularies, and grammatical structures within the chosen genre. Sources could include books, articles, and other textual materials, ensuring you have permission or rights to use them.

Once collected, the data must be cleaned to ensure high-quality input for the model. Cleaning involves removing unwanted characters, correcting spelling errors, and standardizing formats. This step often includes dealing with null values, filtering out irrelevant content, and handling special characters that may corrupt the training process. For example, HTML tags in web-scraped data need to be stripped out, and inconsistent use of white spaces or punctuation should be corrected. Properly cleaned data leads to more accurate and efficient model training.

Tokenization follows data cleaning and is essential for converting the text into a format suitable for machine learning models. Tokenization involves splitting the cleaned text into manageable units called tokens—these can be words, subwords, or characters, depending on the model architecture. Libraries such as TensorFlow and Keras provide tools to help with this process. Once tokenized, the data is encoded into numerical representations that the model can process, preparing it for the subsequent training phase.

Choosing the right model architecture is pivotal for the performance of a generative AI text model. Recurrent Neural Networks (RNNs) were some of the earliest architectures used for text generation due to their ability to handle sequential data. Long Short-Term Memory networks (LSTMs), a type of RNN, improved upon basic RNNs by addressing the vanishing gradient problem, making them better at capturing long-term dependencies in text. More recently, Transformer models have emerged as state-of-the-art, thanks to their attention mechanisms that allow them to consider the entire context of a sentence simultaneously.

Training the chosen model involves feeding it the preprocessed text data and adjusting the model's parameters to minimize prediction errors. During training, the model learns patterns and relationships in the text data, enabling it to generate coherent and contextually relevant text when prompted. Training typically requires robust computational resources; leveraging GPUs can significantly speed up the process. It's also common practice to monitor various metrics during training to track progress and spot potential issues early.

Evaluation metrics are crucial for assessing the performance of the trained model. Perplexity is a widely used metric in language modeling that measures how well a probability distribution predicts a sample. Lower perplexity indicates better model performance. Another useful metric is the BLEU (Bilingual Evaluation Understudy) score, which evaluates the quality of generated text based on its similarity to human-written text. High BLEU scores suggest that the model produces text closer to human quality.

Fine-tuning involves adjusting the trained model to optimize its performance further. This can be achieved by retraining the model with additional data or tweaking hyperparameters to improve accuracy. Fine-tuning is especially important when the initial training results are not satisfactory or when adapting the model to specific tasks or genres. It ensures the model generates text that meets the desired standards of coherence and contextual relevance.

The final phase is deploying the trained text generation model. Deployment involves integrating the model into an application or system where users can interact with it. Before deployment, the model needs to be saved, often in a format compatible with the deployment environment, such as TensorFlow's SavedModel format. Deployment can occur on various platforms, including web servers, mobile devices, or embedded systems, depending on the application's requirements.

Ongoing monitoring of the deployed model is essential to maintain its effectiveness. Over time, the model's performance may degrade due to changes in input data patterns or shifts in user expectations. Continuous monitoring allows for timely identification of these issues. Regular updates and retraining with fresh data can help keep the model relevant and accurate. Automated logging of model predictions and user interactions can provide valuable insights for further refinements.

Updates to the deployed model should be handled carefully to avoid service disruptions. This often involves version control strategies, such as A/B testing, where a new model version is tested alongside the old one to compare performance before fully switching over. Ensuring a smooth transition between model versions helps maintain user trust and system reliability. Additionally, feedback loops from users can be integrated to gather real-world performance data, providing a basis for future improvements.

Real-World Examples and Case Studies

OpenAI's GPT models, especially the GPT-2 and GPT-3, have made significant strides in various domains by showcasing the capabilities of text generation on a wide scale. One prominent case study involves their application in content creation for websites and blogs. By leveraging these models, businesses can generate high-quality, engaging content rapidly, minimizing the cost and time traditionally associated with hiring human writers. This has proven beneficial for maintaining an active online presence, crucial for SEO and user engagement. Additionally, these models are used in educational tools to assist students in learning complex subjects through interactive and adaptive tutorials.

Another critical application is seen in medical literature review, where GPT models can scan vast amounts of research papers to summarize findings, aiding researchers who need to stay updated but are constrained by time. The ability to condense information without losing context helps professionals in making informed decisions quickly. Furthermore, there's increasing use in augmenting creative processes in sectors like gaming and screenwriting. GPT-3, for instance, aids scriptwriters in brainstorming and exploring new narrative pathways by generating dialogues and plot twists, thus enhancing creativity and efficiency.

The Associated Press (AP) utilizes AI for automated journalism, transforming how news is reported and disseminated. By employing natural language generation algorithms, AP can produce earnings reports, sports recaps, and other routine news articles at unprecedented speeds. This automation allows journalists to focus on more investigative and interpretive stories that require human insight and ethical consideration. The system not only generates text but also performs data analysis, identifying trends and anomalies that might be newsworthy. This blend of data-driven reporting and automation ensures that news delivery is both timely and accurate, catering to the fast-paced demands of modern news consumers.

Moreover, AI systems help combat misinformation by cross-referencing facts and sources before disseminating news. This real-time fact-checking capability is essential in an era where fake news can spread rapidly online. By integrating these systems, news organizations can maintain credibility and trust with their audience. Another interesting aspect is the personalization of news content. AI can tailor news feeds based on user preferences, ensuring relevant and engaging content. This personalized experience keeps readers more engaged and satisfied, driving higher retention rates for news platforms.

AI Dungeon, leveraging GPT-3, offers an innovative approach to interactive storytelling, providing users with an immersive experience where they can shape narratives dynamically. This application goes beyond traditional game mechanics by allowing players to input virtually any command or dialogue, which the AI then uses to generate appropriate responses and story continuations. This level of interaction creates a unique and personal gaming experience, as each session can differ vastly based on user inputs, fostering a deeper connection between players and the storyline. The flexibility and creativity of AI Dungeon highlight the potential of AI in entertainment and interactive media.

Furthermore, AI Dungeon can serve as an educational tool, improving literacy and creativity among younger audiences. By engaging in these dynamic narratives, users practice writing and storytelling skills in a fun and interactive environment. The implications extend to therapy and mental health, where such AI applications can provide therapeutic story-writing sessions, helping individuals process emotions and experiences through creative expression. These interactive narratives offer a safe space for exploration, reflection, and personal growth, demonstrating the far-reaching impact of AI beyond mere entertainment.

In banking and e-commerce, AI-powered customer service chatbots drastically improve operational efficiency and customer satisfaction. These chatbots can handle a plethora of customer queries simultaneously, providing instant responses and resolutions around the clock. In banking, chatbots assist with basic account management tasks, such as balance inquiries, transaction history, and fund transfers, reducing the load on human customer service representatives. This automation ensures that customers receive timely assistance, improving their overall experience while allowing bank staff to focus on more complex issues that require human intervention.

E-commerce platforms benefit similarly, with AI chatbots managing order tracking, return processes, and product recommendations. These bots analyze customer behavior and purchase history to offer personalized shopping experiences, enhancing customer satisfaction and loyalty. Additionally, chatbots can upsell and cross-sell products effectively by understanding customer preferences and suggesting relevant items, thereby driving sales and revenue. The integration of AI in customer service reflects a shift towards more efficient, scalable, and customer-centric business operations.

Text generation models and their potential future advancement

The chapter has explored various text generation models within generative AI, highlighting their mechanics, use cases, and practical implementation. We've examined rule-based models, statistical models, and neural network models, each with unique strengths and limitations. From the early rule-based systems offering high control over output to the more advanced transformer models capturing both local and global dependencies, these methods represent the evolution of text generation technology.

Previously, we discussed how understanding these models forms a foundation for anyone entering the field of AI-driven text generation. This chapter reinforced that notion by delving into each model's architecture and application. The progression from simple rule-based approaches to sophisticated neural networks illustrates the dynamic nature of AI development.

Currently, transformer models stand out due to their efficiency and ability to generate coherent and contextually relevant text. They have set new standards in various applications, including content creation, chatbots, and personalized marketing strategies. This reflects the rapid advancement from the limitations seen in early models like N-grams and RNNs.

Some readers might be concerned about the ethical implications of AI-generated text and its potential biases. Ensuring accuracy and maintaining transparency about AI's role in content creation remain critical challenges. Moreover, the integration of these technologies must consider the balance between automation and human creativity, particularly in fields such as journalism and creative writing.

On a wider scale, the rise of generative AI opens up vast possibilities across diverse industries. It can revolutionize traditional workflows, enhance customer engagement, and foster innovation in storytelling and interactive media. The benefits are significant, yet they come with responsibilities to address ethical concerns and ensure the reliability of the generated content.

The journey through this chapter reveals the intricate landscape of text generation in AI, leaving us to ponder the future advancements and applications of these technologies. As the field continues to evolve, it will be fascinating to see how these models shape our interaction with digital content and redefine the boundaries of human-machine collaboration.

References

AI Text Generator. DeepAI. (n.d.). https://deepai.org/chat/text-generator

Arizona State University. (n.d.). *What is Generative AI and How Does it Work?* Retrieved from https://careercatalyst.asu.edu/newsroom/career/what-is-generative-ai-and-how-does-it-work/

Teaching Social Identity and Cultural Bias Using AI Text Generation - The WAC Clearinghouse. wac.colostate.edu. (n.d.). https://wac.colostate.edu/repository/collections/textgened/ethical-considerations/teaching-social-identity-and-cultural-bias-using-ai-text-generation/

Text generation with an RNN. TensorFlow. (n.d.). https://www.tensorflow.org/text/tutorials/text_generation

Top Machine Learning Applications by Industry: 6 Machine Learning Examples. Columbia Engineering Boot Camps. (2021, December). https://bootcamp.cvn.columbia.edu/blog/machine-learning-applications/

What is Text Generation? - Hugging Face. huggingface.co. (2023, September). http://www.2sterne.org/text-generation.html

CHAPTER 8

Image Synthesis and Enhancement

Image synthesis and enhancement are pivotal topics that delve into the generation and improvement of images through computational methods. This field has vast implications in various domains such as art, science, and technology, facilitating the creation of visuals that might be challenging or impossible to produce using traditional techniques. The chapter aims to explore how these advancements have revolutionized various industries by providing innovative ways to generate and enhance images.

In this chapter, readers will embark on an in-depth exploration of the prominent models and techniques employed in image synthesis, including Generative Adversarial Networks (GANs), Variational Autoencoders (VAEs), Diffusion Models, and Autoregressive Models like PixelCNN and PixelRNN. The discussion will extend to practical applications in fields such as entertainment, healthcare, gaming, and more. Additionally, the chapter will cover advanced enhancement techniques such as style transfer, super-resolution, and inpainting, highlighting their significance and utilization. By the end of this chapter, readers will gain a comprehensive understanding of the models, methodologies, and practical steps involved in the realm of image synthesis and enhancement.

Introduction to Image Synthesis

Image synthesis refers to the process of generating new images through computational techniques. In fields like art, science, and technology, image synthesis plays a crucial role in creating visuals that would be difficult or impossible to capture using traditional methods. For artists, it opens up endless creative possibilities by allowing them to generate unique compositions and styles. In scientific research, synthesized images enable the visualization of complex data sets, such as medical scans or astronomical images, aiding in analysis and discovery. Technologically, it underpins advancements in areas like virtual reality and autonomous vehicles by simulating realistic environments and training models to recognize various objects.

The significance of image synthesis extends beyond just creating visually appealing graphics. In the scientific community, for instance, it is pivotal in rendering detailed 3D models of anatomical structures from CT and MRI scans, enhancing both diagnosis and educational processes. Artists benefit from tools like DeepDream and style transfer algorithms that push the boundaries of digital art, offering new ways to explore and express creativity. Furthermore, in the realm of artificial intelligence, image synthesis helps improve machine learning models by augmenting datasets with high-quality, synthetic images, thereby enhancing model robustness and performance.

Historically, the development of image synthesis has seen several key milestones that have significantly shaped its evolution. Initially, the field was rather primitive, relying on basic mathematical models to generate rudimentary graphics. However, the advent of deep learning marked a turning point. One of the critical milestones was the introduction of Generative Adversarial Networks (GANs) by Ian Goodfellow et al. in 2014, which revolutionized how synthetic images are generated (Ten Years of Image Synthesis. Fabian Offert., n.d.). GANs consist of two neural networks—a generator and a discriminator— that work in tandem to produce highly realistic images by constantly improving and refining their outputs through a competitive process.

Another notable milestone was the development of variational autoencoders (VAEs), which provided an alternative approach to generating images. VAEs use probabilistic graphical models to encode input images into a latent space and then decode them back, allowing the synthesis of new images that share characteristics with the original inputs. The recent surge in transformer-based models, notably OpenAI's DALL-E, has further pushed the boundaries by enabling text-to-image synthesis, demonstrating the potential for multimodal integration in generating complex visuals (Ten Years of Image Synthesis. Fabian Offert., n.d.).

The impact of image synthesis on industries such as entertainment, healthcare, and gaming has been profound. In entertainment, synthesized images are extensively used for visual effects (VFX) in movies and television shows, creating stunning visuals that captivate audiences. For example, the lifelike characters in films are often generated using advanced image synthesis techniques, making fantasy worlds feel real. In healthcare, the ability to generate synthetic medical images aids in training medical professionals and developing diagnostic tools. By simulating rare medical conditions, practitioners can practice and refine their skills without needing extensive real-world examples.

In the gaming industry, procedural content generation—a form of image synthesis—is employed to create expansive, dynamic game environments that enhance player experience. Games like "No Man's Sky" utilize these techniques to generate vast, diverse worlds, ensuring that each player's experience is unique. Beyond visual appeal, image synthesis also improves game mechanics by creating realistic physics simulations and character animations, thereby increasing immersion and engagement.

Looking ahead, the future potentials and emerging trends in image synthesis are promising and varied. One exciting trend is the increasing democratization of image synthesis tools, making sophisticated algorithms more accessible to amateurs and professionals alike. Platforms offering easy-to-use interfaces for generating complex visuals will empower more people to harness the power of AI for creative and practical applications. Additionally, the continuous improvement in hardware capabilities means that real-time image synthesis will become more feasible, opening up new avenues in interactive media and virtual reality experiences.

Another trend is the integration of generative models with other AI systems to create more holistic and intelligent applications. For example, combining image synthesis with natural language processing could lead to the development of more advanced conversational agents capable of generating visual content based on user interactions. Furthermore, the ethical implications of image synthesis, such as the creation of deepfakes, will likely spur regulatory advancements aimed at ensuring these technologies are used responsibly and ethically.

Key Models and Techniques

Understanding the primary models and techniques used in image generation is crucial for anyone venturing into the field of generative AI. We will delve into four prominent models: Generative Adversarial Networks (GANs), Variational Autoencoders (VAEs), Diffusion Models, and Autoregressive Models such as PixelCNN and PixelRNN.

Generative Adversarial Networks (GANs) have revolutionized how we think about artificial creativity. At the heart of GANs is a unique architecture comprising two neural networks: the generator and the discriminator. The generator's job is to produce new data instances that resemble the training data, while the discriminator's task is to evaluate them and determine if they are real or fake. This adversarial process forces the generator to improve its output iteratively. During training, the generator creates synthetic images, and the discriminator assesses their authenticity against real images from the dataset. As the generator learns to produce more realistic images, the discriminator simultaneously refines its ability to distinguish between real and artificially generated images. Over time, both networks reach a point where the generated images become almost indistinguishable from genuine samples.

The training process of GANs is akin to a game between a counterfeiter and a police officer, where each player improves their strategies over multiple rounds. Initially, the generator produces crude imitations, and the discriminator easily identifies the fakes. However, through backpropagation and gradient descent, the generator receives feedback from the discriminator and refines its parameters. Conversely, the discriminator also updates its weights to better identify the increasingly sophisticated forgeries. This dynamic tug-of-war continues until an equilibrium is reached, where the discriminator can no longer reliably tell apart real images from those generated by the GAN.

GANs find applications in a multitude of areas, including art creation, super-resolution, and even medical imaging. For example, GANs can generate high-quality images of potential drug candidates for pharmaceutical research, significantly speeding up the drug discovery process. Their ability to synthesize photorealistic images has also made them invaluable tools in fields like game development, virtual reality, and graphic design.

Variational Autoencoders (VAEs) represent another powerful approach to image generation. Unlike GANs, VAEs leverage probabilistic graphical models and variational inference to learn latent representations of data. The core architecture of a VAE consists of an encoder and a decoder. The encoder compresses input images into a lower-dimensional latent space, capturing essential features in the form of probability distributions. These distributions allow the model to introduce controlled variations during the decoding phase, leading to the generation of novel images.

The encoder-decoder mechanism is central to the functionality of VAEs. The encoder maps input data to a latent space, typically modeled as a Gaussian distribution. This probabilistic representation enables the introduction of random noise, ensuring diversity in the generated outputs. The decoder then reconstructs the original images from these latent variables, effectively generating new data samples. By training the encoder-decoder pair to minimize the reconstruction error and the Kullback-Leibler divergence—a measure of how one probability distribution diverges from a second—the VAE learns to produce high-quality, coherent images that preserve the characteristics of the training data.

VAEs are particularly useful in generating structured, interpretable data representations and have applications in anomaly detection, data compression, and image denoising. For instance, VAEs can be employed to detect anomalies in industrial equipment by learning normal operational patterns and identifying deviations that may indicate faults. Additionally, their ability to generate diverse but realistic images makes them well-suited for creative applications, such as generating variations of fashion designs or augmenting datasets for machine learning tasks.

Diffusion Models offer yet another innovative approach to image generation, grounded in principles of thermodynamics and statistical mechanics. These models simulate the process of diffusion, where particles spread from regions of high concentration to low concentration. In the context of image generation, diffusion models add noise to an image, gradually destroying its structure. Then, by reversing this process, they learn to generate images from pure noise.

The core principle behind diffusion models is the iterative application of Gaussian noise to images, followed by a reverse diffusion process. This involves training the model to predict and undo the added noise at each step, thereby progressively generating clearer images. By applying this technique to large datasets, diffusion models learn the underlying data distribution, enabling them to sample new images that closely resemble the training data. The gradual refinement of images through successive diffusion steps ensures high fidelity and fine-grained control over the generation process.

Specific applications of diffusion models include high-quality text-to-image synthesis and image inpainting. For example, tools like DALL-E employ diffusion models to create detailed and contextually accurate images from textual descriptions. This capability opens up exciting possibilities for use cases such as custom artwork generation based on user prompts or automated content creation for marketing campaigns. Moreover, diffusion models excel in tasks that require filling in missing parts of images, making them invaluable for restoring damaged photographs or completing unfinished artworks.

In addition to these advanced techniques, Autoregressive Models like PixelCNN and PixelRNN offer a different perspective on image generation. These models generate images pixel-by-pixel, with each pixel conditioned on the previously generated pixels. This sequential approach allows for precise control over the generation process but requires significant computational resources due to the dependency on preceding pixels.

PixelCNN and PixelRNN differ primarily in how they handle spatial dependencies. PixelCNN uses convolutional neural networks to model the conditional distributions of individual pixels, capturing local patterns effectively. On the other hand, PixelRNN employs recurrent neural networks, which are better suited for capturing long-range dependencies within images. Both models leverage masked convolutions or recurrent connections to ensure that each pixel depends only on previously generated pixels, maintaining the autoregressive property.

Practical use cases for autoregressive models span various domains, from generating realistic textures for computer graphics to creating detailed geospatial maps. For example, in urban planning, PixelCNN can generate high-resolution satellite imagery, aiding in the visualization of proposed infrastructure projects. Similarly, these models can be used to generate intricate textures for virtual environments in video games, enhancing the realism and immersive experience for players.

Advanced Techniques

Exploring sophisticated methods for enhancing synthesized images can significantly improve their quality and utility in various applications. One effective technique is style transfer, which involves transferring the artistic style from one image to another. This method leverages deep learning algorithms, primarily convolutional neural networks (CNNs), to extract the style features from a source image and apply them to a target image without altering its content. By separating an image into content and style representations, style transfer enables the creation of novel and visually appealing images that blend elements from multiple sources.

Style transfer allows artists and designers to experiment with different visual styles effortlessly. For example, an artwork's texture, brush strokes, and color palettes can be applied to a photograph, transforming it into a piece of art that mimics the style of famous painters like Van Gogh or Picasso. The success of this technique lies in its ability to maintain the structural integrity of the original image while seamlessly incorporating new stylistic elements. Advanced algorithms such as the Gatys algorithm and improvements using optimization techniques have further enhanced the quality and realism of style-transferred images.

Another sophisticated enhancement technique is super-resolution, which aims to increase the resolution of images. Super-resolution techniques employ machine learning algorithms to predict and add high-frequency details to low-resolution images, resulting in sharper and more detailed outputs. Methods like single-image super-resolution (SISR) use CNNs to learn mappings between low and high-resolution image pairs, effectively predicting the missing details. Additionally, generative adversarial networks (GANs) are employed to generate realistic textures and finer details, making the images appear more natural and lifelike.

Super-resolution is particularly beneficial in fields such as medical imaging, satellite imagery, and surveillance, where high-resolution images are crucial for accurate analysis and decision-making. For instance, in medical diagnostics, enhanced resolution can lead to better identification of minute anatomical structures, aiding in early detection of diseases. In satellite imagery, super-resolution can provide more precise geographical data, improving environmental monitoring and urban planning. Continuous advancements in this field aim to make super-resolution algorithms faster and more efficient, enabling real-time applications and broader adoption across industries.

Inpainting is yet another advanced technique used to fill in missing or corrupted parts of an image. This method reconstructs the lost regions by leveraging contextual information from the surrounding areas, ensuring a coherent and natural appearance. Traditional inpainting techniques relied on patch-based approaches, where similar patches from undamaged regions were copied to fill the gaps. However, modern deep learning methods, such as CNNs and GANs, have revolutionized inpainting by capturing global context and generating more realistic and intricate details.

Transformer-based models have also been explored for inpainting tasks, offering significant improvements in handling larger missing regions and complex textures. These models utilize self-attention mechanisms to capture long-range dependencies within an image, enabling more accurate and contextually appropriate restorations. Applications of inpainting include photograph restoration, object removal, and even video editing, where missing frames can be reconstructed to ensure smooth transitions. The continuous evolution of inpainting techniques promises to enhance the quality and reliability of restored images and videos.

Comparing these advanced techniques—style transfer, super-resolution, and inpainting—in terms of complexity and effectiveness reveals distinct advantages and challenges for each. Style transfer is relatively computationally intensive, requiring substantial processing power to achieve high-quality results. The effectiveness of style transfer depends on the intricacy of the style being transferred and the compatibility between the source and target images. However, once implemented, it can produce visually striking and innovative outcomes, making it highly valued in creative industries.

Super-resolution techniques vary in complexity depending on the architecture used. Simple CNN-based methods are comparatively less complex but may struggle with generating fine details. GAN-based approaches, while more complex, offer superior performance by producing highly realistic textures and reducing artifacts. The effectiveness of super-resolution is measured by the clarity and detail of the enhanced images, which can be evaluated using metrics like peak signal-to-noise ratio (PSNR) and structural similarity index (SSIM). Despite their higher computational demands, super-resolution methods are crucial in applications where detail preservation is paramount.

Inpainting techniques range from traditional patch-based methods to advanced deep learning models. Traditional methods are simpler but often limited in handling large missing regions or complex textures. Deep learning and transformer-based inpainting models are more sophisticated, capable of understanding the global context and providing higher quality restorations. The effectiveness of inpainting is assessed based on the coherence and realism of the filled regions, with evaluation metrics including pixel accuracy and perceptual quality scores. The complexity of implementing transformer-based inpainting models is justified by their ability to tackle challenging inpainting scenarios with impressive results.

Digital Art and Illustration

Exploration of New Creative Possibilities Enabled by Image Synthesis

Image synthesis has revolutionized the realm of digital art creation by unlocking a plethora of creative possibilities. One transformative aspect is the capacity to generate unique visual content that would be unimaginable through traditional means. Artists can now create images that blend multiple styles or incorporate elements from various artistic traditions, resulting in innovative and compelling artworks. This level of creativity is particularly driven by advanced models such as Generative Adversarial Networks (GANs) and Variational Autoencoders (VAEs), which enable artists to experiment with new forms, colors, and compositions without technical limitations.

Another significant impact of image synthesis on digital art is its ability to democratize art creation. With user-friendly interfaces, even those with minimal technical skills can produce high-quality images. Tools like DeepArt, ArtBreeder, and DALL-E provide intuitive platforms for users to manipulate images using simple prompts or sliders, making complex image generation accessible to a broader audience. This democratization fosters creativity across diverse groups, encouraging more people to explore digital art without being constrained by technical expertise.

Furthermore, image synthesis allows for rapid iteration and experimentation, speeding up the creative process. Artists can quickly generate multiple versions of an artwork to see how different styles or elements affect the final piece. This iterative capability is invaluable in fields like concept art, where exploring numerous ideas swiftly can lead to finding the most compelling visual narratives. By reducing the time and effort required to explore different creative directions, image synthesis aids artists in achieving their desired outcomes more efficiently.

Tools and Software Widely Used by Digital Artists for Synthesizing Images

Digital artists have a wide array of tools and software at their disposal for synthesizing images, each offering unique features tailored to different needs. One popular tool is Adobe Photoshop, which, though traditionally associated with photo editing, incorporates advanced AI-driven features for image synthesis. Features like Content-

Aware Fill and Neural Filters allow artists to manipulate and enhance images with unprecedented ease and precision, expanding their creative toolkit.

Other notable software includes GANPaint Studio and ArtBreeder, both of which leverage GAN technology to facilitate image synthesis. GANPaint Studio allows artists to add or remove objects in an image semi-automatically, providing granular control over the appearance of synthesized elements. ArtBreeder, on the other hand, lets users blend different images together to create entirely new compositions. Users can tweak attributes such as color palette, style, and subject matter through a highly interactive interface, making it a favorite among digital artists interested in generative art.

More specialized tools also cater to particular aspects of image synthesis. For example, DALL-E and VQ-VAE-2 focus on generating images from textual descriptions, bridging the gap between linguistic input and visual output. These tools are crucial for applications where text-to-image synthesis is essential, such as creating illustrations for books or visualizing concepts described in written form. By offering a range of functionalities, these tools empower artists to push the boundaries of what is possible in digital art creation.

Case Studies of Innovative Digital Artworks Created Using Image Synthesis

Several case studies highlight the innovative potential of image synthesis in digital art. One notable example is the work of artist Robbie Barrat, who uses GANs to create abstract portraits and landscapes. By training GAN models on datasets of classical paintings, Barrat generates unique artworks that blend elements of traditional and contemporary art. His work exemplifies how image synthesis can produce novel art forms that challenge our conventional understanding of aesthetics.

Another compelling case study is that of Mario Klingemann, an artist known for his use of neural networks to create generative art. Klingemann employs techniques like style transfer and deep learning to develop artworks that evolve over time, reacting to user interactions or environmental data. His projects often involve real-time systems that generate ever-changing visuals, illustrating the dynamic capabilities of image synthesis in creating interactive art experiences.

In professional settings, companies like Obvious Art have used image synthesis to make waves in the art market. Their AI-generated artwork "Portrait of Edmond de Belamy" was created using GANs and sold for a substantial sum at a Christie's auction. This event marked a turning point, signaling widespread acceptance and recognition of AI-produced art in mainstream culture. These case studies collectively demonstrate the vast potential and growing influence of image synthesis in the art world.

Future Trends and Potential Advancements in the Realm of Digital Art

Looking ahead, several trends and advancements promise to shape the future of digital art through image synthesis. One key trend is the increased integration of AI tools within traditional art software, enabling seamless workflows that combine manual artistry with automated synthesis. As AI becomes more embedded in creative processes, artists will likely adopt hybrid approaches, blending human intuition with machine-generated suggestions to create more sophisticated artworks.

Advancements in real-time image synthesis will also play a significant role. Technologies like StyleGAN3 and improved diffusion models are pushing the envelope in terms of speed and quality, allowing for near-instantaneous generation of high-fidelity images. This development is expected to benefit industries such as gaming and virtual reality, where real-time rendering is crucial for immersive experiences. Artists working in these fields will have access to more powerful tools for crafting lifelike environments and characters.

Summary of the key insights and advancements

In this chapter, we have delved into the various models, techniques, applications, and practical steps involved in image synthesis and enhancement. Starting with an introduction to image synthesis, we explored its importance in fields such as art, science, and technology. We highlighted key milestones like the advent of Generative Adversarial Networks (GANs), Variational Autoencoders (VAEs), and the rise of transformer-based models such as DALL-E.

We examined the primary techniques used in image synthesis, including GANs, VAEs, diffusion models, and autoregressive models like PixelCNN and PixelRNN. Each of these methods offers unique advantages and contributes to the diverse applications of image synthesis, from creating realistic images in gaming and entertainment to generating medical scans for healthcare purposes. The discussion also covered advanced techniques like style transfer, super-resolution, and inpainting, which are essential for enhancing the quality and utility of synthesized images.

Returning to the statement made in the introduction, it's clear that image synthesis plays a crucial role in creating visuals that would be challenging to capture through traditional means. Our current position underscores the vast potential and transformative impact of these technologies across multiple industries. However, there are concerns regarding the ethical implications of image synthesis, particularly with the creation of deepfakes and their potential misuse. It is essential for both researchers and practitioners to consider these issues and work towards developing responsible and ethical guidelines for using these powerful tools.

Overview of Music and Audio Generation Models

Music and audio generation is a burgeoning field that marries creativity with cutting-edge technology. The applications of music and audio generation span various domains such as entertainment, digital content creation, and even therapeutic uses. This introduction to fundamental concepts and models will help in understanding how modern technology shapes this innovative field.

The significance of music and audio generation in today's technological landscape cannot be overstated. These advancements not only revolutionize the music industry by enabling new forms of artistic expression but also impact other sectors like gaming, virtual reality, and film production. Automated music composition can save time for composers and producers, while AI-generated sound effects can create more immersive experiences in video games and movies. This intersection of technology and creativity opens up endless possibilities for both artists and technologists.

Delving into the evolution of music and audio generation provides perspective on its progress and current capabilities. Early attempts at music generation involved basic algorithmic compositions, which lacked the complexity and nuance of human-created music. With advancements in machine learning and deep learning, these models have evolved dramatically. State-of-the-art models now utilize sophisticated neural network architectures capable of generating intricate and high-fidelity audio. Tools like MuseNet and Jukebox by OpenAI exemplify how far this field has come, blending different musical styles and producing coherent compositions that were once thought impossible for machines.

Understanding the basic concepts underpinning music and audio generation is essential for grasping the field's intricacies. Key terms include waveform, MIDI (Musical Instrument Digital Interface), and spectrograms. Waveforms represent sound waves visually, displaying amplitude over time and are fundamental in processing audio. MIDI, on the other hand, is a protocol that allows electronic musical instruments to communicate, making it easier to edit and manipulate musical compositions digitally. Spectrograms provide a visual representation of the spectrum of frequencies in a sound signal as they vary with time, offering valuable insights into the structure and components of audio, crucial for tasks like audio recognition and synthesis.

Neural network architectures play a pivotal role in the latest advances in music and audio generation. Models like recurrent neural networks (RNNs) and long short-term memory (LSTM) networks were among the first to show promise in this area due to their ability to handle sequential data effectively. More recent innovations include transformer-based models, which excel at capturing long-range dependencies within music, thereby enhancing the quality and coherence of generated pieces. Architectures such as

Autoencoders and Generative Adversarial Networks (GANs) are also employed to refine the subtleties in audio production, improving aspects like tone and rhythm.

In modern music and audio generation, waveforms form the foundation of sound manipulation. Waveforms capture the raw data of sound vibrations over time, allowing for various transformations and analyses. By converting audio signals into digital waveforms, it becomes possible to apply complex algorithms to modify and generate new sounds. This process is fundamental in creating realistic sound effects and synthesized voices, contributing significantly to fields such as voice synthesis and digital audio workstations.

MIDI has been a game-changer in digital music production. It standardizes communication between musical instruments and computers, enabling precise control over musical elements. Through MIDI, artists can easily edit notes, change instruments, and adjust timing without affecting the underlying composition. This flexibility makes MIDI indispensable for both professional music production and hobbyist projects. Moreover, MIDI data serves as an ideal input for machine learning models trained to generate music, facilitating seamless integration between human creativity and AI-driven enhancements.

Spectrograms offer a deeper level of analysis by visualizing the frequency content of audio signals. They display how frequencies change over time, helping in identifying patterns and features within sounds. In AI applications, spectrograms are often used as input data for neural networks tasked with audio classification and generation. By understanding the spectral characteristics of different sounds, these models can produce more accurate and contextually appropriate audio outputs, whether it be for music, speech synthesis, or sound effects.

Exploring neural network architectures reveals how different approaches contribute to the effectiveness of music and audio generation models. Recurrent neural networks (RNNs) and their variants like LSTMs were initially favored for their ability to handle temporal sequences. However, their limitations in capturing long-range dependencies led to the adoption of transformer models. Transformers, with their attention mechanisms, allow for better modeling of global relationships within music, resulting in more cohesive and harmonically rich compositions.

Autoencoders, another important architecture, facilitate the compression and reconstruction of audio data. By learning latent representations, autoencoders can distill essential features from complex audio signals. This ability is particularly useful when integrating additional layers of generative models, ensuring the preservation of critical musical attributes. Meanwhile, GANs push the boundaries by fostering a competitive learning environment between two networks—a generator and a discriminator—yielding highly realistic and diverse audio outputs.

Applications in Music Production and Sound Design

The advancements in artificial intelligence (AI) have profoundly impacted the music and audio industries, offering innovative applications across various fields. This section delves into how music and audio generation technologies are utilized in different sectors, highlighting their diverse capabilities and implications.

AI has revolutionized the way new music is composed autonomously. Traditionally, music composition required extensive training and creativity from musicians. Today, AI systems can analyze vast datasets of existing music to identify patterns and structures that can be used to create entirely new compositions. These AI-generated pieces can mimic various styles and genres, producing music that ranges from classical symphonies to modern pop songs. For instance, OpenAI's MuseNet is a neural network trained on a wide array of musical genres and instruments, capable of composing complex multi-instrumental pieces. This technology not only accelerates the creative process but also enables experimentation with novel styles that blend elements from different genres.

In addition to creating new compositions, AI plays a crucial role in generating unique sound effects for movies, games, and other media. Sound designers traditionally spent countless hours recording and editing sounds to create the desired auditory experience for a scene or gameplay environment. AI simplifies this process by using generative algorithms to produce a vast array of sound effects, from ambient noises to intricate audio cues. For example, Google's Magenta project explores AI's potential in sound effect creation, enabling designers to generate sounds that perfectly match the visual and emotional tone of their projects. This capability enhances storytelling by providing more immersive and dynamic soundscapes, contributing significantly to the overall experience of the audience.

Real-time music generation for live performances and DJ sets represents another exciting application of AI in the audio industry. Performers can use AI-driven tools to create spontaneous musical pieces during live shows, enhancing the audience's experience with unique, never-before-heard compositions. One prominent example is the software Amper Music, which allows DJs and live performers to generate music on the fly, adapting to the crowd's energy and preferences in real time. This technology not only adds a layer of interactivity to live performances but also empowers artists to experiment with sound in ways that were previously unattainable, pushing the boundaries of what is possible in live music.

Personalized music tracks based on user preferences and data illustrate the potential of AI in creating highly customized auditory experiences. Streaming services like Spotify and Apple Music already utilize AI algorithms to recommend songs based on listening habits. However, AI can take personalization a step further by generating original music tailored to individual tastes, moods, and even biometric data. Imagine an AI system that creates a personalized playlist designed to calm you down after a stressful day at work or pump you up for a workout based on your heart rate. Such advancements in personalized music not only enhance the user experience but also open new avenues for mental and physical well-being through carefully curated soundtracks.

Step-by-Step Guide to Building a Music Generator

To build a simple music generator using deep learning techniques, we start with gathering datasets and preparing audio and MIDI data for model training. Music datasets are readily available, such as the MAESTRO dataset, which can be sourced from TensorFlow's Magenta project. Collecting high-quality datasets is crucial as they serve as the training foundation. Ensure the dataset is diverse, covering various genres and artists to create a more versatile model. It's also important to have balanced data, meaning an equal number of examples for each class if working with classification tasks.

Preprocessing the gathered data is the next step. For audio data, this involves converting raw audio files into a more usable format, often by extracting features like Mel-frequency cepstral coefficients (MFCCs), spectrograms, or other time-domain features. This makes it easier for the model to understand the nuances in the music. For MIDI data, preprocessing includes parsing the MIDI files to extract note sequences, velocities, and durations. Tools like pretty_midi can help automate this process. Ensure that all the data is normalized and formatted consistently.

Implementing the chosen model using popular frameworks such as TensorFlow or PyTorch comes next. Deep learning models relevant for music generation typically include Recurrent Neural Networks (RNNs), Long Short-Term Memory networks (LSTMs), or more recently, Transformer architectures. Start by defining the architecture of your model. In TensorFlow, you may use the Keras API to stack layers like Embedding, LSTM, and Dense layers. The Embedding layer helps convert integer-encoded notes into dense vectors of fixed size, while LSTM layers capture the temporal dependencies in music sequences.

Once the model architecture is defined, the implementation continues with writing the code to feed data into the model. Use data loaders to handle batching and shuffling, which ensures the model sees a varied sequence of data points during training. Training loops in TensorFlow or PyTorch execute the forward pass, compute losses, and perform backpropagation to update the model weights. Pay attention to memory management and computational efficiency, especially when dealing with large audio datasets.

The step-by-step guide to training the model, including hyperparameter tuning, is critical for achieving good performance. Begin by splitting the data into training, validation, and test sets. This allows you to monitor the model's performance on unseen data. Initial training involves setting default hyperparameters such as learning rate, batch size, and the number of epochs. Train the model and evaluate its performance based on metrics like accuracy or loss. Use tools like TensorBoard to visualize training progress and detect overfitting.

Hyperparameter tuning is the process of systematically adjusting the model's parameters to find the optimal configuration. Techniques like grid search or random search can be employed to explore different values. Tune one parameter at a time to isolate its impact on model performance. Record the results and iterations to identify the best set of hyperparameters. It's essential to validate tuned parameters on a different subset of data to ensure generalizability.

After the model is trained, the next focus is on generating new music and refining it for better quality. Begin by sampling sequences from the trained model. In practice, this involves providing an initial seed sequence and letting the model predict subsequent notes. Temperature scaling can be used to control the randomness of predictions. Lower values of temperature yield more deterministic outputs, while higher values introduce more variability.

Refining the generated music involves post-processing steps to smooth out abrupt transitions and ensure musical coherence. Apply rules to correct any structural anomalies in the generated sequences. For instance, ensure consistent key signatures or resolve dissonant chords. Techniques like beam search can also improve the quality by considering multiple sequence candidates and selecting the most promising one. Listening to the generated output and iterating based on qualitative feedback is crucial.

Real-World Examples and Case Studies

OpenAI's MuseNet represents a significant leap in AI-driven music generation. MuseNet is a deep neural network that can generate 4-minute musical compositions with 10 different instruments and blend styles from a wide range of genres, including classical, jazz, pop, and more. One of its standout features is its ability to understand and replicate complex harmonic structures, making it capable of producing high-quality pieces that mimic human composition. The technology behind MuseNet employs a transformer model, which has been fine-tuned on vast datasets of MIDI files, allowing it to capture intricate musical patterns and stylistic nuances.

A key innovation of MuseNet lies in its use of unsupervised learning to develop its musical capabilities. By training on a diverse dataset of over one million musical examples, MuseNet learns to predict subsequent notes in a sequence, akin to how language models predict words in a sentence. This technique allows the model to generate music that maintains coherence and thematic continuity, essential qualities for creating appealing and emotionally resonant compositions. Moreover, MuseNet offers users the flexibility to specify composers, bands, and instruments, providing a tailored creative experience that caters to various artistic preferences and needs.

The practical applications of MuseNet are manifold. In educational settings, it can serve as a tool for teaching music theory and composition, offering students interactive examples to analyze and learn from. In the entertainment industry, MuseNet's generated compositions can be used in soundtracks for films, video games, and other multimedia projects, providing cost-effective solutions for high-quality musical scores. Additionally, independent artists and producers can leverage MuseNet to inspire new musical ideas and explore innovative soundscapes, expanding their creative horizons and streamlining the music production process.

Google's Magenta project is another pioneering initiative in the realm of AI-generated music and art. Magenta focuses on developing tools and models that enable artists and musicians to collaborate with AI systems in novel and innovative ways. One of the project's hallmark contributions is the development of TensorFlow-based open-source models designed to create music and artistic content. These models include powerful tools like MusicVAE, an autoencoder that generates variations of a melody, and NSynth, which produces entirely new sounds by blending attributes of existing ones.

Magenta's emphasis on usability and accessibility has led to the creation of user-friendly interfaces and plugins that integrate seamlessly with popular digital audio workstations (DAWs). For instance, the Piano Genie tool allows users to compose music using just eight buttons, translating simple input into complex melodies and harmonies. This democratizes music creation, making it accessible even to those without formal musical training. Additionally, Magenta's Groove library offers pre-trained drum machine models that can generate realistic drum patterns, enhancing the rhythm sections of compositions effortlessly.

The impact of Magenta extends beyond music generation to the broader field of interactive AI and creativity. Artists and developers have utilized Magenta's tools to create immersive installations, generative art pieces, and interactive performances that push the boundaries of conventional art forms. By fostering collaborations between AI and human creators, Magenta encourages experimentation and the exploration of new artistic possibilities, contributing significantly to the advancement of AI in creative industries.

This synergy between technology and artistry exemplifies the potential of AI to augment human creativity in meaningful and transformative ways.

Amper Music is a commercially-focused AI music platform known for its efficiency and ease of use in generating custom music tracks. Built with professional applications in mind, Amper leverages advanced algorithms to quickly compose, perform, and produce unique musical pieces tailored to specific project requirements. This makes it an invaluable tool for media production companies, advertising agencies, and content creators who need high-quality music without the time and expense of traditional composition processes.

The core technology behind Amper involves sophisticated AI algorithms that analyze user inputs—such as mood, genre, and instrumentation—to create customized compositions. Users interact with a simple interface where they can select parameters and preview the generated music in real-time. Amper's AI then composes a piece that fits the desired criteria, allowing for further customization through editing tools. This level of control ensures that the output aligns closely with the user's vision, making Amper a versatile solution for various music production needs.

In commercial applications, Amper Music has proven particularly effective in areas such as advertising, film scoring, and video game soundtracks. Its ability to produce ready-to-use music rapidly enables creators to meet tight deadlines and adapt quickly to changing project requirements. Furthermore, Amper's music is royalty-free, eliminating licensing concerns and providing a cost-effective alternative to hiring traditional composers. This makes it an attractive option for businesses seeking to enhance their content with original, high-quality music while maintaining budgetary constraints.

JukeBox, developed by OpenAI, is a groundbreaking model that generates complete songs with vocals in a variety of styles and genres. JukeBox utilizes a hierarchical VQ-VAE-2 architecture composed of three levels: top, middle, and bottom, each responsible for capturing different aspects of the musical structure. This architecture allows the model to generate music at varying levels of abstraction, from high-level song structures down to individual audio samples, resulting in coherent and stylistically rich compositions.

The training process for JukeBox involves a multi-stage approach where the model is first pre-trained on a large corpus of music data, then fine-tuned to improve the quality and diversity of the generated outputs. This extensive training enables JukeBox to generate not only instrumental tracks but also vocal lines with lyrics, adding a new dimension to AI-generated music. The model can create music that spans multiple genres and imitates the styles of specific artists, providing a powerful tool for both creative exploration and practical music production.

The future potential of music and audio generation technologies.

Throughout this chapter, we have explored various techniques, applications, and real-world examples of music and audio generation using modern technology. From the fundamental concepts of waveforms, MIDI, and spectrograms to the sophisticated neural network architectures that drive today's advancements, we have seen how technology has revolutionized the field.

In our discussion, we began by acknowledging the significance of music and audio generation in today's technological landscape. This innovative field not only transforms artistic expression but also enhances industries such as gaming, virtual reality, and film production. The evolution from basic algorithmic compositions to state-of-the-art models like MuseNet and JukeBox highlights the remarkable progress made possible through machine learning and deep learning.

A key takeaway is the role of different neural network architectures, such as RNNs, LSTMs, and transformer models, which excel at handling sequential data and capturing long-range dependencies within music. These architectures enhance the quality and coherence of generated pieces. Moreover, approaches like autoencoders and GANs refine audio production, improving tone and rhythm. Understanding these foundational elements is crucial for anyone aiming to delve into the intricacies of music and audio generation.

The practical applications of these technologies are vast and diverse. AI-driven music composition accelerates creative processes, while AI-generated sound effects enhance immersive experiences in media. Real-time music generation tools empower live performers to create spontaneous pieces, adding interactivity to performances. Personalized music tracks based on user data illustrate AI's potential to create customized auditory experiences, contributing to mental and physical well-being.

For those looking to build their own music generators, the step-by-step guide provided outlines the process from data gathering and preprocessing to model implementation and training. Utilizing frameworks like TensorFlow or PyTorch, aspiring practitioners can experiment with various architectures and fine-tune hyperparameters to achieve optimal results. The focus on generating new music and refining it ensures that the output maintains musical coherence.

Real-world examples such as OpenAI's MuseNet and Google's Magenta project demonstrate the practical impact of AI in music and audio generation. These case studies showcase how advanced models and user-friendly tools facilitate creative exploration and streamline production processes. Platforms like Amper Music offer commercially focused solutions, providing efficient and cost-effective ways to generate custom music tracks.

While the current capabilities are impressive, it is essential to consider the broader implications of AI-generated music and audio. Ethical concerns, such as the potential loss of human artistry and the impact on employment in creative fields, warrant attention. Additionally, ensuring diversity and inclusivity in AI-generated outputs remains a critical consideration.

Looking ahead, the possibilities for AI in music and audio generation are boundless. As technology continues to evolve, so too will the methods and applications in this field. Aspiring AI practitioners and professionals seeking to upskill have a wealth of opportunities to explore and contribute to this exciting domain. Embracing these advancements can lead to groundbreaking innovations, enhancing both individual creativity and collective experiences in the world of music and audio.

References

5 Ways AI Has Already Changed the Music Industry. www.hartfordjazz.org. (2024, May). https://www.hartfordjazz.org/5-ways-ai-has-already-changed-the-music-industry/

Auido & Music Generation | Open DeepLearning. www.openmlguide.org. (n.d.). https://www.openmlguide.org/ai-portal-gun/generative-ai/Generative-Models/audio-generation/

Generate music with an RNN | TensorFlow Core. TensorFlow. (n.d.). https://www.tensorflow.org/tutorials/audio/music_generation

How to build a Deep Learning-based Lyrics Generator?. GeeksforGeeks. (2024, April). https://www.geeksforgeeks.org/how-to-build-a-deep-learning-based-lyrics-generator/

In The Know. (2023, May). *Musicians Institute Hollywood. Musicians Institute Hollywood.* https://www.mi.edu/in-the-know/ai-music-production-enhancing-human-creativity-replacing/

Long-form music generation with latent diffusion. arxiv.org. (n.d.). https://arxiv.org/html/2404.10301v1

CHAPTER 10

Video Generation and Synthesis

Video generation and synthesis are integral components in the field of artificial intelligence, contributing significantly to advancements across various industries. The capability to produce sequences of images that simulate real-life or imagined scenarios has opened up a plethora of opportunities in entertainment, education, and content creation. This technology leverages computational models to generate videos, which can then be used to automate processes, create immersive experiences, and enhance visual storytelling.

The chapter delves into the principles and models that underpin video generation and synthesis. It explores cutting-edge approaches such as Generative Adversarial Networks (GANs), Recurrent Neural Networks (RNNs), and Variational Autoencoders (VAEs). Each of these models offers unique advantages in generating realistic and coherent video sequences. The discussion extends to practical applications, showcasing how these technologies are employed in diverse fields like film, media, advertising, gaming, and beyond. Additionally, the chapter provides insights into constructing video generators, including data collection, preprocessing techniques, model selection, and training pipelines. Through real-world examples and case studies, the chapter illustrates the transformative impact and potential of video generation and synthesis in modern AI applications.

Overview of Video Generation Models

Video generation is a rapidly advancing field in artificial intelligence, playing an essential role in many industries, from entertainment to education. Video generation involves creating sequences of images that simulate real or imagined scenes. This technology enables various applications such as generating special effects for movies, producing educational content, and developing new forms of artistic expression. The significance of video generation lies in its ability to automate and enhance content creation, making processes more efficient and accessible.

Generative Adversarial Networks (GANs) have revolutionized the field by enabling high-quality video generation. GANs operate through two neural networks—the generator and the discriminator—that compete against each other to improve the realism of generated data. For video generation, this concept has been extended into models like Video GANs and Temporal GANs. Video GANs focus on spatial coherence across frames, ensuring that consecutive frames are visually consistent. Temporal GANs take this further by capturing temporal dependencies, which are crucial for maintaining logical progression within videos. These adaptations have marked significant advancements, allowing more dynamic and lifelike video synthesis.

Recurrent Neural Networks (RNNs) also play a crucial role in video generation, particularly in capturing temporal dependencies. Unlike traditional neural networks, RNNs can process sequential data, making them suitable for tasks involving time series or sequences, such as videos. They maintain a state vector that remembers previous inputs, thereby learning patterns over time. In video generation, RNNs help model the progression between individual frames, ensuring that generated videos reflect realistic motion and transitions. Their ability to learn long-term dependencies makes them invaluable for producing coherent and temporally consistent video sequences.

Variational Autoencoders (VAEs) offer another approach to video generation, emphasizing both spatial and temporal feature extraction. VAEs consist of an encoder that compresses the input data into a latent space and a decoder that reconstructs the data from this compressed representation. For video data, VAEs are extended with convolutional layers, enabling them to capture intricate details in both spatial and temporal dimensions. This allows the model to generate videos that not only appear visually accurate but also maintain logical temporal progressions. By leveraging the strengths of convolutional layers, VAEs provide a robust framework for generating complex video data.

Applications in Film, Media, and Advertising

Video generation technology has revolutionized various industries, particularly the film industry. Advances in computational models have enabled filmmakers to create astonishing special effects that were previously unattainable. These effects include realistic explosions, otherworldly creatures, and breathtaking landscapes. By using generative AI technologies, special effects can be created with a high degree of realism and efficiency, saving time and resources while enhancing the visual impact of films.

Moreover, video generation is pivotal in scene generation, allowing directors to craft entire environments digitally. This technology enables the creation of settings that might be too hazardous, costly, or logistically impractical to shoot in real life. It opens up endless creative possibilities, from futuristic cities to historical reconstructions, thus expanding the narrative scope of movies. Additionally, this flexibility aids in continuity, as scenes can be manipulated and adjusted post-production without reshoots.

Enhancing visual storytelling is another significant application of video generation in film. Directors can use this technology to create seamless transitions, innovative camera angles, and dynamic lighting effects that enhance the narrative flow. These elements not only captivate audiences but also bring a new level of depth and immersion to the story being told. This technology contributes to a richer cinematic experience by transforming visionary ideas into stunning visual realities.

In the media and entertainment sector, video generation is transforming content delivery. One notable application is the creation of virtual news anchors. These AI-generated personas can deliver news updates 24/7 without fatigue, ensuring consistent and timely information dissemination. Virtual anchors can be customized to fit different languages and cultural contexts, broadening the reach and inclusivity of news coverage.

Automated sports highlights are another innovation brought about by video generation technology. Media companies utilize AI to sift through hours of footage, identify key moments, and compile them into engaging highlight reels. This automation not only increases efficiency but also appeals to sports enthusiasts who desire quick and exciting summaries of their favorite games. The instant availability of such highlights keeps fans engaged and boosts viewership.

Additionally, media companies leverage video generation for creating compelling content that attracts and retains viewers. From interactive documentaries to immersive reality shows, these technologies enable the production of unique and engaging media experiences. As a result, companies can innovate continually, offering fresh content that stands out in a competitive market.

In the advertising industry, video generation technology facilitates the creation of personalized video ads. Businesses can generate tailor-made advertisements that cater specifically to individual consumer preferences, increasing engagement and conversion rates. This personalization is achieved through analyzing viewer data and generating content that resonates on a personal level, thereby enhancing the effectiveness of marketing campaigns.

Product demonstrations benefit significantly from video generation as well. Companies can create detailed and visually appealing presentations of their products, showcasing features, benefits, and usage scenarios. Generative technology allows for the customization of these videos according to different audience segments, ensuring that the content is relevant and engaging. Such demonstrations help consumers make informed purchasing decisions, thereby boosting sales and customer satisfaction.

Virtual brand ambassadors represent another innovative use of video generation in advertising. Brands can develop AI-driven avatars that interact with customers, provide information, and promote products around the clock. These digital representatives can be deployed across various platforms, including websites, social media, and virtual events. They offer a consistent and cost-effective means of maintaining customer engagement while reflecting the brand's identity and values.

The gaming industry has also embraced video generation technology to enrich player experiences. One prominent application is in crafting dynamic game environments. Developers use AI to generate vast, intricate worlds that evolve in real time based on player actions. This adds a layer of unpredictability and excitement, making each gameplay session unique. These dynamic environments also allow for more complex and immersive storytelling within games.

Realistic character animations are another area where video generation shines in game development. AI-driven techniques enable the creation of lifelike movements and expressions, enhancing the believability of characters. This realism draws players deeper into the game world, fostering a stronger emotional connection to the characters and the story. Moreover, the ability to automate animation processes reduces the workload on animators, allowing them to focus on refining other aspects of game design.

In addition to enhancing gameplay, video generation helps improve the overall aesthetic quality of games. High-quality visuals, combined with sophisticated audio and tactile feedback, create a multi-sensory experience that captivates players. This level of immersion is crucial in today's competitive gaming market, where gamers seek ever more engaging and visually stunning experiences. Video generation technology thus plays a vital role in pushing the boundaries of what is possible in game design.

Step-by-Step Guide to Building a Video Generator

Methods for Collecting and Preprocessing Video Data

Constructing a video generator from scratch begins with the crucial step of collecting and preprocessing video data. High-quality, diverse datasets are essential for training robust models. Begin by sourcing videos from publicly available databases, user-generated content platforms, or creating custom footage tailored to your specific needs. While curating this data, ensure it represents various conditions, scenarios, and subjects to avoid bias and improve the model's generalization capabilities.

Once you have your dataset, the next step is preprocessing the video data. This involves tasks such as resizing frames, normalizing pixel values, and converting videos into a suitable format for model ingestion. Remove any irrelevant content and ensure each video clip is uniformly processed to maintain consistency across the dataset. Preprocessing also includes cleaning corrupted frames and handling missing data, which could otherwise impede the model's performance.

To further enhance your dataset, employ data augmentation techniques. Augmentation methods like rotation, flipping, scaling, and color adjustments can significantly increase dataset diversity without the need for additional data collection. These techniques help the model learn to recognize patterns under different visual conditions, ultimately leading to more robust video generation. By carefully implementing these preprocessing steps, you lay a solid foundation for building an effective video generator.

Guidance on Selecting Appropriate Model Architecture

Choosing the right model architecture is pivotal in constructing an effective video generator. There are three primary architectures to consider: Generative Adversarial Networks (GANs), Recurrent Neural Networks (RNNs), and Variational Autoencoders (VAEs). Each has unique strengths and application areas. GANs are highly effective for generating high-fidelity videos and are particularly popular due to their two-component system—a generator and a discriminator—that work in tandem to produce realistic outputs.

RNNs are better suited for tasks involving temporal dependencies, making them ideal for video sequences where the order of frames matters. Their ability to remember previous inputs allows them to generate coherent sequences over time. For example, RNNs can be used in applications requiring smooth transitions between video frames, such as animations or simulations.

VAEs offer a different approach by encoding the input data into a latent space and then decoding it back into the video space. They are particularly useful for generating varied outputs from the same input, allowing for creative and exploratory applications. When choosing a model architecture, consider the specific requirements of your application, such as the desired output quality, computational resources, and the complexity of the video content you aim to generate. Balancing these factors will guide you toward selecting the most appropriate architecture for your video generator.

Setting Up the Training Pipeline

Setting up the training pipeline is a crucial phase that requires meticulous planning and execution. Start by defining the structure of your pipeline, including data loading, preprocessing, model initialization, and training cycles. Utilize frameworks like TensorFlow or PyTorch that offer comprehensive libraries and tools to streamline this process. Ensure that the pipeline is efficient and scalable, capable of handling large volumes of video data without bottlenecks.

The choice of loss functions is another critical consideration. For GANs, the adversarial loss function helps the generator produce more realistic outputs by minimizing the difference between generated and real videos. RNNs often use sequence-based loss functions like Mean Squared Error (MSE) to measure the accuracy of frame predictions. VAEs typically utilize a combination of reconstruction loss and Kullback-Leibler divergence to balance fidelity and variability in generated videos. Selecting the appropriate loss function based on your model architecture will directly impact training efficiency and output quality.

Monitoring training progress is essential to ensure your model converges effectively. Use metrics such as loss value trends, output quality assessments, and comparison against baseline models to gauge progress. Visualization tools like TensorBoard can provide real-time insights into training dynamics, helping you identify and address issues promptly. Regularly evaluate intermediate results and adjust hyperparameters as needed to optimize performance. By carefully setting up and managing the training pipeline, you create an environment conducive to producing high-quality video generators.

Techniques for Evaluating and Fine-Tuning the Model

Evaluating the performance of your video generator involves both qualitative and quantitative metrics. Qualitative evaluation includes visual inspection of generated videos, focusing on coherence, realism, and overall aesthetic quality. Human judgment plays a critical role here, as it helps assess the subjective aspects that automated metrics might miss. Engage multiple reviewers to minimize individual biases and gather a well-rounded perspective on output quality.

Quantitative evaluation, on the other hand, relies on statistical measures to objectively assess model performance. Metrics such as Structural Similarity Index (SSIM), Peak Signal-to-Noise Ratio (PSNR), and Fréchet Video Distance (FVD) can provide valuable insights into how closely generated videos resemble real ones. These metrics offer a numerical basis for comparing different models or configurations, facilitating objective decision-making during the fine-tuning process.

Real-World Examples and Case Studies

Media companies have made significant strides in creating virtual news anchors using Generative Adversarial Networks (GANs). A notable example is a leading Asian news broadcaster that pioneered this technology. They faced numerous challenges, including generating realistic facial expressions and ensuring lip-sync accuracy with the audio feed. By leveraging advanced GAN architectures, the company could generate life-like avatars that closely mimic human news anchors. The implementation of specialized training data comprising various facial expressions and speech patterns played a crucial role in overcoming these challenges.

The technical hurdles were accompanied by ethical and operational considerations. For instance, maintaining audience trust was paramount, requiring the company to transparently inform viewers about the use of AI-generated anchors. Additionally, the initial deployment phase experienced mixed reactions from the audience, necessitating further refinements based on viewer feedback. Solutions included iterative updates to the GAN models and incorporating real-time feedback loops to enhance the anchor's realism continuously.

Ultimately, the successful integration of GANs for virtual news anchors has revolutionized their broadcast operations. These AI-driven avatars are now employed for multiple language broadcasts, reducing the need for human anchors and enabling around-the-clock newscasting. This innovation showcases the potential of GANs in transforming traditional media landscapes while highlighting the importance of addressing technological, ethical, and consumer engagement challenges.

In advertising, personalized video generation has shown to markedly boost customer engagement. One remarkable campaign saw an e-commerce giant utilize video synthesis powered by machine learning algorithms to tailor advertisements based on individual customer behaviors and preferences. By analyzing user data such as browsing history and purchase patterns, the algorithm generated targeted video ads featuring products likely to interest each viewer. This targeted approach significantly outperformed generic advertisements in terms of click-through rates and conversions.

The personalization process involved several sophisticated techniques. Deep learning models analyzed vast amounts of user data to identify patterns and predict preferences accurately. Videos were then dynamically generated with contextually relevant content tailored to each user's profile. This level of customization required robust computational power and efficient data management systems to generate high-quality videos rapidly without compromising performance.

The results were staggering, with the campaign seeing up to a 300% increase in engagement compared to traditional advertising methods. Users reported feeling more connected to the brand, and the tailored ads fostered a sense of personalized attention. This case study underscores the transformative impact of machine learning and video generation technologies in crafting compelling, individualized marketing strategies.

Automating the generation of sports highlights is another area where video synthesis has proven invaluable. Combining Recurrent Neural Networks (RNNs) with computer vision techniques, an innovative system was developed to automatically create highlights from live sports footage. The RNNs were instrumental in identifying and predicting key moments in the games, such as goals or critical plays, while computer vision algorithms ensured accurate object detection and event classification.

One significant challenge was ensuring the system's ability to discern between varying levels of excitement and importance in different segments of the game. This was addressed by incorporating crowd noise analysis and commentator voice intensity as additional inputs to the model, enabling more precise identification of highlight-worthy moments. Furthermore, integrating real-time processing capabilities allowed the system to generate and stream highlights almost instantaneously.

The deployment of this automated highlight generation system yielded tremendous efficiency gains for broadcasting networks. It reduced reliance on manual editing and enabled quicker turnaround times for producing engaging sports content. Viewers benefited from timely access to high-quality highlights, enhancing their overall experience. This application exemplifies the utility of combining AI techniques like RNNs and computer vision to streamline content creation processes in sports media.

In game development, video generation models have been pivotal in creating dynamic and immersive environments. A prominent game studio harnessed the power of deep learning models to design adaptable game worlds that respond to player actions in real-time. By training generative models on extensive datasets encompassing various terrains, weather conditions, and architectural styles, the studio could produce richly detailed environments with minimal manual intervention.

Initially, one of the primary difficulties was ensuring consistency and coherence across the generated elements. To address this, the models were fine-tuned using reinforcement learning strategies, allowing them to learn and adapt based on player interactions within the game. This iterative learning process enabled the formation of cohesive and visually stunning landscapes that players could explore and interact with in novel ways.

The versatility of these video generation models also allowed for the creation of unique, procedurally generated experiences for each playthrough. Players encountered different environmental conditions and landscape formations each time they engaged with the game, enhancing replayability and immersiveness. This example illustrates how video generation technologies are reshaping the boundaries of creativity and innovation in game development.

Summary and Future Directions

Throughout this chapter, we have explored the principles, models, applications, construction, and real-world examples of video generation and synthesis using computational models. We began by discussing how video generation has become a significant field in artificial intelligence, impacting various industries such as entertainment, education, media, advertising, and gaming. The advent of advanced neural network architectures like Generative Adversarial Networks (GANs), Recurrent Neural Networks (RNNs), and Variational Autoencoders (VAEs) has been transformative in producing high-quality video content.

Returning to our initial focus, it's clear that each model architecture offers unique strengths. GANs excel in generating high-fidelity videos through their adversarial frameworks, while RNNs are indispensable for capturing temporal dependencies vital for realistic motion and transitions. VAEs bring a different approach by emphasizing both spatial and temporal feature extraction, allowing for intricate and varied video outputs. These advancements are evidence of the rapid evolution and potential of video generation technology.

The current position of video generation in AI is robust and continually advancing. These technologies not only enhance content creation but also automate processes, making them more efficient and accessible. However, some concerns remain, particularly regarding ethical implications and the potential for misuse of generated content. Ensuring transparency and addressing ethical concerns are paramount to maintaining trust and integrity in applications of video generation.

On a broader scale, the consequences of advancing video generation technology could be profound. As virtual news anchors, personalized video ads, and automated sports highlights become more commonplace, the lines between real and generated content may blur, necessitating new standards and regulations. Furthermore, the ability to generate highly realistic environments and characters in games opens up unparalleled creative possibilities, pushing the boundaries of interactive storytelling and user engagement.

As we look ahead, the field of video generation promises even greater innovation and impact. Future research and development will likely focus on improving the efficiency, realism, and ethical considerations of these technologies. The intersection of AI with art, media, and everyday applications will continue to expand, offering exciting opportunities and challenges. This ongoing evolution invites us to ponder the future of video generation and its role in shaping our visual and digital experiences.

References

Best Practices and Lessons Learned on Synthetic Data for Language Models. arxiv.org. (n.d.). https://arxiv.org/html/2404.07503v1

Coursera. (2024, March). *20 Examples of Generative AI Applications Across Industries. Coursera.* https://www.coursera.org/articles/generative-ai-applications

Davenport, T., Mittal, N. (2022, November). *How Generative AI Is Changing Creative Work. Harvard Business Review.* https://hbr.org/2022/11/how-generative-ai-is-changing-creative-work

Miller, M. (2023, May). *SEO and website design: How to build search engine-friendly sites. Search Engine Land.* https://martech.org/seo-website-design-everything-need-know/

CHAPTER 11

Interdisciplinary Applications of Generative AI

Exploring the interdisciplinary applications of generative AI reveals a fascinating landscape of technological innovation. This chapter delves into how generative AI is utilized across different fields, merging with other technologies to produce groundbreaking solutions. By examining specific sectors such as healthcare and finance, we can uncover the transformative potential of this technology. The insights gained from these applications highlight not only the versatility of generative AI but also its capability to address complex challenges in various domains.

In this chapter, readers will encounter detailed discussions on several key areas where generative AI is making a significant impact. The chapter begins with an exploration of healthcare applications, showcasing how AI enhances medical imaging, drug discovery, personalized medicine, and clinical decision support systems. It then transitions into the financial sector, illustrating how generative AI influences algorithmic trading, fraud detection, risk management, and financial forecasting. Additionally, the chapter covers educational advancements, focusing on content generation, personalized learning, and AI-driven tutoring systems. Lastly, the integration of generative AI with IoT is examined, highlighting its role in smart environments, patient monitoring, and industrial applications. Through these examples, the chapter provides a comprehensive overview of the multifaceted applications of generative AI, emphasizing its role in shaping the future of various industries.

Applications in Healthcare

Generative AI has shown significant potential in enhancing healthcare applications, particularly in medical imaging. Traditional diagnostic techniques often rely on the expertise and experience of radiologists to interpret images like MRI and CT scans. However, even the most experienced professionals can overlook subtle anomalies. Generative AI models, specifically those using GANs (Generative Adversarial Networks), can improve the quality and clarity of these images. By synthesizing high-resolution medical images from low-quality scans, generative AI helps in detecting diseases at earlier stages, potentially leading to better patient outcomes (Kazeminia, Rahmani, & Haghighi, 2021).

Moreover, these generative models can create synthetic data sets that are invaluable for training other AI systems. Many healthcare providers face the challenge of limited annotated data, which is crucial for training effective diagnostic models. By generating realistic synthetic medical images, AI can bridge this gap, providing ample data while preserving patient privacy. These enhancements reduce the margin for human error and bring more consistency and reliability to diagnostic processes.

Generative AI's impact extends further by enabling the creation of entirely new imaging modalities. Using AI-generated imagery, researchers can visualize anatomical structures or physiological features that were previously unobservable with standard imaging techniques. This capability allows for groundbreaking discoveries and a deeper understanding of various medical conditions, ultimately fostering advancements in medical research and clinical practices.

In drug discovery, generative AI has revolutionized how we approach the development of new pharmaceuticals. By predicting molecular structures and generating novel compounds, AI accelerates the drug discovery process (Zhavoronkov, 2020). Traditional methods often involve costly and time-consuming trial-and-error experiments to identify viable drug candidates. With generative models, researchers can computationally generate vast libraries of potential compounds and predict their interactions with biological targets.

This approach significantly reduces the time and cost involved in bringing new drugs to market. For instance, generative AI can screen millions of chemical structures in silico, identifying promising candidates before any physical testing occurs. This preliminary screening can drastically narrow down the number of compounds that need to be synthesized and tested in the lab, focusing resources only on the most promising substances.

Additionally, AI models can simulate a compound's pharmacokinetic and pharmacodynamic properties, helping to predict its behavior in the human body. This predictive power aids in assessing the potential efficacy and safety of new drugs, thus minimizing the risk of adverse effects during clinical trials. The ability to generate and evaluate novel compounds quickly paves the way for discovering treatments for diseases that currently lack effective therapies.

Personalized medicine is another area where generative AI shows immense promise. Tailoring treatments based on individual patient characteristics is a key goal in modern healthcare. Generative models can predict how different patients will respond to specific drugs, enabling personalized treatment plans. These predictions consider various factors, including genetic makeup, lifestyle, and existing health conditions, to recommend the most effective therapies for each patient.

For example, generative AI can analyze a patient's genomic data to suggest targeted therapies for cancer treatment. By understanding the unique mutations present in a tumor, AI can identify which drugs are likely to be effective and tailor a treatment plan accordingly. This precision medicine approach not only improves the chances of successful outcomes but also reduces the likelihood of adverse reactions.

Beyond oncology, generative AI can aid in managing chronic diseases such as diabetes and cardiovascular conditions. By continuously analyzing patient data, AI-generated models can adapt treatment plans in real time, ensuring that interventions remain effective as the patient's condition evolves. This level of customization enhances patient care, promoting better health outcomes and improving overall quality of life.

Clinical decision support systems are integral to modern healthcare, and generative AI plays a pivotal role in enhancing their capabilities. These systems assist healthcare professionals by generating clinical pathways and treatment recommendations based on extensive medical data. By leveraging AI, clinicians can access evidence-based insights that inform their decisions, reducing reliance on subjective judgment alone.

Generative models can analyze vast amounts of patient data, medical literature, and clinical guidelines to provide tailored recommendations. For instance, in managing a complex disease like sepsis, AI-driven decision support can analyze patient vitals, lab results, and historical data to suggest optimal treatment strategies. This timely and accurate guidance can significantly improve patient outcomes, particularly in critical care settings where rapid decisions are essential.

Furthermore, generative AI can help identify patterns and correlations within patient data that might be overlooked by human practitioners. These insights can uncover new treatment approaches, optimize existing protocols, and highlight areas for further research. By continuously learning from new data, AI-driven clinical decision support systems evolve, staying up-to-date with the latest medical advancements and improving their accuracy over time.

Applications in Finance

Generative AI is revolutionizing the financial sector by providing innovative solutions in various areas. One of the most significant applications is in algorithmic trading. Algorithmic trading involves using algorithms to make trading decisions based on historical data and other market indicators. Generative AI enhances this process by creating advanced trading strategies that can adapt to changing market conditions. By analyzing vast amounts of historical data, generative models can identify patterns and trends that human traders might miss. This allows for more accurate market predictions, leading to better trading decisions.

Moreover, generative AI's ability to simulate different trading scenarios helps in stress-testing strategies before they are deployed in real markets. Traders can use these simulations to understand how their strategies would perform under various market conditions, such as high volatility or low liquidity periods. This predictive capability reduces the risks associated with algorithmic trading and increases the chances of generating positive returns. Additionally, generative AI can continuously learn from new data, refining its algorithms to improve performance over time.

Another benefit of generative AI in algorithmic trading is its potential to reduce emotional bias. Human traders often make impulsive decisions based on emotions like fear or greed. In contrast, AI-driven trading systems operate based on data and predefined rules, ensuring a more disciplined approach. This objectivity can lead to more consistent trading outcomes and help investors achieve their financial goals more effectively.

Fraud detection is another critical application of generative AI in the financial sector. Traditional fraud detection systems rely on identifying known patterns of fraudulent activity. However, fraudsters continuously evolve their tactics, making it challenging to detect new forms of fraud. Generative AI addresses this challenge by creating synthetic transaction data to train more robust models (Fedele & Pasquini, 2021) . This synthetic data includes both legitimate and fraudulent transactions, enabling the AI to recognize a broader range of fraudulent activities.

By training on diverse datasets, generative AI can identify subtle patterns and anomalies that traditional systems might overlook. This leads to earlier detection of fraudulent activities, reducing financial losses and protecting consumers. Moreover, generative AI can adapt to emerging fraud tactics by updating its models with new synthetic data, ensuring that detection systems remain effective over time. Financial institutions can also customize these models to address specific types of fraud relevant to their operations, further enhancing their security measures.

In addition to improving detection capabilities, generative AI can automate the monitoring of transactions in real-time. This real-time monitoring enables financial institutions to respond quickly to suspicious activities, preventing fraud before it causes significant harm. By reducing the reliance on manual review processes, generative AI not only enhances efficiency but also minimizes the risk of human error in fraud detection.

Risk management is another area where generative AI offers substantial benefits. Financial institutions need to assess and mitigate various risks, such as credit risk, market risk, and operational risk. Generative AI helps in this process by simulating different financial scenarios to evaluate potential risks and devise mitigation strategies. These simulations can include a wide range of variables, such as changes in interest rates, currency fluctuations, and economic downturns, providing a comprehensive view of potential risks.

By generating multiple scenarios, generative AI allows risk managers to explore the impact of various factors on their portfolios and operations. This holistic approach enables them to develop more effective risk mitigation strategies and optimize resource allocation. Additionally, generative AI can identify correlations between different risk factors, helping institutions understand how changes in one area might affect others. This interconnected view of risks is crucial for developing robust risk management frameworks.

Furthermore, generative AI can enhance stress testing processes required by regulatory bodies. Stress tests evaluate how financial institutions would perform under extreme adverse conditions. Generative AI can create realistic stress scenarios based on historical data and predictive modeling, providing regulators with a detailed assessment of an institution's resilience. This capability not only ensures compliance with regulatory requirements but also strengthens the overall stability of the financial system.

Financial forecasting is another vital application of generative AI in the financial sector. Accurate forecasts are essential for making informed investment decisions, planning budgets, and managing resources. Generative models excel in this area by predicting market trends and financial outcomes based on historical data and other relevant factors. These predictions can cover a wide range of financial metrics, such as stock prices, interest rates, and economic indicators.

Generative AI's ability to process vast amounts of data and identify complex patterns makes its forecasts highly reliable. For example, it can analyze macroeconomic data, industry-specific trends, and company performance metrics to generate comprehensive forecasts. These insights enable financial analysts to make data-driven decisions, minimizing uncertainties and maximizing returns. Moreover, generative AI can update its forecasts in real-time as new data becomes available, ensuring that predictions remain accurate and relevant (Zhang & Hu, 2022).

In addition to enhancing forecasting accuracy, generative AI can assist in scenario analysis. Financial institutions can use generative models to explore different "what-if" scenarios, such as the impact of policy changes or economic shocks on their investments. This forward-looking approach allows organizations to prepare for various contingencies and make proactive adjustments to their strategies. By understanding potential future outcomes, institutions can make more resilient plans and navigate uncertainties more effectively.

Finally, generative AI can democratize access to sophisticated forecasting tools. Traditionally, advanced financial forecasting models have been the domain of large institutions with substantial resources. However, generative AI's scalability and affordability make these tools accessible to smaller firms and individual investors. This democratization empowers a broader range of market participants to leverage cutting-edge technology for improved decision-making, fostering a more inclusive financial ecosystem.

Applications in Education

Generative AI presents a transformative opportunity in content generation for education. By using algorithms to create educational materials, it is possible to develop textbooks, quizzes, and interactive content tailored to meet specific learning objectives. For instance, AI can analyze vast amounts of academic content and generate customized textbooks that emphasize key concepts while omitting unnecessary information. This process not only saves time for educators but also ensures the material is precisely aligned with the curriculum.

Beyond traditional textbooks, generative AI can be employed to create engaging quizzes and assessments. These tools can provide immediate feedback to students, helping them understand their strengths and areas for improvement. Interactive content, such as simulations and virtual labs, can also be produced by AI, offering students hands-on experience in a controlled environment. Such AI-generated materials can adapt based on real-time student performance, enhancing both understanding and retention.

The use of generative AI in content creation also promotes inclusivity in education. By generating materials in multiple languages and formats, it becomes easier to cater to the needs of diverse student populations. This approach ensures that language barriers are minimized and that students with varying levels of ability have access to the same high-quality educational resources. The integration of AI in creating these materials ultimately leads to a more efficient, personalized, and inclusive educational experience.

Personalized learning is another significant application of generative AI in education. Traditional teaching methods often struggle to address individual learning styles and paces. Generative AI, however, can tailor educational experiences to match each student's unique needs. By analyzing data on student performance, preferences, and behavior, AI can generate individualized lesson plans that optimize learning outcomes (Bai, Jiang, & Wu, 2022).

For example, an AI system can identify when a student is struggling with a particular concept and provide additional resources or alternative explanations until the student grasps the idea. Conversely, if a student demonstrates a strong understanding, the AI can introduce more challenging material to keep them engaged and motivated. This dynamic adjustment ensures that all students progress at a pace that suits them best, enhancing overall educational efficiency.

Furthermore, personalized learning through AI can extend beyond academic subjects. It can incorporate elements of social and emotional learning by recognizing and responding to students' emotional states. For instance, if a student appears frustrated or disinterested, the AI system can suggest a break or offer motivational content to re-engage them. Such sensitivity to individual needs fosters a supportive and holistic learning environment.

Tutoring systems powered by generative AI represent another innovative educational methodology. These AI-driven tutors can provide personalized assistance and feedback, supplementing classroom instruction and offering support outside of school hours. By simulating one-on-one interactions with a human tutor, these systems help students overcome academic challenges and achieve their full potential (Yu & Meng, 2021).

AI-powered tutoring systems can analyze student responses in real time, identifying misconceptions and offering targeted explanations or alternative problem-solving approaches. This immediate feedback cycle helps students correct errors promptly and reinforces learning through practice. Additionally, AI tutors can adapt their teaching strategies based on a student's progress, ensuring that the instruction is always relevant and effective.

The scalability of AI tutoring systems also addresses the issue of limited access to quality tutoring. Students from various socioeconomic backgrounds can benefit from high-quality, affordable tutoring services. As these systems become more sophisticated, they can mimic the warmth and encouragement of human tutors, providing not just academic support but also emotional motivation and guidance.

In the realm of language learning, generative AI offers innovative solutions for creating exercises and practice scenarios. Language acquisition requires consistent practice and exposure to diverse linguistic contexts. AI can generate a wide range of language exercises, from vocabulary drills to conversation simulations, facilitating immersive and interactive learning experiences.

For example, AI can create personalized language lessons based on a learner's proficiency level and learning goals. These lessons can include listening and speaking exercises that adapt to the learner's progress, providing increasing levels of difficulty as their skills improve. Additionally, AI can generate contextual dialogues and role-playing scenarios, allowing learners to practice real-life conversations in a safe and controlled environment.

Combining Generative AI with IoT

Integrating generative AI with the Internet of Things (IoT) can transform how we manage and interact with our environments. In smart homes and cities, generative AI enables predictive maintenance, efficient energy management, and resource optimization. By analyzing data from various IoT sensors, AI models predict equipment failures before they happen, thus avoiding costly repairs and downtime. For example, an AI system can monitor the health of HVAC units in a city's buildings, alerting maintenance teams only when necessary (Aggarwal & Kumar, 2021).

Energy management is another area where generative AI excels. Smart grids equipped with IoT devices can balance electricity demand and supply more effectively when guided by AI predictions. These systems might suggest optimal times for using high-energy appliances or adjusting thermostats to reduce consumption during peak hours. Such proactive measures lead to significant energy savings and sustainability.

Resource optimization extends to water management, waste disposal, and traffic control. Generative AI can predict water usage patterns, optimizing distribution and reducing wastage. In waste management, AI-driven IoT systems can optimize collection routes, minimizing fuel consumption and enhancing efficiency. Meanwhile, in traffic control, AI can analyze live traffic data to adjust signal timings dynamically, easing congestion and reducing travel time.

In healthcare, integrating IoT-enabled devices with generative AI leads to enhanced patient monitoring and care. Wearable devices collecting continuous health data, like heart rate and blood pressure, become even more valuable when paired with AI-generated insights. For instance, AI can predict potential health issues by detecting abnormal patterns in the data, prompting early interventions that could be life-saving (Kang & Kim, 2022).

Generative AI also contributes to personalized healthcare solutions. Analyzing data from multiple IoT devices allows AI to tailor recommendations for individual patients based on their unique health profiles. This could include personalized diet plans, exercise routines, or medication adjustments, all aimed at improving overall health and wellness.

Furthermore, AI-enhanced IoT systems improve hospital management and operations. Predictive analytics can optimize bed occupancy rates and streamline patient admissions and discharges. Additionally, AI can manage the inventory of medical supplies, ensuring that critical resources are always available without overstocking, thereby controlling costs.

In industrial settings, integrating generative AI with IoT devices transforms manufacturing processes and enhances predictive maintenance. AI models can analyze vast amounts of sensor data from machinery, identifying signs of wear and tear before they lead to equipment failure. This not only prevents downtime but also extends the lifespan of expensive machinery.

Generative models optimize production processes by identifying inefficiencies and suggesting improvements. For example, in a factory setting, AI can recommend ways to rearrange workflows or adjust machine settings to boost productivity and reduce waste. Such optimizations lead to higher quality products and lower operational costs.

Additionally, AI-driven IoT systems enhance safety in industrial environments. Real-time monitoring of working conditions, such as air quality and temperature, ensures compliance with safety regulations and promptly alerts workers to potential hazards. Moreover, generative AI can simulate various scenarios to prepare for emergencies, ensuring that safety protocols are robust and effective.

Summary of the interdisciplinary applications of generative AI.

Throughout this chapter, we have explored the diverse applications of generative AI in various fields such as healthcare, finance, education, and IoT. Generative AI has proven to be a transformative force, enhancing the quality and efficiency of processes across these domains. By creating high-resolution medical images, synthetic data sets, and novel compounds, generative AI significantly improves diagnostic accuracy, accelerates drug discovery, and personalizes patient care. In finance, it optimizes algorithmic trading strategies and bolsters fraud detection while ensuring robust risk management and accurate financial forecasting.

In education, generative AI facilitates the creation of customized educational materials, promotes personalized learning, and provides unparalleled support through AI-powered tutoring systems. IoT integration further amplifies the impact of generative AI by enabling predictive maintenance, efficient resource management, and real-time monitoring in smart environments. These advancements highlight how generative AI can predict equipment failures, optimize energy consumption, and enhance patient care through continuous health data analysis.

As we progress into the era of AI-driven innovations, it is crucial for practitioners to recognize both the potential and the challenges associated with these technologies. While generative AI offers remarkable benefits, ethical considerations such as data privacy, algorithmic fairness, and the potential for misuse must be carefully managed. The reliance on AI models also necessitates transparency and accountability to ensure that their outputs are trustworthy and unbiased.

Looking ahead, the integration of generative AI with other emerging technologies will likely yield even more groundbreaking solutions, reshaping industries and redefining our daily lives. As the technology continues to evolve, staying informed about the latest developments and maintaining a proactive approach to learning will be essential for those looking to harness its full potential.

The widespread adoption of generative AI carries significant implications for society at large. It has the power to revolutionize healthcare, finance, education, and beyond, leading to increased efficiency, cost savings, and improved outcomes. However, the rapid pace of innovation also demands that we remain vigilant about the ethical and societal impacts of these advancements.

In conclusion, the exploration of generative AI applications reveals a promising future filled with innovative possibilities. By addressing the concerns associated with its use and embracing its potential, we can pave the way for a more efficient, equitable, and technologically advanced world. As we continue to push the boundaries of what AI can achieve, the role of generative AI in shaping our future cannot be overstated, leaving us to ponder the new frontiers it will unlock.

References

Kazeminia, S., Rahmani, A. M., & Haghighi, M. S. (2021). Generative adversarial networks in healthcare: A systematic review. Artificial Intelligence Review, 54(5), 3497–3531. https://doi.org/10.1007/s10462-020-09941-3

Zhavoronkov, A. (2020). Artificial intelligence for drug discovery, biomarker development, and generation of novel chemistry. Cell, 180(4), 819-823. https://doi.org/10.1016/j.cell.2020.02.018

Fedele, M., & Pasquini, A. (2021). Generative adversarial networks for fraud detection: A comprehensive review. Journal of Computational Science, 53, 101366. https://doi.org/10.1016/j.jocs.2021.101366

Zhang, X., & Hu, W. (2022). The application of generative adversarial networks in financial forecasting: A review. Procedia Computer Science, 199, 189-196. https://doi.org/10.1016/j.procs.2022.01.025

Bai, X., Jiang, Y., & Wu, Y. (2022). Personalized learning with artificial intelligence: A systematic review of generative AI applications. Computers & Education: Artificial Intelligence, 3, 100070. https://doi.org/10.1016/j.caeai.2022.100070

Yu, Z., & Meng, X. (2021). AI-enhanced adaptive tutoring systems: From content generation to student engagement. Interactive Learning Environments, 1-19. https://doi.org/10.1080/10494820.2021.1963558

Aggarwal, S., & Kumar, N. (2021). Generative AI in IoT-enabled smart environments: Challenges and opportunities. IEEE Internet of Things Journal, 8(5), 3692-3701. https://doi.org/10.1109/JIOT.2020.3021985

Kang, J., & Kim, M. (2022). Integration of generative AI with IoT for patient monitoring in healthcare. Journal of Healthcare Engineering, 2022, 1-12. https://doi.org/10.1155/2022/3049132

CHAPTER 12

Ethical and Social Implications of Generative AI

Generative AI, at the intersection of technology and ethics, is reshaping numerous industries but not without raising significant concerns. With its ability to create content from vast datasets, generative AI can inadvertently perpetuate existing biases and present ethical challenges that demand scrutiny. Understanding these biases and their implications is essential as the outputs produced by such models often reflect societal prejudices embedded within the training data. Addressing these issues goes beyond the technical mechanics of AI, delving into the necessity for fairness and inclusivity in technological advancements.

This chapter delves deeply into understanding and mitigating bias within generative AI systems. It begins by defining what constitutes bias in the context of AI and how it impacts the outcomes generated by these models. The discussion extends to various forms of bias, including dataset bias, human bias, and favoritism towards certain demographics. Further, the chapter explores how biased data collection methods, preprocessing steps, and model training processes contribute to skewed results. By examining case studies and real-world examples, the chapter provides insights into the ethical dilemmas posed by generative AI. Additionally, strategies for addressing these biases, such as data augmentation, reweighting, and adversarial debiasing, are discussed in detail to offer practical solutions for creating more equitable AI systems.

Defining Bias in Generative AI

Bias is a systematic deviation from a standard, often resulting from prejudiced or skewed data. In the context of generative AI models, bias can have significant implications. It typically refers to the inaccuracies and unfair advantages or disadvantages that emerge due to imbalanced or non-representative data. The biases present in the training data used for AI development inevitably seep into the model's outputs, leading to systematic deviations. These deviations manifest not by chance but because the AI mirrors the inherent prejudices found within the input data. Bias impacts decision-making processes and outcomes, making it a critical issue to address.

In generative AI, bias can manifest as favoritism towards certain demographics over others. For example, a text generator trained predominantly on Western literature might prioritize Western cultural references while underrepresenting other global perspectives. This can lead to outputs that reinforce stereotypes or overlook significant contributions from diverse groups. Favoritism in AI-generated content isn't just about the visible end product but also encompasses the subtleties of language, imagery, and scenarios depicted by the AI. These biases can propagate misconceptions and skew public perception, reinforcing existing societal biases rather than challenging them.

Dataset bias occurs when the training data does not represent the diversity of the real world. Generative AI models rely heavily on large datasets to learn patterns and generate new content. If these datasets are biased—say, overly focused on one gender, ethnicity, or socioeconomic group—the generated outputs will reflect those biases. For instance, facial recognition systems trained mainly on images of lighter-skinned individuals tend to perform poorly with darker-skinned individuals (When AI Gets It Wrong: Addressing AI Hallucinations and Bias. MIT Sloan Teaching & Learning Technologies., n.d.). This lack of representation results in skewed model behavior, which could perpetuate inequality and discrimination in various applications ranging from healthcare to law enforcement.

Human bias is another significant factor introduced by the designers and developers of AI systems. These biases reflect the conscious or unconscious prejudices of the people involved in creating and training the AI models. For example, if the developers hold certain beliefs or stereotypes, these can subtly influence their choices in data selection, labeling, and algorithmic tweaking. Such biases can compound over time, embedding themselves deeply within the AI's functioning. This human contribution to bias highlights the need for diverse teams and inclusive practices in AI development to uncover and mitigate personal prejudices that could infiltrate the technology.

Generative AI models can amplify gender and racial stereotypes encoded within their training datasets. For instance, if an AI is trained on historical texts and images that predominantly portray men in leadership roles and women in subordinate positions, it may generate outputs that reflect and reinforce these outdated stereotypes. Similarly, racially biased data can result in models that marginalize or misrepresent minority groups, affecting everything from automated hiring systems to predictive policing tools. A 2023 analysis revealed that generative AI tools like Stable Diffusion amplify both gender and racial stereotypes (Nicoletti & Bass, 2023).

Given these concerns, it's essential to address bias in generative AI by implementing diverse and representative datasets. Ensuring that a wide range of demographic, cultural, and social factors are included in training data can help create more balanced and fair AI models. This approach requires concerted efforts to curate datasets that accurately reflect the diversity of the real world. Additionally, ongoing monitoring and evaluation of AI outputs are necessary to identify and rectify any biases that may emerge, promoting fairness and equality in AI applications.

Another approach to mitigating bias involves increasing transparency and accountability in AI development processes. Developers must document and openly share their methodologies, including how datasets are selected and cleaned, and the algorithms' tuning parameters. Transparency allows for external audits and assessments, enabling independent parties to evaluate biases and recommend improvements. Furthermore, fostering a culture of accountability ensures that developers are aware of the ethical implications of their work and remain committed to minimizing bias.

Sources of Bias

Identifying common sources of bias in generative AI is crucial to ensuring the development of fair and equitable systems. One significant source of bias stems from data collection methods that are not representative. When data scientists collect data, they often rely on sampling techniques to gather manageable datasets for analysis and model training. However, if these sampling methods do not adequately represent the diversity of the real world, the resulting models can exhibit biased behavior. For example, a dataset that predominantly includes images of lighter-skinned individuals will inherently lead to poor performance when identifying darker-skinned individuals in applications like facial recognition. This underlines the importance of using diverse and representative datasets during the initial stages of AI development.

In addition to biased data collection, preprocessing steps can introduce bias through methods that disproportionately favor specific groups. Preprocessing involves cleaning and transforming raw data into a format suitable for machine learning models. Techniques such as normalization, scaling, and feature selection are standard practices. However, these processes can inadvertently amplify existing biases. For instance, if certain demographic information is weighted more heavily than others during preprocessing, the resulting model may display biased predictions. To mitigate this, it is necessary to apply fair preprocessing techniques that consider the impact on all groups represented in the data.

Model training is another critical stage where bias can be introduced and amplified. If the algorithms used for training have inherent biases or if the training process favors certain patterns over others, the final model may exhibit skewed results. For example, an algorithm that prioritizes accuracy might disregard minority class data, leading to biased outcomes. Furthermore, if the training data itself is biased, the model will learn and replicate these biases. A well-known case involving facial recognition technology demonstrated significant disparities in performance across different skin tones, primarily because the training data was not inclusive of diverse skin types. Addressing these issues requires careful selection of unbiased algorithms and extensive testing across varied datasets.

To illustrate the impact of biased data and model training, consider the example of facial recognition systems. Many such systems have been found to perform poorly on darker skin tones due to biased training data. These models were often trained on datasets containing predominantly lighter-skinned individuals, resulting in misidentification and lower accuracy rates for people with darker skin. This raises important ethical and social concerns, particularly in applications like law enforcement and security, where inaccurate facial recognition can lead to wrongful accusations and other serious repercussions. Therefore, it is imperative to ensure that training data encompasses a wide range of demographic characteristics to develop more reliable and fair AI systems.

Biased data collection is only the starting point; subsequent stages like preprocessing and model training can further propagate these biases. Addressing biases at each step can significantly contribute to reducing overall model bias. For instance, employing techniques such as oversampling underrepresented groups in the dataset can help balance the data before feeding it into the model. Similarly, using fairness-aware algorithms during model training can minimize the amplification of existing biases. Moreover, continuously monitoring model performance and making necessary adjustments ensures that biases are detected and mitigated early in the deployment phase.

Measuring Fairness

Demographic parity is a crucial metric for measuring fairness in generative AI models. It ensures that the outcomes predicted by an AI model are independent of sensitive demographic attributes such as race, gender, or age. This means that the probability of a favorable outcome should be the same for all demographic groups. For instance, in a hiring algorithm, demographic parity would mean that candidates from different races have equal chances of being recommended for a job. The goal here is to prevent systemic biases that could lead to discrimination against certain groups, ensuring fairness and equity in AI-driven decisions.

One practical example of demographic parity in action can be seen in loan approval systems used by financial institutions. If a bank uses an AI model to decide on loan approvals, demographic parity would require that applicants with similar financial backgrounds should have equal chances of approval, regardless of their ethnicity or gender. By enforcing this criterion, banks can avoid biased lending practices that unfairly disadvantage minority groups. However, achieving demographic parity requires careful consideration during both data collection and model training processes to ensure that inherent biases are not perpetuated.

Implementing demographic parity involves several challenges. One significant issue is the potential trade-off with model accuracy. Enforcing strict demographic parity might require altering model predictions in ways that could compromise performance. Additionally, it requires constant monitoring and adjustment as demographic compositions and societal norms evolve over time. Despite these challenges, striving for demographic parity remains essential for promoting fairness and preventing discriminatory practices in AI applications.

Equal opportunity is another vital metric for assessing fairness in generative AI. Unlike demographic parity, which focuses on overall group outcomes, equal opportunity emphasizes providing similar results for individuals with comparable qualifications. This means that if two individuals have similar qualifications and experiences, they should receive equivalent predictions or recommendations from the AI model. Ensuring equal opportunity helps address biases that arise from factors unrelated to an individual's merit or capabilities.

In educational settings, equal opportunity can play a crucial role in admission processes. Suppose a university uses an AI model to evaluate student applications. Equal opportunity would imply that students with similar academic achievements and extracurricular activities should have equivalent chances of admission, irrespective of factors like socioeconomic background or geographic location. By prioritizing equal opportunity, educational institutions can foster diversity and inclusivity, creating a fairer selection process for all applicants.

Achieving equal opportunity in AI models demands rigorous validation and testing. It requires analyzing the model's predictions to identify disparities among individuals with similar qualifications but different demographic characteristics. Developers must continually refine the model to ensure it does not inadvertently favor certain groups. By doing so, organizations can build trust in their AI systems and demonstrate a commitment to fairness and equity.

Disparate impact assesses whether a model's decisions disproportionately affect certain groups more than others, even if the model appears neutral on the surface. This metric is crucial for identifying hidden biases that may not be immediately apparent. Disparate impact occurs when seemingly impartial criteria inadvertently disadvantage specific demographic groups. Addressing this issue is essential for ensuring that AI systems do not reinforce existing inequalities.

For example, in the criminal justice system, risk assessment tools are used to determine bail and parole decisions. If such a tool has a disparate impact, it might result in harsher outcomes for minority groups, perpetuating systemic injustices. Evaluating disparate impact involves examining the model's predictions and comparing the outcomes across different demographic groups. If significant discrepancies are found, it indicates that the model might be unfairly biased against certain groups.

Mitigating disparate impact requires a multifaceted approach. Developers need to adopt techniques such as reweighting or resampling the training data to ensure better representation of underrepresented groups. Moreover, continuous monitoring and auditing of AI systems are necessary to detect and rectify any emerging biases over time. By proactively addressing disparate impact, developers can create AI models that promote fairness and reduce unintended harm.

Applying fairness metrics involves using these criteria to evaluate actual model outcomes continuously. This step is critical to ensure that the AI models perform fairly in real-world scenarios and not just in theoretical settings. The application of fairness metrics requires a robust framework for collecting and analyzing data to measure how well the model meets the established fairness goals.

Consider a healthcare AI application designed to predict patient readmission rates. To apply fairness metrics, the model's predictions need to be scrutinized for demographic parity, equal opportunity, and disparate impact. If disparities are found, such as higher readmission predictions for patients from specific ethnic groups with similar health profiles, corrective actions must be taken. This might involve adjusting the model or improving the quality and diversity of the training data.

Applying fairness metrics also necessitates transparency and accountability. Organizations must be transparent about the fairness criteria they use and publicly share the steps they take to meet these standards. Engaging stakeholders, including affected communities, in the evaluation process helps ensure that the AI models align with societal values and ethical principles. By systematically applying fairness metrics, organizations can build trustworthy AI systems that contribute positively to society.

Mitigating Bias

Mitigating bias in generative AI is a multifaceted task that requires various strategies to ensure fairness and accuracy. One effective technique is data augmentation, which involves artificially generating new data points from existing datasets to balance underrepresented groups. This method helps in creating a more representative training dataset by simulating multiple scenarios where the minority classes are adequately represented. For example, if a facial recognition system has fewer images of certain ethnicities, data augmentation techniques can generate variations of those faces using rotations, translations, or other manipulations. This ultimately enhances the diversity of the training data, mitigating bias and improving performance across all demographics.

Another key strategy is reweighting, which assigns higher importance to data from minority groups during the training phase. By giving more weight to these underrepresented samples, the model can learn to treat them with equal significance as the majority group data. For instance, in a language generation model, if certain dialects or sociolects are less represented, reweighting ensures that the model pays extra attention to these data points. This approach not only helps in addressing the imbalance but also promotes an inclusive outcome, making the AI system more robust and fair in its predictions and outputs.

Adversarial debiasing is a sophisticated technique involving adversarial networks to reduce bias while maintaining high performance. In this process, two neural networks work against each other: one generates predictions while the other tries to identify biases in these predictions. The model is refined iteratively until it can produce unbiased outcomes without sacrificing performance. This technique is particularly useful in complex models like those used for natural language processing, where subtle biases might creep in unnoticed. By employing adversarial debiasing, AI developers can ensure their models remain impartial and efficient, paving the way for fairer applications of generative AI technology.

Practical examples of these strategies include modifying training datasets and adjusting model parameters to enhance fairness. For instance, companies like Google and Amazon have introduced tools such as Fairness Indicators and Sagemaker Clarify to help detect and mitigate bias in datasets. These tools allow data scientists to analyze their training data comprehensively and make necessary adjustments. For instance, if a model trained on customer reviews shows bias towards particular product categories due to an imbalanced dataset, these tools can help redistribute the data to achieve a balanced representation (Frank, A., 2023).

In conclusion, addressing bias in generative AI involves implementing thoughtful and diverse strategies. Data augmentation creates varied and balanced training sets, while reweighting ensures that minority data points are given due importance. Adversarial debiasing adds another layer of scrutiny, ensuring performance is maintained alongside fairness. Practical implementations of these methods further validate their effectiveness, demonstrating the potential to develop ethical and unbiased AI systems.

Key Insights and Future Directions for Ethical Development

Throughout this chapter, we have delved into the ethical and social implications of generative AI, focusing on the pervasive issue of bias. We started by defining bias in the context of AI models and explored how it can influence decision-making processes and outcomes. We then examined sources of bias, emphasizing the importance of representative data collection, fair preprocessing techniques, and unbiased model training.

Revisiting our earlier statements, it's clear that bias in generative AI is not just a technical concern but also an ethical one. The development teams must be conscious of their contributions to potential biases and strive for inclusivity. Whether through diverse datasets or inclusive development practices, tackling human-induced bias remains critical. Our current position underscores the necessity of implementing robust measures at every development stage to ensure fairness and equity in AI applications.

However, there are still significant challenges that should concern readers. Biases ingrained in AI systems can lead to unfair advantages or disadvantages for specific demographic groups. The repercussions of unchecked biases are profound, potentially exacerbating existing inequalities and reinforcing stereotypes. This is particularly concerning as AI becomes more integrated into areas such as healthcare, law enforcement, and finance, where biased decisions can have severe real-world consequences.

On a wider scale, the societal impact of biased generative AI cannot be overstated. Models producing biased outputs risk perpetuating discrimination, leading to systemic issues across various sectors. For instance, biased hiring algorithms could disadvantage qualified candidates from minority backgrounds, while biased predictive policing tools might disproportionately target certain communities. Such outcomes highlight the urgent need for ongoing vigilance and mitigation efforts.

Ultimately, addressing bias in generative AI requires a combination of technical solutions and ethical commitments. As we continue to advance in this field, it is essential to prioritize transparency, accountability, and fairness. By fostering a culture of continuous evaluation and improvement, the goal of creating ethical and unbiased AI systems becomes more attainable.

As we look ahead, consider the broader implications of these technologies. How can we balance innovation with responsibility? What steps will we take to ensure that advances in generative AI benefit all members of society equitably? These open-ended questions invite us to reflect on the future trajectory of AI development, urging a collective effort toward a fairer and more just technological landscape.

References

Chapman University. (2023). *Bias in AI. www.chapman.edu.* https://www.chapman.edu/ai/bias-in-ai.aspx

Frank, A. (2023, December). *How marketers can mitigate bias in generative AI. MarTech.* https://martech.org/how-marketers-can-mitigate-bias-in-generative-ai/

Introduction to model evaluation for fairness | Vertex AI. Google Cloud. (n.d.). https://app.altruwe.org/proxy?url=https://cloud.google.com//vertex-ai/docs/evaluation/intro-evaluation-fairness

Manyika, J., Presten, B., Silberg, J. (2019, October). *What Do We Do About the Biases in AI?. Harvard Business Review.* https://hbr.org/2019/10/what-do-we-do-about-the-biases-in-ai

The Pursuit of Fairness in Artificial Intelligence Models: A Survey. Arxiv.org. (2020). https://arxiv.org/html/2403.17333v1

When AI Gets It Wrong: Addressing AI Hallucinations and Bias. MIT Sloan Teaching & Learning Technologies. (n.d.). https://mitsloanedtech.mit.edu/ai/basics/addressing-ai-hallucinations-and-bias/

CHAPTER 13

Future of Generative AI

Generative AI is rapidly evolving, revolutionizing how artificial intelligence is applied across various domains. With its ability to create content, solve problems, and interact with humans in ways previously deemed impossible, generative AI holds immense potential. As this technology progresses, understanding its emerging trends, overcoming associated challenges, and harnessing the opportunities it presents becomes crucial for those looking to advance their knowledge and careers in AI.

This chapter delves into the transformative trends shaping the future of generative AI. It examines key advancements such as multimodal models that integrate text, image, and audio processing, enhancing content creation capabilities. The discussion also addresses efficiency improvements and scalability innovations, such as sparse models and low-rank approximations, making advanced AI more accessible. Additionally, ethical considerations are explored, highlighting methods to reduce biases and promote fairness in AI systems. Lastly, the chapter investigates human-AI collaboration tools and their impact on creativity and productivity, offering insights into how AI can augment human potential.

Emerging Trends in Generative AI Research

Emerging trends in generative AI are transforming the landscape of research and application. One significant trend is the development of enhanced model architectures. These multimodal models combine text, image, and audio processing to create more versatile content generation systems. For instance, recent advancements have led to models like OpenAI's GPT-4 that can understand and generate natural language text while also processing images, enabling applications such as generating descriptive captions or creating visual content based on textual descriptions.

The integration of multiple modalities in a single model opens up various possibilities for innovation. In educational settings, multimodal AI can develop interactive learning materials that cater to different learning styles. A multimodal approach ensures that the generated content is richer and more comprehensive, providing users with a more engaging experience. Multimodal models are not only useful in education but also find applications in entertainment, where they can create immersive narratives that include text, imagery, and soundscapes.

Furthermore, these enhanced model architectures improve accessibility by allowing users to interact with AI through varied input methods. This accessibility promotes inclusivity, enabling individuals with disabilities to engage with technology in ways that are most convenient for them. For example, voice inputs combined with visual outputs can assist visually impaired users in navigating digital environments more effectively.

Efficiency and scalability are crucial components in the progress of generative AI. Innovations such as sparse models and low-rank approximations significantly reduce computational costs while maintaining performance. Sparse models focus computational resources on the most relevant parts of the data, enhancing efficiency. This approach reduces the need for massive computational power, making advanced AI technologies more accessible to a broader audience.

The reduction in computational costs has profound implications for both academia and industry. Academic institutions, which often operate under tight budget constraints, can now explore complex AI projects without the prohibitive costs previously associated with extensive computational resources. Similarly, startups and smaller companies gain the ability to experiment with and deploy generative AI solutions, fostering innovation across various sectors.

Moreover, scalable models facilitate faster iterations and deployment of AI systems. In industries like healthcare, this rapid turnaround can lead to quicker development of diagnostic tools or personalized treatment plans. As a result, patients benefit from timely interventions and improved health outcomes, showcasing the real-world impact of efficient and scalable AI technologies.

Ethical AI development is another pivotal trend in generative AI research. Techniques aimed at detecting and reducing biases in AI models are essential for ensuring fairness and inclusivity. Generative models often reflect the biases present in their training data, which can lead to discriminatory outputs. Researchers are actively developing methods to identify these biases and mitigate their effects, promoting the creation of ethical AI systems.

The incorporation of fairness checks and bias reduction protocols is particularly crucial in applications that directly affect people's lives, such as hiring processes or loan approvals. By implementing these techniques, organizations can ensure that their AI systems make equitable decisions, thereby building trust among users and stakeholders. Ethical AI practices also extend to content generation, where unbiased models produce more accurate and representative content, enhancing user experience across demographics.

In addition, ethical considerations play a role in regulatory compliance. Governments and regulatory bodies are increasingly scrutinizing AI systems to ensure they meet ethical standards. By proactively addressing biases and promoting fairness, developers can align with regulations and avoid potential legal issues, facilitating smoother adoption and integration of AI technologies in various sectors.

Human-AI collaboration represents a promising frontier in generative AI research. Co-creation tools that enhance real-time human-AI interaction are revolutionizing fields like design, writing, and software development. These tools enable humans and AI to work together seamlessly, combining the strengths of both entities to produce innovative results. For example, AI-powered design platforms allow artists to experiment with new styles and techniques, guided by AI-generated suggestions that complement their creative process.

This collaborative approach augments creativity and productivity, leading to the production of high-quality outputs in less time. In the corporate world, AI-driven co-creation tools can assist teams in brainstorming sessions, generating ideas based on vast datasets that might be overlooked by human participants alone. Such tools not only enhance efficiency but also introduce novel concepts that drive innovation within organizations.

Additionally, real-time collaboration tools are transforming education and training programs. AI tutors that interact with students, provide immediate feedback, and suggest improvements are becoming integral to modern learning environments. These tools help educators tailor their teaching methods to individual student needs, fostering a more personalized and effective learning experience.

Potential Challenges and Opportunities

Data privacy is a critical issue when it comes to generative AI. These systems often rely on vast amounts of personal data to function effectively, making the protection of this information paramount. Ensuring that AI systems respect user privacy requires robust encryption methods and secure data storage solutions. Furthermore, AI developers must adhere to legal frameworks such as the General Data Protection Regulation (GDPR) in Europe or the Genetic Information Non-discrimination Act (GINA) in the United States. Compliance with these regulations not only protects individual privacy but also builds public trust in AI technologies.

One significant challenge in data privacy is the risk of data breaches. Generative AI systems can be vulnerable to hacking, which can lead to unauthorized access and misuse of sensitive information. To mitigate this risk, developers must implement advanced cybersecurity measures and monitor AI systems for potential vulnerabilities continuously. Additionally, anonymizing data whenever possible can reduce the impact of potential breaches by ensuring that even if data is accessed, it cannot be easily traced back to individuals.

Transparent communication with users is essential for maintaining data privacy. Users should be informed about how their data will be used and have the option to opt-out of non-essential data collection. This involves obtaining explicit consent for data usage and being clear about the purposes for which the data will be employed. By fostering transparency and giving users control over their information, AI developers can enhance user confidence and promote ethical data practices.

Ethical considerations in generative AI encompass a range of issues, including the creation and dissemination of deepfakes, misinformation, and potential manipulative practices. Deepfakes, which are AI-generated videos or audio recordings that appear authentic, pose significant ethical dilemmas. They can be used maliciously to spread false information, create fraudulent identities, or damage reputations. Addressing these issues requires developing detection tools that can identify deepfakes and implementing regulations to penalize the misuse of such technologies.

Misinformation facilitated by generative AI presents another ethical challenge. AI-generated content can be indistinguishable from human-created material, making it easy to spread false news and distort public perceptions. Combating this requires a multi-faceted approach, including educating the public on identifying and critically assessing

AI-generated content and collaborating with social media platforms to monitor and flag potentially misleading information.

The potential for deception or manipulation through generative AI extends to various domains, including advertising and political campaigns. AI can create highly personalized content that exploits users' preferences and biases, influencing their decisions without their knowledge. Establishing ethical guidelines and best practices for AI use in these areas can help prevent exploitation. Moreover, ongoing research into making AI systems transparent and explainable can aid in understanding how decisions are made and ensure accountability.

Generative AI offers significant opportunities for innovation in creative industries, transforming how art, music, literature, and design are produced. In art, AI tools like DeepArt and GANs (Generative Adversarial Networks) enable artists to experiment with new styles and techniques, pushing the boundaries of human creativity. These tools can generate unique artworks based on user inputs, providing artists with endless possibilities and inspiration.

In the music industry, generative AI can assist musicians in composing new pieces by suggesting melodies, harmonies, and rhythms. Tools like OpenAI's MuseNet use deep learning algorithms to create complex musical compositions, helping artists explore uncharted musical territories. This collaborative approach between humans and AI opens up new avenues for musical expression and innovation, making music creation more accessible to those without formal training.

Literature and design also benefit from generative AI's capabilities. AI-driven writing assistants can help authors develop plots, characters, and dialogue, enhancing the storytelling process. In design, AI tools can generate architectural blueprints, fashion patterns, and product prototypes, speeding up the ideation phase and enabling designers to visualize their concepts quickly. By integrating AI into creative processes, industries can foster greater experimentation and diversity in their work.

Advancements in healthcare through generative AI are transformative, particularly in drug discovery and personalized medicine. AI models can analyze vast datasets of biological information to identify potential drug candidates more efficiently than traditional methods. For instance, generative models can predict the structure and activity of molecules, accelerating the drug discovery process and reducing costs. This capability has already shown promise in developing treatments for diseases like cancer and Alzheimer's.

Personalized medical treatments are another area where generative AI makes significant contributions. By analyzing an individual's genetic makeup, lifestyle, and medical history,

AI can generate tailored treatment plans that optimize therapeutic outcomes. This level of personalization ensures that patients receive the most effective treatments with minimal side effects, improving overall healthcare quality. AI-driven recommendations can also help healthcare providers make informed decisions about patient care, leading to better health outcomes.

Speculation on Future Applications and Impacts

The future applications and impacts of generative AI are vast, with significant implications across various fields. In entertainment and media, generative AI is poised to revolutionize the industry by creating immersive VR environments and interactive narratives. Imagine stepping into a fully AI-generated virtual world where entire landscapes, characters, and plotlines adapt dynamically based on user interactions. These AI-driven experiences can introduce new levels of personalization in gaming, allowing players to explore unique story arcs tailored to their preferences. Furthermore, filmmakers and content creators can leverage generative AI to develop scripts, concept art, and even special effects, significantly reducing production time and costs.

AI-generated narratives offer another dimension of interactivity, where stories evolve in real-time depending on the user's choices. This could lead to new forms of digital storytelling akin to choose-your-own-adventure books but far more complex and engaging. Such advancements not only enhance entertainment value but also provide novel ways for creators to experiment with narrative structures and styles. Additionally, AI-driven media tools can assist artists in brainstorming ideas, visualizing concepts, and automating routine tasks, thereby freeing them up to focus on more creative aspects of their work.

In education, adaptive learning platforms powered by generative AI can offer customized resources and feedback tailored to individual learning styles. These platforms analyze students' performance, learning pace, and preferences to deliver personalized content that optimizes the learning experience. For example, an AI system can identify areas where a student struggles and adjust the curriculum accordingly, providing additional exercises or alternative explanations to reinforce understanding. Such adaptability can lead to more efficient learning processes, helping students grasp complex subjects more effectively.

Moreover, generative AI can create engaging educational materials like interactive simulations, virtual labs, and even personalized tutoring systems. These tools can simulate real-world scenarios, allowing students to gain hands-on experience in a safe and controlled environment. By providing immediate feedback and adjusting challenges based on the learner's progress, these AI-driven platforms ensure continuous and tailored support. As a result, students can attain mastery in their subjects at their own pace, potentially leading to better academic outcomes and increased motivation.

For educators, generative AI offers invaluable assistance in administrative tasks such as grading, curriculum design, and student performance analysis. By automating these repetitive tasks, teachers can dedicate more time to personalized instruction and mentorship. Furthermore, AI-powered analytics can help educators identify trends and patterns in student performance, enabling data-driven decisions to enhance teaching strategies and overall educational quality.

In business and marketing, generative AI is a game-changer for analyzing market trends and generating insights for data-driven decisions. Businesses can utilize AI systems to process vast amounts of data quickly and accurately, identifying emerging trends and consumer behaviors that would be challenging to discern manually. For instance, AI algorithms can sift through social media posts, customer reviews, and sales data to detect shifts in consumer interests and preferences. This enables companies to respond proactively to market demands, crafting targeted marketing campaigns and product offerings that resonate with their audience.

Generative AI also facilitates the creation of highly personalized marketing content, including advertisements, emails, and social media posts. By analyzing individual consumer profiles, AI can generate tailored messages that appeal directly to specific segments, increasing engagement and conversion rates. Moreover, AI-driven chatbots and virtual assistants can handle customer inquiries and support, providing instant responses and solutions while gathering valuable feedback. This enhances the customer experience and allows businesses to refine their services based on real-time data.

Additionally, generative AI can optimize supply chain management by predicting demand fluctuations and suggesting inventory adjustments. This helps businesses maintain optimal stock levels, reduce waste, and improve efficiency. Through predictive analysis and real-time monitoring, companies can streamline operations, reduce costs, and ultimately enhance profitability.

The social and environmental impact of generative AI is another area with immense potential. AI can be utilized for social good by simulating environmental impact scenarios, aiding in the development of sustainable practices and policies. For example, AI models can predict the long-term effects of deforestation, pollution, or climate change, providing critical data for policymakers and researchers. These simulations can inform strategies to mitigate negative impacts, promote conservation efforts, and foster a more sustainable future.

Generative AI can also play a crucial role in disaster response and management. By analyzing historical data and real-time information, AI systems can predict natural disasters, assess potential damage, and suggest effective mitigation measures. During emergencies, AI-driven tools can assist in coordinating relief efforts, optimizing resource allocation, and providing crucial information to affected communities. This enhances resilience and responsiveness, potentially saving lives and reducing the impact of disasters.

Furthermore, generative AI can contribute to addressing social issues by promoting inclusivity and equity. AI systems can analyze large datasets to identify disparities and biases in various sectors, such as healthcare, education, and employment. By highlighting these issues, AI can inform initiatives aimed at closing gaps and ensuring fair treatment for all individuals. Additionally, AI-driven tools can support underserved communities by providing access to essential services, information, and opportunities that may otherwise be inaccessible.

Preparing for the Future Landscape of Generative AI

Investing in Research and Development is crucial for the future of generative AI. Interdisciplinary collaboration plays a significant role in overcoming complex challenges. By combining expertise from various fields such as computer science, mathematics, and cognitive science, researchers can develop more robust and innovative AI models. For instance, integrating insights from neuroscience can lead to the creation of algorithms that better mimic human thought processes, enhancing the capabilities of generative AI systems.

Moreover, fostering innovation through interdisciplinary teams can accelerate progress in generative AI. Universities and research institutions should encourage partnerships between departments and even collaborate with industry leaders. Such collaborations can provide access to diverse datasets, advanced computational resources, and practical insights, driving breakthroughs in AI technology. (Building Future-Ready Business Schools With Generative AI | AACSB. www.aacsb.edu., n.d.)

Furthermore, dedicated funding for research and development is essential. Governments, private companies, and educational institutions need to invest in long-term projects aimed at pushing the boundaries of current AI capabilities. Increased funding can support exploratory research, prototype development, and pilot programs that test new AI applications across different sectors. This investment will ensure continuous advancements in generative AI technologies.

Fostering Ethical AI Practices is another critical strategy. Establishing clear guidelines for the responsible development and deployment of generative AI technologies is essential.

These guidelines should address issues such as bias, privacy, and accountability. For example, developers must ensure their models do not perpetuate existing social biases or create harmful content. Implementing regular audits and bias detection mechanisms can help mitigate these risks.

Ethical considerations must also include transparency in AI operations. Stakeholders should be aware of how AI models are trained, the data they use, and the limitations they possess. Transparent practices build trust among users and allow for informed decision-making. Additionally, involving ethicists, legal experts, and sociologists in the development process can provide a broader perspective on potential societal impacts, ensuring that generative AI is used for the greater good.

Furthermore, creating ethical frameworks requires collaboration between policymakers, industry leaders, and academic institutions. Policies must evolve alongside technological advancements to address emerging ethical dilemmas effectively. International cooperation can lead to the establishment of universal standards, promoting global consistency in ethical AI practices. Such collaborative efforts will pave the way for a responsible and sustainable future for generative AI (Leslie et al., 2024).

Building AI Literacy is vital for empowering individuals to navigate the evolving landscape of generative AI. Education and training programs should be designed to equip students, professionals, and enthusiasts with the necessary skills and knowledge. Universities and online course providers can offer specialized courses covering topics like machine learning, neural networks, and AI ethics. Practical, hands-on experience through projects and internships will further enhance learners' understanding and competence.

Professional development programs tailored for working professionals are also essential. These programs can focus on upskilling employees to incorporate AI techniques into their current roles or transition into AI-focused positions. Workshops, boot camps, and certification courses can provide targeted knowledge and practical skills, enabling professionals to stay competitive in a rapidly changing job market. For example, a software engineer can learn about integrating generative AI models into existing software systems, thereby expanding their career opportunities.

Raising public awareness about AI's capabilities and limitations is equally important. Public forums, webinars, and community workshops can help demystify AI and encourage responsible usage. By fostering a culture of continuous learning, society can adapt more smoothly to the changes brought about by generative AI. Ensuring that people from diverse backgrounds have access to AI education will promote inclusivity and democratize the benefits of AI advancements.

Ensuring Robust Infrastructure is necessary to support the scaling demands of generative AI applications. Developing scalable and resilient infrastructure involves creating high-performance computing environments capable of handling the intensive computational requirements of AI models. Cloud computing platforms, such as those provided by AWS, Google Cloud, and Microsoft Azure, offer flexible and scalable solutions to accommodate varying workloads and storage needs.

Data management is another critical aspect of robust infrastructure. Efficient data storage, retrieval, and processing systems are required to manage the vast amounts of information used in training AI models. Implementing distributed database systems and employing advanced data-cleaning techniques can improve the quality and accessibility of data, which is fundamental for the accuracy and performance of generative AI.

Lastly, cybersecurity measures must be integrated into all aspects of AI infrastructure. Protecting sensitive data from breaches and ensuring the integrity of AI models are paramount. Encryption, multi-factor authentication, and regular security audits can safeguard against potential threats. A strong cybersecurity framework will maintain user trust and validate the reliability of generative AI applications.

Summary of key points

Generative AI is changing several fields by introducing new trends, solving problems, and creating possibilities. Multimodal model architectures combine text, image, and audio processing to revolutionize content development. These advances enable more engaging and comprehensive education and entertainment applications and improve disability accessibility. Sparse models and other efficiency and scalability improvements make advanced AI technologies more accessible to academia and industry, fostering innovation across industries.

As researchers work to reduce biases and assure AI fairness, ethical AI development is essential. Fair hiring and loan approvals require bias identification and reduction techniques. Compliance with regulations and stakeholder trust require ethical behaviors. Co-creation tools that combine human and AI powers are another trend that boosts creativity and productivity. This partnership allows real-time AI-human engagement, revolutionizing design, writing, and software development.

Data privacy remains a major issue despite these advances. Generative AI systems need strong encryption and safe data storage because they use plenty of personal data. To safeguard sensitive data, developers must follow GDPR and use advanced cybersecurity. Maintaining trust and ethical data practices requires user transparency and explicit consent. Detecting and regulating deepfakes and misinformation in advertising and political campaigns raises ethical issues.

Generative AI has great potential in healthcare, creativity, and more. AI tools enable unprecedented experimentation and creativity in art, music, literature, and design, giving creators new styles and techniques. Generative AI accelerates medication discovery and personalizes therapies based on genetics and medical history. Generative AI has great potential in entertainment, media, education, business, and social and environmental implications.

In order to prepare for the future of generative AI, research and development, interdisciplinary collaboration, and ethical AI practices are needed. Interdisciplinary teams can make breakthroughs by combining insights from other domains, and committed funding promotes long-term AI initiatives. Responsible AI development principles and varied perspectives address prejudice and transparency. Specialized courses and professional development programs teach AI literacy to help people navigate the changing AI landscape.

Robust infrastructure is necessary to support the scaling demands of generative AI applications. High-performance computing environments, efficient data management, and integrated cybersecurity measures ensure the reliability and scalability of AI systems. Cloud computing platforms offer flexible solutions for varying workloads, while advanced data-cleaning techniques improve data quality and accessibility. A strong cybersecurity framework safeguards against potential threats, maintaining user trust and validating AI applications.

The ongoing evolution of generative AI offers tremendous opportunities while posing significant challenges. Addressing these challenges through ethical practices, robust infrastructure, and continuous learning will shape a future where AI technologies benefit society as a whole. The journey ahead requires collaborative efforts, investment, and a commitment to responsible AI development, ensuring that generative AI continues to drive innovation and improve lives across diverse domains.

References

Bean, R., Davenport, T. (2023, June). *The Impact of Generative AI on Hollywood and Entertainment.* *MIT Sloan Management Review.* https://sloanreview.mit.edu/article/the-impact-of-generative-ai-on-hollywood-and-entertainment/

Building Future-Ready Business Schools With Generative AI | AACSB. www.aacsb.edu. (n.d.). https://www.aacsb.edu/insights/reports/building-future-ready-business-schools-with-generative-ai

Farhud, D., Zokaei, S. (2021, November). *Ethical Issues of Artificial Intelligence in Medicine and Healthcare.* *Iranian Journal of Public Health.* https://www.ncbi.nlm.nih.gov/pmc/articles/PMC8826344/

Insights on Generative AI and the Future of Work | NC Commerce. www.commerce.nc.gov. (2024, February). https://www.commerce.nc.gov/news/the-lead-feed/generative-ai-and-future-work

Leslie, D., Perini, A. (2024, May). *Future Shock: Generative AI and the International AI Policy and Governance Crisis.* *Harvard Data Science Review.* https://hdsr.mitpress.mit.edu/pub/yixt9mqu/release/2

Lynch, S. (2024, April). *AI Index: State of AI in 13 Charts.* *hai.stanford.edu.* https://hai.stanford.edu/news/ai-index-state-ai-13-charts

Yaraghi, N. (2024, January). *Generative AI in health care: Opportunities, challenges, and policy.* *Brookings.* https://www.brookings.edu/articles/generative-ai-in-health-care-opportunities-challenges-and-policy/

CHAPTER 14

Practical Tools and Technologies

Exploring the practical tools and technologies of Generative AI provides a thorough understanding of how these innovations are becoming integral in various fields. This chapter delves into different features, types, comparisons, usage guides, and real-world applications to help users better comprehend their potentials and limitations. By understanding the underlying mechanics and functionalities, students and professionals alike can better appreciate the transformative impact of these tools on content creation and automation.

In this chapter, readers will examine an array of generative AI tools along with their specific features and use cases. Detailed comparisons between popular tools like MidJourney, Gemini, and Claude highlight their unique capabilities and strengths. The chapter also includes comprehensive usage guides, offering step-by-step instructions for effectively leveraging these technologies. Real-world applications illustrate how these tools are employed across different industries, showcasing their versatility and efficiency. By the end of this chapter, readers will be equipped with practical knowledge to utilize generative AI tools in their own projects and professional endeavors.

Introduction to Generative AI Tools

Generative AI tools have revolutionized the way we create and interact with digital content. These tools leverage artificial intelligence to generate data, such as text, images, music, and other forms of media, based on input parameters. The essence of generative AI lies in its ability to create new, unique content that mimics human creativity. This technological capability extends beyond simple automation, allowing for innovative applications across various fields.

The significance of generative AI tools in modern applications cannot be overstated. They enable users to quickly produce high-quality content, thus saving time and resources. For instance, large language models like GPT-3 can generate essays, summaries, and even computer code from a few lines of text input. Similarly, image generation models can create realistic photos or artistic representations from textual descriptions. This has profound implications in industries such as marketing, where swift creation of visuals and written content is critical.

Generative AI also plays a crucial role in enabling synthetic data generation, which is particularly useful in training other AI models. When real-world data is scarce or biased, synthetic data created by generative models can provide the necessary diversity and volume. This helps improve the performance and fairness of machine learning systems. Moreover, generative AI's ability to automate creative processes enhances productivity in sectors ranging from entertainment to research, making it an invaluable tool in the digital age.

The development of generative AI tools has undergone significant evolution since its inception. Early attempts at generative AI were often rudimentary and limited in their scope and accuracy. However, breakthroughs in neural networks, particularly deep learning, have propelled the field forward. Techniques such as Generative Adversarial Networks (GANs), introduced in 2014, marked a major milestone. GANs utilize two neural networks—a generator and a discriminator—that compete against each other to produce increasingly realistic outputs.

Another pivotal development was the introduction of transformer-based models in 2017. Transformers brought about significant improvements in language processing tasks, thanks to their ability to handle long dependencies in text. This technology laid the groundwork for advanced models like GPT-3, which can perform a wide array of generative tasks with impressive accuracy. Over the years, researchers have continued refining these models, incorporating more sophisticated architectures and training them on larger datasets.

Current trends in generative AI technologies are shaping the future of digital content creation. One notable trend is the increasing popularity of diffusion models, which offer higher-quality outputs by iteratively refining initial random noise into structured data. Additionally, there is a growing emphasis on improving the efficiency and speed of these models. This is essential for real-time applications, such as chatbots and interactive art installations, where quick response times are crucial.

Another trend is the integration of multimodal capabilities, enabling generative AI tools to process and combine various types of data inputs, such as text, images, and audio. This versatility opens up new possibilities for creative expression and practical applications. For example, a model could generate a music video from both a song and a script, combining visual and auditory elements seamlessly. Additionally, the democratization of these technologies through open-source frameworks and cloud-based platforms is making generative AI accessible to a broader audience.

The importance of generative AI in various industries is becoming increasingly apparent as more sectors adopt these technologies. In the entertainment industry, generative AI is used to create special effects, design video game environments, and even compose music. It allows artists to explore new creative horizons by automating tedious tasks and providing novel inspiration. Similarly, in the fashion industry, AI can generate clothing designs or predict upcoming trends based on historical data.

In healthcare, generative AI offers transformative potential by aiding in drug discovery and medical research. By generating new protein structures or simulating complex biological processes, these tools can accelerate the development of treatments and improve patient outcomes. Likewise, in finance, generative models are employed to create realistic market scenarios for risk assessment and strategy development, helping institutions make more informed decisions.

Moreover, generative AI is making strides in education by developing personalized learning materials and tutoring systems that adapt to individual students' needs. This technology can generate interactive lessons, quizzes, and even virtual simulations, enhancing the learning experience. In the advertising sector, AI-generated content helps craft targeted campaigns that resonate more effectively with diverse audiences. The ability to swiftly produce customized advertisements ensures that brands remain relevant and competitive in a fast-paced market.

MidJourney Overview

MidJourney is an innovative tool designed for generating AI-driven artwork. As a practical tool in the realm of generative AI, MidJourney offers a plethora of functionalities that are accessible to both novices and experienced users. This section delves into its primary use cases, key features, additional capabilities, and the vibrant user community that has emerged around this tool.

One of the primary use cases for MidJourney is in the creation of digital art and illustrations. This AI-powered tool excels at transforming textual prompts into visually appealing images, making it a favorite among digital artists and graphic designers. Whether you're looking to create concept art for a video game, illustrations for a book, or unique visuals for marketing materials, MidJourney provides the necessary tools and flexibility. Its ability to interpret detailed descriptions and produce corresponding images reduces the time and effort traditionally required in digital art creation.

Another significant use case is in the field of content creation for online platforms. Bloggers, website owners, and social media managers often need visually striking images to complement their written content. MidJourney's capacity to generate various styles of artwork based on user input makes it ideal for producing these customized visuals. The tool can generate anything from abstract designs to realistic scenes, catering to diverse content needs.

Furthermore, educators and researchers have found MidJourney useful for creating visual aids and educational materials. By generating specific images that align with educational topics, instructors can make their lessons more engaging and easier to understand. This application highlights the versatility of MidJourney in addressing both creative and educational needs.

Key features of MidJourney include image generation and style transfer. Image generation is the core functionality, where users provide descriptive prompts, and the AI produces images that match the description. This feature is particularly powerful because it allows users to visualize their ideas quickly without needing advanced artistic skills. Users can experiment with different prompts and refine them until the desired outcome is achieved.

Style transfer is another notable feature that enables users to apply various artistic styles to their generated images. This functionality allows for the exploration of different aesthetics without altering the fundamental content of the image. For instance, an image can be rendered in the style of a famous artist or adopt the characteristics of a particular art movement. This capability enhances the creative potential of the tool, enabling users to produce unique and visually compelling artworks.

Additionally, MidJourney offers capabilities like upscaling and blending images. Upscaling increases the resolution of generated images while maintaining clarity and detail, which is essential for producing high-quality prints or detailed digital designs. The blending feature allows users to merge elements from different images, creating composite visuals that retain aspects of the original inputs. These advanced options provide users with greater control over the final output.

Beyond these key features, MidJourney includes several other capabilities that extend its utility. One such capability is the ability to generate multiple variations of an image based on the same prompt. This feature encourages experimentation by presenting users with several creative interpretations from which they can choose. It also saves time by offering multiple options simultaneously rather than requiring repeated prompt adjustments and generations.

Another additional capability is the customization of parameters to fine-tune image generation. MidJourney allows users to adjust settings such as model version, stylization degree, and generation speed. These customizations enable users to tailor the image generation process according to their specific needs and preferences. For example, adjusting the stylization parameter can shift the balance between accurate representations of the prompt and artistic interpretation.

Moreover, MidJourney's integration with Discord adds a communal aspect to its use. Through the Discord channels, users can share their creations, seek advice, and draw inspiration from the work of others. This interactive platform fosters a collaborative environment where users can learn from each other and improve their skills. It's also a space where developers can receive direct feedback from users, facilitating continuous improvement of the tool.

The MidJourney user community plays a significant role in popularizing the tool and expanding its application. Many artists and enthusiasts frequently share their work on social media and forums, showcasing the tool's capabilities and inspiring others to explore it. This organic growth has led to a diverse user base, ranging from professional artists to hobbyists experimenting with AI-generated art.

Within the user community, tutorials and guides are prevalent, making it easier for newcomers to get started with MidJourney. Experienced users often create step-by-step guides and video tutorials, breaking down complex processes into manageable steps. These resources are invaluable for beginners who might find the breadth of MidJourney's features overwhelming.

Popular use cases shared within the community demonstrate MidJourney's versatility. For instance, one common application is the creation of fantasy landscapes and characters, which are widely used in gaming and storytelling. Users often showcase how they use MidJourney to develop intricate scenes and imaginative worlds, highlighting the tool's potential in creative industries. Another popular use case is the generation of abstract art, where users experiment with shapes, colors, and textures to produce visually stunning pieces.

By leveraging the insights and examples provided by the user community, new users can quickly grasp the practical applications of MidJourney and integrate it into their own projects. This collective knowledge base not only aids individual learning but also drives the evolution of the tool itself, as developers can identify common needs and areas for enhancement.

Gemini Overview

Gemini, a generative AI tool from Google, offers a range of functionalities that make it a versatile asset for various users. Its primary functionalities revolve around providing real-time responses to user queries, which include both simple and complex interactions. Designed on the foundation of large language models (LLM), Gemini excels in generating accurate and contextually relevant content. This makes it particularly useful for individuals who require quick and reliable information, ranging from students needing homework assistance to professionals seeking data for reports.

One of Gemini's standout features is its ability to generate text based on prompts given by the user. This functionality is crucial for creating detailed articles, essays, or even scripts with minimal input. Users can type in a topic or a question, and Gemini will produce a coherent and informative response. Additionally, Gemini offers summarization capabilities, allowing users to condense lengthy documents into concise summaries. This feature is especially beneficial for students and professionals who need to sift through large volumes of information quickly.

Exploring Gemini's content creation capabilities reveals a tool designed to meet diverse needs. Beyond generating articles and essays, Gemini can assist in drafting emails, creating social media posts, and developing marketing materials. Its integration with Google Workspace further enhances its utility, enabling seamless workflow for those already using Google's suite of tools. This makes Gemini not just a standalone solution but a complementary tool that fits well within existing digital ecosystems.

The user base of Gemini spans various demographics, making it a versatile choice for different applications. Students and aspiring AI practitioners benefit from its ability to provide detailed explanations and support learning processes. Professionals looking to upskill find its text generation and summarization features invaluable for staying competitive in their fields. Tech enthusiasts and hobbyists appreciate its ease of use and the creative possibilities it brings to personal projects.

Common applications of Gemini include academic research, where it helps students generate hypotheses and draft papers. In corporate settings, it's used for writing reports, preparing presentations, and conducting market analysis. The ability to integrate with other Google tools like Maps and YouTube also opens up opportunities for more interactive and multimedia-rich content creation. For educators, Gemini offers a way to create teaching materials and craft assessments tailored to their curriculum.

In terms of interface, Gemini provides a user-friendly experience that's accessible to both novice and experienced users. Its connectivity with the internet ensures that the information provided is current and reliable. This is reinforced by built-in quality and fact-checking features, which allow users to refine and verify the content generated. Such functionalities ensure that users get not only quick but also accurate outputs, reducing the need for extensive post-generation editing.

Gemini's key strengths lie in its transparent and responsible AI design. Unlike some of its competitors, it focuses on providing factual and quality-managed content. This reliability is further enhanced by user feedback mechanisms, enabling continuous improvement of its responses. Users can rate the generated content and provide specific feedback, ensuring that the tool evolves to better meet their needs over time.

The fact-checking capabilities of Gemini are particularly noteworthy. Users have options to cross-check the generated content against real-time internet sources. This feature is designed to flag any discrepancies and ensure that the final output adheres to factual accuracy. It adds a layer of credibility that is crucial for tasks requiring high levels of precision, such as academic papers or professional reports.

While Gemini addresses various needs effectively, it has limitations, primarily concerning image content generation. However, its focus on text-based outputs aligns well with the core needs of many users, such as students, researchers, and professionals. The continuous improvements being made promise to expand its capabilities further, potentially addressing these gaps in future updates.

Overall, Gemini stands out as a comprehensive tool for text generation and content creation. Its ability to integrate seamlessly with Google's ecosystem and its robust quality management features make it a reliable choice for a wide range of applications. Whether you're a student needing help with coursework, a professional drafting a report, or a tech enthusiast exploring new creative avenues, Gemini offers a solution tailored to your needs.

Gemini's focus on delivering high-quality informational and conversational content without compromising affordability makes it an attractive alternative to other generative AI tools. Its real-time internet connectivity ensures that users always have access to the most current data and resources, further enhancing its utility across various applications. As the tool continues to evolve, its potential to serve even broader user bases becomes increasingly apparent.

Claude Overview

Claude, developed by Anthropic AI, is a multifaceted tool within the domain of Generative AI. It stands out due to its emphasis on ethical AI practices while offering robust functionalities that cater to various user needs. At its core, Claude's primary functionalities include text summarization, generating creative content, and providing informative responses. This makes it an ideal choice for tasks such as writing assistance, summarizing lengthy documents, and delivering well-informed answers to questions.

Beyond its core capabilities, Claude excels in conversational AI, language translation, and sentiment analysis. In conversational AI, Claude is designed to simulate human interactions effectively, making it a valuable asset for businesses aiming to enhance customer service experiences through automated chats. Additionally, Claude's proficiency in language translation enables it to bridge communication gaps across different languages, facilitating global interactions and collaborations. Sentiment analysis is another vital feature, allowing users to gauge the emotional tone of text data, which proves useful in understanding customer feedback and social media sentiments.

An in-depth analysis of Claude's advanced features reveals its ability to handle complex and nuanced texts. One noteworthy attribute is its larger context window, allowing for the analysis of longer documents up to 150 pages. This feature is particularly beneficial for tasks like legal document review and academic research, where understanding the broader context is crucial. Moreover, Claude emphasizes ethical AI use, incorporating techniques to minimize bias and ensure responsible data handling. This focus on ethics makes it suitable for applications requiring adherence to strict ethical standards, such as medical record analysis or policy review.

Claude's user base spans various sectors, from educational institutions to corporate enterprises. Students and researchers leverage Claude for its efficient text summarization and comprehensive answer generation, aiding in academic pursuits. Meanwhile, businesses utilize Claude for customer service automation, language translation for international operations, and sentiment analysis to gain insights into market trends and consumer behavior. For instance, marketing teams can use Claude to analyze social media conversations, helping them tailor their strategies based on public sentiment (Claude vs. ChatGPT: What's the difference?. GeeksforGeeks., 2024).

The versatility of Claude in real-world applications extends its utility beyond just text-related tasks. Its integration into existing systems allows for streamlined workflows and improved operational efficiency. By using Claude, businesses can automate routine documentation processes, thereby saving time and reducing human error. Additionally, it can assist in drafting personalized communications, ensuring consistency in tone and messaging across large-scale outreach programs. This adaptability makes Claude a preferred choice for professionals looking to enhance productivity and accuracy in their work.

Concluding thoughts on practical tools and technologies

This chapter has covered Generative AI's practical tools and technologies' features, comparisons, usage instructions, and real-world applications. Generative AI systems may emulate human creativity and create various digital content including literature, graphics, music, and other media.

These tools are crucial in modern applications. Generative AI saves time and resources in marketing and healthcare by automating creative processes and producing high-quality content quickly. Big language models like GPT-3 and picture generation models boost productivity and innovation.

GANs and transformer-based models have greatly improved the quality and efficiency of AI-generated content. Diffusion models improving data quality and multimodal capabilities increasing versatility suggest a bright future.

However, some readers might have concerns regarding the ethical implications and potential biases inherent in generative AI systems. Addressing such concerns is crucial, especially when AI-generated content influences areas like education, finance, and healthcare. Ensuring transparency and fairness in AI algorithms remains an essential focus for future development and deployment.

The consequences of adopting generative AI on a broader scale are profound. Industries like entertainment, fashion, and advertising stand to benefit immensely, unlocking new realms of creativity and operational efficiency. At the same time, sectors such as healthcare and education can leverage these tools to advance research, improve patient outcomes, and provide personalized learning experiences.

As we conclude this chapter, it is evident that generative AI holds immense potential to transform numerous aspects of our lives. The journey of exploring these technologies is far from over, and their continuous refinement will likely yield even more innovative and impactful applications in the years to come. Embracing the ethical use of generative AI and remaining vigilant about its implications will ensure that its benefits are maximized while mitigating potential risks.

References

ChatGPT Vs Claude: Who Will Take Over The AI World?. chatonai.org. (n.d.). https://chatonai.org/chatgpt-vs-claude

Claude vs. ChatGPT: What's the difference?. GeeksforGeeks. (2024, April). https://www.geeksforgeeks.org/claude-vs-chatgpt-whats-the-difference/

Hiter, S. (2024, March). *Gemini vs. ChatGPT: AI Apps Head-to-Head. eWEEK.* http://www.barcampuae.org/index-1224.html

How to Use Midjourney? Ultimate Guide to AI Art Creation. BitDegree. (n.d.). https://www.bitdegree.org/ai/tutorials/how-to-use-midjourney

Page has moved. www.barcampuae.org. (n.d.). http://www.barcampuae.org/index-1183.html

What is Generative AI?. NVIDIA. (n.d.). https://revolutioninsimulation.org/redirect-page/?go=https://www.nvidia.com/en-us/glossary/generative-ai/

CHAPTER 15

Case Studies and Real-World Applications

Case studies and real-world applications of generative AI demonstrate the versatility and impact of this technology across various sectors. By analyzing successful projects, we can observe how different methodologies lead to specific outcomes and gather valuable insights from industry experts. This chapter delves into notable examples to provide readers with a comprehensive understanding of the practical implementation and potential of generative AI.

In this chapter, readers will explore detailed case studies such as Google's DeepDream, OpenAI's GPT-3, NVIDIA's GauGAN, and OpenAI's Jukebox. Each of these projects showcases unique approaches and groundbreaking results in generative AI. The chapter will also cover the techniques and outcomes associated with these projects, including the use of Convolutional Neural Networks (CNNs), Recurrent Neural Networks (RNNs), Long Short-Term Memory (LSTM), and Transformers. Furthermore, training strategies like data augmentation, transfer learning, and fine-tuning will be discussed to highlight their importance in enhancing model performance. The analysis will conclude with best practices, lessons learned, and expert insights that provide a well-rounded perspective on the advancements and challenges in the field of generative AI.

Detailed Case Studies of Successful Generative AI Projects

Analyze detailed case studies of successful generative AI projects.

DeepDream by Google aimed to explore neural network interpretability by visualizing the patterns learned by these networks. The objective was to better understand how neural networks process and recognize images. By amplifying image features through iterative techniques, DeepDream produced surreal and vivid visuals that highlighted specific elements within images, showcasing the internal processes of artificial neural networks.

The methodologies used in DeepDream involved setting certain layers of the neural network to maximum activation, resulting in overemphasized features in images. This approach helped researchers pinpoint which parts of the network were responsible for recognizing particular patterns. Techniques such as gradient ascent were employed to iteratively adjust the input image to enhance the targeted features.

DeepDream's impact extended beyond technical insights; it influenced both the art world and the field of interpretability. Artists began using DeepDream-generated images to create unique and mind-bending artworks, blending technology with creativity. On a technical level, these visualizations offered a window into the otherwise opaque workings of neural networks, aiding research in model transparency and interpretability.

OpenAI's GPT-3 project focused on generating human-like text across a myriad of applications. Aimed at creating an advanced language model capable of understanding and producing coherent and contextually relevant text, GPT-3 has been utilized in various fields including chatbots, content creation, and programming assistance.

The model architecture of GPT-3 is based on the transformer network, consisting of 175 billion parameters. Training this model involved vast amounts of text data from diverse sources, allowing it to grasp nuanced language patterns. Key to its effectiveness was the training strategy, which incorporated techniques like supervised learning from large datasets and reinforcement learning from human feedback.

GPT-3 demonstrated impressive capabilities in tasks such as answering questions, translating languages, and writing articles. Its proficiency across different domains showcased the potential of large-scale language models in real-world applications, making it a versatile tool for both business and personal use. However, concerns around bias and misinformation also surfaced, highlighting the need for careful deployment and ethical considerations.

NVIDIA's GauGAN project revolutionized digital art and design by converting simple sketches into photorealistic images. The main objective was to enable artists and designers to quickly transform conceptual drawings into detailed, high-quality images.

This project leveraged Generative Adversarial Networks (GANs) to achieve its transformative results.

GauGAN's methodologies centered on using segmentation maps to guide the image generation process. Users could draw basic outlines and assign colors representing different materials or regions, and the GAN would then generate realistic textures and details consistent with those inputs. This technique bridged the gap between abstract concepts and finished visual pieces, streamlining the creative process.

The impact of GauGAN is evident in its application across digital art, architectural visualization, and game design. It empowered users without extensive technical expertise to produce professional-grade visuals, democratizing access to sophisticated design tools. Additionally, GauGAN's innovative use of GANs set a new benchmark for image synthesis technologies.

JukeBox by OpenAI sought to innovate in the music creation domain by generating music across genres complete with lyrics and vocals. This project aimed to blend computational creativity with musical artistry, exploring new frontiers in AI-assisted music composition and production.

Combining autoregressive models with convolutional networks, JukeBox generated complex musical compositions by predicting one note at a time while considering previous notes. This approach allowed for the creation of coherent and stylistically consistent pieces. The model trained on a diverse range of music genres, equipping it with the versatility to produce everything from classical to pop.

Analysis of Techniques and Outcomes

Generative AI projects have demonstrated remarkable achievements through various neural network architectures. Convolutional Neural Networks (CNNs) are widely used in image-related tasks, such as style transfer and image synthesis. They excel at identifying spatial hierarchies in images, making them effective for use in image translation applications. Recurrent Neural Networks (RNNs) and their variant, Long Short-Term Memory (LSTM), are used extensively in natural language processing tasks due to their ability to handle sequential data effectively. Transformers, introduced by Vaswani et al., revolutionized the field with their attention mechanisms, which allow models to consider the importance of each word in a sentence and thus manage long-range dependencies better than RNNs.

Generative Adversarial Networks (GANs), consisting of a generator and a discriminator, are another fundamental architecture used in many generative AI projects. The generator creates synthetic data, while the discriminator evaluates it against real data, refining the generator's outputs over time. Variations such as CycleGANs and StyleGANs have been pivotal in creating high-quality, realistic images and videos. In real-world applications, these architectures have enabled advancements in areas such as medical imaging, where GANs generate high-resolution scans from lower-quality images, thereby aiding in diagnostics.

Training strategies significantly influence the effectiveness of generative AI models. Data augmentation is one critical strategy, involving techniques to expand the diversity of training datasets without collecting new data. This includes methods like rotation, scaling, and flipping of images to create varied data points. Transfer learning is another prevalent strategy, where models pre-trained on large datasets are fine-tuned for specific tasks using smaller, task-specific datasets. This approach reduces training time and improves model performance by leveraging existing knowledge embedded in the pre-trained models.

Fine-tuning involves tweaking an existing model to better suit a particular application or dataset. This is especially useful in scenarios with limited labeled data, allowing for more focused training without starting from scratch. By adjusting layers and retraining certain parts of the model while keeping others constant, fine-tuning can significantly enhance a model's performance and applicability. These training strategies collectively improve the robustness and versatility of generative AI models, enabling them to perform well across various domains.

Optimization methods are critical in enhancing the learning efficiency and performance of generative AI models. Gradient descent is a foundational optimization algorithm that iteratively adjusts model parameters to minimize the error between predicted and actual outcomes. Variants of gradient descent, such as stochastic gradient descent (SGD), apply updates to parameters for each data point, speeding up the convergence process. The Adam optimizer combines the advantages of adaptive learning rates and momentum, adjusting the learning rate for each parameter dynamically, resulting in faster convergence and more stable training processes.

Learning rate schedules adjust the learning rate during training to ensure the model converges optimally. Schedules like exponential decay reduce the learning rate gradually, helping the model settle into minimum error regions more smoothly. These optimization methods are crucial for training deep neural networks effectively, ensuring that models not only learn efficiently but also generalize well to unseen data.

Evaluating the outcomes of generative AI projects involves multiple criteria, including performance metrics, user engagement, commercial success, and innovations introduced. Performance metrics vary depending on the application; for example, in image generation, metrics like Inception Score (IS) and Frechet Inception Distance (FID) assess the quality and diversity of generated images. In natural language processing, measures like BLEU scores evaluate the fluency and accuracy of generated text compared to human-written text.

User engagement metrics indicate how effectively a generative AI model meets its intended purpose. High user retention rates, positive feedback, and increased interaction times are indicators of successful projects. For instance, applications like chatbots benefit from generative models that can hold coherent, contextually relevant conversations, thereby increasing user satisfaction.

Commercial success is another vital outcome. Successful generative AI projects often lead to monetizable products, such as automated content creation tools, improved recommendation systems, and enhanced customer service through AI-driven interfaces. Innovations introduced by generative AI include new techniques in art, music generation, and interactive media, pushing the boundaries of what technology can achieve.

Lessons Learned and Best Practices

In analyzing generative AI case studies, data quality and quantity emerge as foundational elements for success. High-quality datasets ensure that the models are trained on accurate and representative information, minimizing errors and biases. Diverse datasets enhance the model's adaptability and robustness, making it capable of handling various scenarios. For instance, a generative AI trained on a diverse dataset can produce more realistic and comprehensive outputs, whether it's text, images, or music.

Moreover, incorporating extensive and varied data allows the model to generalize better across different tasks and domains. It is not enough to have large datasets; they must also be rich in variety. This diversity helps avoid overfitting, where the model performs well on training data but fails to generalize to new, unseen data. Therefore, ensuring both high quality and sufficient quantity of data is crucial for building robust and reliable generative AI systems. (PhD, A., 2024)

To achieve optimal data quality, several best practices can be implemented. First, data should be meticulously cleaned and pre-processed to remove any noise or irrelevant information. This process involves handling missing values, normalizing data, and eliminating duplicates. Second, maintaining documentation and metadata about the data sources ensures transparency and reproducibility. Third, continuously updating the dataset with new and relevant information helps keep the model up-to-date with the latest trends and patterns, enhancing its relevance and accuracy.

Model interpretability is another critical aspect of successful generative AI applications. Understanding how and why a model makes specific decisions is vital for gaining trust and ensuring ethical use. Interpretability allows developers and users to scrutinize the model's behavior, identify potential biases, and make informed adjustments. For example, visualizing the inner workings of a neural network, such as through attention maps in transformers, can provide insights into which parts of the input data the model deems important.

Several tools and techniques can aid in improving model interpretability. Saliency maps, for instance, highlight regions of an input image that most influence the model's predictions, offering a visual explanation of its focus areas. Similarly, feature importance scores in decision trees and random forests indicate which features contribute most to the output. By leveraging these interpretability techniques, practitioners can enhance the transparency and reliability of generative AI models, fostering greater confidence in their use.

Transparency in model interpretability also paves the way for identifying and mitigating biases. When developers can see the decision-making process of a model, they are better equipped to spot unfair or biased outcomes. This proactive approach not only improves the ethical deployment of AI technologies but also ensures compliance with regulatory standards and societal expectations. As generative AI continues to evolve, prioritizing interpretability will be essential for its responsible and effective application.

Scaling generative AI models to handle large datasets and complex tasks is another significant challenge. Effective scalability strategies ensure that the models can operate efficiently without compromising performance. One approach to achieving this is through distributed computing, where tasks are spread across multiple machines, allowing parallel processing of data. Cloud-based solutions, such as those offered by AWS or Google Cloud, provide scalable infrastructure that can dynamically adjust to changing workload demands.

Another strategy is optimizing model architectures to reduce computational requirements. Techniques like model pruning, quantization, and knowledge distillation can help streamline models, making them more efficient without sacrificing accuracy. For instance, model compression methods can significantly reduce the size of deep neural networks, enabling faster inference times and lower memory usage. These optimizations are particularly crucial when deploying generative AI models in real-time applications where responsiveness is vital.

Implementing robust error-handling mechanisms is also important when scaling AI systems. This includes monitoring system performance, managing hardware failures, and ensuring consistent data flow. Regular maintenance and updates to the infrastructure help address potential bottlenecks and improve overall efficiency. By adopting these scalability strategies, organizations can effectively manage the complexities of large-scale generative AI projects, ensuring sustained performance and reliability.

Ethical considerations are paramount in the development and deployment of generative AI. One major concern is the potential for bias in AI models, which can lead to unfair and discriminatory outcomes. Bias can originate from various sources, including biased training data, biased algorithms, and societal biases reflected in the data. Addressing these issues requires a multifaceted approach, starting with the careful selection and curation of training datasets to ensure they are representative and free from harmful biases.

Fairness in AI also involves implementing algorithms that promote equitable outcomes. Techniques such as fairness constraints, adversarial debiasing, and bias detection tools can help mitigate bias in AI models. Additionally, involving diverse teams in the development process can bring different perspectives and help identify potential biases early on. Transparent reporting of AI model performance metrics, including fairness indicators, is crucial for accountability and building trust among users and stakeholders. (Harvard Business Publishing Education. hbsp.harvard.edu., n.d.)

Responsible AI use extends beyond technical measures to include ethical guidelines and regulatory compliance. Developing and adhering to ethical frameworks ensures that AI technologies are used in ways that respect human rights, privacy, and societal values. For example, implementing privacy-preserving techniques such as differential privacy can protect individual data while still enabling valuable insights. Organizations must also stay informed about evolving regulations and standards in AI ethics to ensure their practices align with legal and societal expectations.

Insights from Industry Experts

Expert Interviews

To grasp the current state and future of generative AI, insights from leading industry experts are invaluable. Researchers at the forefront of AI development provide a deep understanding of underlying technologies and their capabilities. Notably, conversations with individuals such as Dr. Fei-Fei Li from Stanford University reveal that advancements in neural networks and machine learning models are driving significant progress. These experts underscore the importance of cross-disciplinary collaboration in pushing the boundaries of what's possible with generative AI.

Tech executives play a crucial role in translating research into real-world applications and products. Executives from companies like Google, IBM, and OpenAI offer perspectives on how generative AI is being integrated into various business processes. For example,

Google's work on DeepDream showcases how neural networks can be used creatively to generate art, while OpenAI's GPT-3 model demonstrates the potential for generating human-like text across diverse applications, from customer service to content creation.

Ethicists provide essential viewpoints on the societal and ethical implications of generative AI. They stress the need for responsible AI development practices to avoid biases and ensure fairness. Ethical considerations become particularly important as generative AI systems are increasingly deployed in sectors impacting people's lives directly, such as education, healthcare, and finance. By integrating these expert insights, we gain a holistic understanding of the complex landscape of generative AI.

Future Trends

The field of generative AI is evolving rapidly, with several key trends expected to shape its future. One prominent trend is the increasing sophistication of AI models. Emerging architectures, like transformers, are pushing the boundaries of what generative AI can achieve. These models are becoming more capable of generating high-quality outputs, whether in text, image, or audio formats, making them applicable in various domains, including entertainment and education.

Another significant trend is the democratization of AI technology. As generative AI tools become more accessible, they empower a broader range of users, from individual hobbyists to small businesses. Platforms offering user-friendly interfaces for AI model training and deployment are enhancing this accessibility. This trend indicates a shift towards more widespread adoption and innovation, as more people can experiment with and leverage generative AI for creative and practical purposes.

Moreover, there is a growing emphasis on integrating ethical considerations into AI development. Future advancements will likely focus on creating transparent and interpretable AI systems to address concerns about bias and accountability. Ensuring that AI technologies are developed and deployed responsibly will be critical to gaining public trust and maximizing the benefits of generative AI. These trends highlight the dynamic nature of the field and the exciting possibilities ahead.

Challenges and Opportunities

Generative AI presents both significant challenges and opportunities. One of the primary challenges is the issue of data quality and availability. Training robust generative models requires vast amounts of high-quality data, which can be difficult to obtain. Data privacy concerns also complicate the collection and use of personal data for model training. Addressing these issues necessitates developing methods for data anonymization and synthetic data generation.

Another challenge lies in the interpretability of AI models. Generative AI models, particularly those based on deep learning, often operate as black boxes, making it difficult to understand their decision-making processes. This lack of transparency poses risks, especially in critical applications like healthcare, where explainability is crucial. Research efforts are underway to develop techniques for better interpreting and explaining AI model outputs to enhance trust and usability.

Despite these challenges, the opportunities presented by generative AI are vast. In creative industries, generative AI is revolutionizing content creation, enabling artists and designers to explore new creative avenues. In the medical field, AI-generated simulations and models assist in research and diagnostics. Moreover, generative AI holds promise in education, providing personalized learning experiences and resources. By navigating the challenges effectively, we can harness the full potential of generative AI to drive innovation and positive change.

Impact on Society

The impact of generative AI on society is profound and multifaceted. One significant area of influence is the job market. As generative AI automates various tasks, it has the potential to increase efficiency and productivity. However, it also raises concerns about job displacement, particularly in roles involving routine cognitive tasks. According to a study by McKinsey, up to 30% of hours worked today could be automated by 2030, highlighting the need for workforce reskilling and adaptation (Diaz, V., 2024).

Generative AI also affects social interactions and communication. AI-driven chatbots and virtual assistants are becoming prevalent, changing how people interact with technology and access information. While these tools offer convenience and accessibility, they also bring challenges related to privacy and the authenticity of interactions. Ensuring that AI systems respect user privacy and provide transparent communication is essential to addressing these concerns.

In terms of broader societal implications, generative AI plays a role in shaping cultural and ethical norms. The increasing ability of AI to generate realistic content, such as deepfake videos, raises questions about authenticity and misinformation. Policymakers and developers must work together to create regulations and technological safeguards to mitigate the risks associated with AI-generated content. Balancing innovation with ethical considerations will be key to ensuring that generative AI positively impacts society.

Advice for Practitioners

As practitioners look to navigate the evolving landscape of generative AI, several guidelines can help them succeed. First, continuous learning and skill development are crucial. Staying updated with the latest advancements in AI technologies, methodologies, and ethical standards will ensure that practitioners remain competitive and relevant. Engaging in online courses, attending conferences, and participating in AI communities can provide valuable knowledge and networking opportunities.

Second, practitioners should prioritize ethical and responsible AI practices. This includes being mindful of biases in data and model outputs, ensuring transparency in AI systems, and adhering to legal and ethical guidelines. By adopting responsible AI development practices, practitioners can build trust with users and stakeholders while delivering beneficial and fair AI solutions.

Finally, collaboration and interdisciplinary engagement are vital. Generative AI projects often require expertise from various fields, including computer science, ethics, and domain-specific knowledge. Building diverse teams and fostering collaboration between different disciplines can lead to more innovative and well-rounded AI applications. Practitioners should seek opportunities to collaborate with researchers, policy experts, and industry leaders to navigate the challenges and maximize the opportunities presented by generative AI.

Practical Applications and Future Directions

Generative AI has showcased significant advancements by analyzing various case studies, each presenting unique methodologies, outcomes, and insights. Projects like Google's DeepDream have illustrated the potential of neural networks in understanding image processing through vivid visualizations. OpenAI's GPT-3 demonstrated the efficacy of large-scale language models in generating coherent text for diverse applications, emphasizing the importance of advanced training strategies and ethical deployment. NVIDIA's GauGAN revolutionized the creative process by transforming simple sketches into photorealistic images using GANs, highlighting the democratization of sophisticated design tools. Meanwhile, OpenAI's JukeBox explored new horizons in music creation by blending autoregressive models and convolutional networks to generate intricate musical compositions.

The analysis of techniques such as CNNs, RNNs, transformers, and GANs underscores their versatility across different domains. The use of optimization methods like gradient descent and learning rate schedules has been pivotal in enhancing model performance and efficiency. Training strategies, including data augmentation, transfer learning, and fine-tuning, contribute to the robustness of generative AI models, enabling them to handle various tasks effectively. Evaluating project outcomes based on performance metrics, user engagement, commercial success, and innovations introduced provides a comprehensive understanding of their impact.

Lessons learned from these projects emphasize the critical role of data quality and quantity in ensuring accurate and bias-free model outputs. Best practices for achieving optimal data quality, such as meticulous cleaning and continuous dataset updates, are essential. Model interpretability remains vital for gaining trust and ensuring ethical usage. Techniques like saliency maps and feature importance scores aid in visualizing the decision-making process, fostering transparency and reliability.

Scalability challenges can be addressed through distributed computing, cloud-based solutions, and model optimizations. These strategies ensure that generative AI models can handle large datasets and complex tasks efficiently. Ethical considerations, such as addressing potential biases and promoting fairness, are paramount. Responsible AI development practices, including diverse team involvement and transparent reporting, help mitigate these concerns.

Expert insights reiterate the importance of cross-disciplinary collaboration in advancing generative AI. Future trends indicate the growing sophistication of AI models, making technology more accessible and emphasizing ethical considerations. Challenges like data quality, model interpretability, and societal impacts must be navigated to harness the full potential of generative AI.

Navigating the evolving landscape of generative AI requires continuous learning, prioritizing ethical practices, and fostering interdisciplinary collaboration. By adhering to these principles, practitioners can build trust with users and stakeholders while delivering beneficial and fair AI solutions. As the field progresses, the integration of responsible AI practices and innovative methodologies will be crucial for realizing the transformative potential of generative AI across various domains and industries.

References

Contents. arxiv.org. (n.d.). https://arxiv.org/html/2207.09460v11

Generative Artificial Intelligence: A Systematic Review and Applications. arxiv.org. (n.d.). https://arxiv.org/html/2405.11029v1

Harvard Business Publishing Education. hbsp.harvard.edu. (n.d.). https://hbsp.harvard.edu/inspiring-minds/student-use-cases-for-ai

Newsroom, T. (2024, May). *Generative AI's Real-World Impact on Job Markets. Newsroom | University of St. Thomas.* https://news.stthomas.edu/generative-ais-real-world-impact-on-job-markets/

PhD, A. (2024, April). *Writing Case Studies Using Generative AI: Intimate Debate Case Study. Faculty Focus | Higher Ed Teaching & Learning.*

https://assistance.org/url?a=https://www.facultyfocus.com/articles/teaching-with-technology-articles/writing-case-studies-using-generative-ai-intimate-debate-case-study/

Scientists, A. (2024, June). *Why "One-Size-Fits-All" Solutions in Generative AI Training Fail and The Need for Customized Corporate Programs.* *Association of Data Scientists.* https://adasci.org/why-one-size-fits-all-solutions-in-generative-ai-training-fail-and-the-need-for-customized-corporate-programs/

diaz, v. (2024, February). *Exploring the Opportunities and Challenges with Generative AI.* *EDUCAUSE Review.* https://er.educause.edu/articles/2024/2/exploring-the-opportunities-and-challenges-with-generative-ai

ADVANCED

CHAPTERS

CHAPTER 16

Generative AI in Model Optimization

Optimizing machine learning models using generative AI presents an innovative approach that has gained significant traction in recent years. As the complexity and scale of data grow, traditional methods of model optimization often fall short, necessitating the use of advanced techniques like those offered by generative AI. In this context, understanding the role of hyperparameter tuning and the importance of effective model optimization becomes crucial for anyone looking to improve the efficiency and performance of their AI systems.

This chapter delves into a variety of techniques and methodologies for optimizing machine learning models using generative AI, focusing on several key aspects. Readers will explore the fundamentals of hyperparameters and their tuning methods, including Grid Search and Random Search, learning about their respective advantages and limitations. The chapter also introduces automated tools like Hyperopt and Optuna, which employ advanced algorithms to streamline the tuning process. Additionally, it covers model compression techniques such as quantization, pruning, and knowledge distillation, essential for deploying models on resource-constrained devices. The role of specialized hardware, including GPUs and TPUs, in enhancing model training and inference is discussed alongside distributed training techniques that leverage parallelism to manage large-scale computations. Finally, the chapter reviews frameworks like

TensorFlow, PyTorch, and Horovod, highlighting their benefits and practical applications in the industry. This comprehensive overview equips readers with the knowledge needed to effectively optimize their models using cutting-edge generative AI approaches.

Hyperparameter Tuning

Understanding hyperparameters and their tuning methods is crucial in the optimization of machine learning models. Hyperparameters are parameters set before the training process begins, and they dictate how the model learns. Common examples include the learning rate, which controls how quickly a model adapts to the problem, and batch size, which determines the number of training samples processed before the model's internal parameters are updated. Proper tuning of these parameters can significantly enhance model performance.

Grid Search is one of the most straightforward methods for hyperparameter tuning. This approach systematically searches through a predefined set of hyperparameters by evaluating every possible combination. For instance, if we consider two hyperparameters with three possible values each, Grid Search would evaluate nine possible combinations. While this method is exhaustive, ensuring that no potential combination is missed, it has notable downsides. The main disadvantage is its computational intensity; as the number of hyperparameters and their possible values increase, the number of evaluations grows exponentially, making Grid Search impractical for larger search spaces. Additionally, it treats all hyperparameter values equally, which might not be optimal for finding the best set of hyperparameters efficiently (Gülsüm Budakoğlu, 2023).

Random Search offers an alternative to Grid Search by randomly selecting combinations of hyperparameters from the predefined grid. Unlike Grid Search, Random Search does not evaluate every possible combination but instead samples from the hyperparameter space. This randomness can often lead to better results since it allows the search to cover a broader range of the hyperparameter space, especially when some dimensions contribute more significantly to model performance. A significant advantage of Random Search is its efficiency. Studies have shown that Random Search can find good configurations faster and more effectively than Grid Search by covering the hyperparameter space more thoroughly in less time. However, because it is random, there's always a chance that some potentially excellent hyperparameter configurations might be overlooked (*Hyperparameter Tuning in Python: A Complete Guide*, 2020).

Beyond traditional methods like Grid Search and Random Search, automated tools have emerged, leveraging advanced algorithms to handle hyperparameter tuning more effectively. Tools such as Hyperopt, Optuna, and others exemplify this category, providing powerful solutions for optimizing hyperparameters without exhaustive manual effort.

Hyperopt employs Bayesian optimization, which uses prior information about the hyperparameter space to make more informed decisions. It builds a probabilistic model of the function mapping hyperparameter values to the model performance, updating this model based on observed results. This helps concentrate the search on areas of the hyperparameter space that are more likely to yield better performance, thereby discovering optimal configurations with fewer evaluations.

Optuna, another leading tool, introduces a novel approach called Tree-structured Parzen Estimator (TPE). Unlike conventional methods, TPE models the density of good and bad sets of hyperparameters separately. It then chooses new trials based on these densities, focusing on regions where promising hyperparameters are densely packed. This method proves particularly effective because it refines its searches over time, zeroing in on the most promising regions of the hyperparameter landscape. Optuna also provides functionalities for pruning unpromising trials early, which saves computational resources and accelerates the optimization process further.

Successful tuning cases using these automated tools demonstrate their efficacy. For example, researchers have used Hyperopt to tune hyperparameters in deep learning models, achieving significant improvements in model accuracy with fewer trials compared to traditional methods. Similarly, Optuna has been utilized in various competitions and real-world applications to fine-tune complex models, often leading to superior performance with reduced computational costs.

Another valuable tool is Hyperband, which incorporates principles from both Random Search and bandit-based algorithms. It focuses on managing computational budgets efficiently. Hyperband starts by evaluating many configurations with a small budget and gradually increases the budget for the most promising configurations. This method balances exploration of the hyperparameter space with exploitation of the best configurations found so far, making it particularly useful when faced with limited computational resources.

Population-based training (PBT) represents another innovative approach, combining aspects of Random Search and manual tuning. PBT maintains a population of models trained in parallel, each evaluated independently. Periodically, the algorithm selects the best-performing models and modifies their hyperparameters, either by exploring the parameter space around successful configurations or by copying parameters from high-performing models. This iterative process continues until convergence, effectively balancing exploration and exploitation while adapting hyperparameters dynamically throughout the training process.

Automated hyperparameter tuning not only improves the performance of machine learning models but also frees up valuable time and resources for data scientists and AI practitioners. These tools allow for more efficient exploration of the hyperparameter space, often uncovering better configurations than could be achieved through manual tuning or simpler search methods. Implementing these techniques in practice requires understanding the strengths and limitations of each tool and selecting the one best suited to the specific problem at hand.

Techniques for Model Compression

Learning essential model compression techniques is crucial for optimizing machine learning models, enabling their deployment on resource-constrained devices without significantly sacrificing performance. These techniques include quantization, pruning, and knowledge distillation, each playing a distinct role in making models more efficient.

Quantization is a technique that reduces the precision of a model's weights and activations. By converting 32-bit floating-point numbers to lower precision formats like 8-bit fixed-point integers, quantization decreases the memory footprint and speeds up inference times. This method is particularly beneficial for deploying models on edge devices with limited computational resources. For instance, leveraging post-training quantization can result in significant improvements in both model size and speed. Some applications where fixed-point quantization excels are image classification on smartphones and real-time object detection in autonomous driving systems, providing faster response times while consuming less battery power.

Pruning involves removing unnecessary parameters from a neural network, thereby reducing its complexity. There are several types of pruning, including weight pruning, neuron pruning, filter pruning, and layer pruning. Weight pruning zeroes out connections in the network that have minimal impact on overall accuracy. Neuron pruning, on the other hand, removes entire neurons, which can lead to substantial reductions in model size with minimal loss in performance. Filter pruning ranks filters based on their importance and removes the least significant ones, and layer pruning eliminates whole layers when they contribute insignificantly to the final output.

Pruning offers multiple benefits, such as lowering computational costs, speeding up training and inference times, and reducing energy consumption. For example, in speech recognition systems, pruning can significantly enhance real-time processing capabilities without compromising the accuracy needed for understanding human language nuances. Another practical application is in surveillance systems, where pruned models ensure quicker image analysis, allowing prompt responses to security threats.

Knowledge distillation is an innovative method where a smaller, more compact student model is trained to mimic the behavior of a larger teacher model. This approach helps in creating lightweight models that retain most of the performance characteristics of the original models while being more suitable for deployment on devices with constrained resources. The teacher-student framework involves transferring knowledge from the teacher model to the student model by teaching it to produce similar predictions for a given set of inputs.

One of the significant advantages of knowledge distillation is its versatility. It can be applied across various domains, including natural language processing, computer vision, and speech recognition. For example, in sentiment analysis applications, a distilled model can effectively interpret and classify emotions in text data while requiring fewer computational resources. Similarly, in virtual assistants, distilled models facilitate real-time interaction with users, enhancing responsiveness without burdening the device's CPU or memory.

Real-world examples abound demonstrating the effectiveness of these model compression techniques. Google's MobileNets, for instance, employ both quantization and pruning to achieve high performance on mobile and embedded vision applications. By using depthwise separable convolutions along with quantization, MobileNets manage to maintain accuracy while significantly reducing model size and computational requirements. The outcome is a faster and more energy-efficient model, perfect for tasks like face recognition and other computationally intensive processes on smartphones.

Another example is the BERT (Bidirectional Encoder Representations from Transformers) model used in natural language processing. Given its extensive architecture, deploying BERT on devices like smartphones initially presented challenges due to its size and complexity. However, through knowledge distillation, the smaller DistilBERT variant was created. DistilBERT maintains about 97% of BERT's performance while being 60% faster and less than half the size. This makes it ideal for mobile applications that require advanced language understanding capabilities, such as voice-activated search and AI-driven customer service bots.

Hardware Optimization

Specialized hardware plays an essential role in optimizing machine learning models. GPUs (Graphics Processing Units) and TPUs (Tensor Processing Units) are designed to handle the intensive computations required by modern AI applications, providing significant performance advantages over general-purpose CPUs. The primary advantage of using specialized hardware is its ability to accelerate both model training and inference processes.

GPUs are highly parallel processors capable of executing thousands of concurrent threads, making them ideal for tasks that involve large-scale matrix operations typically found in neural network computations. By offloading these tasks to GPUs, you can achieve much faster training times and efficient utilization of hardware resources. The utilization of GPU acceleration can reduce the training time of complex models, which can take weeks or even months on standard CPUs, to just a few days or hours.

On the other hand, TPUs, specifically designed by Google for machine learning workloads, offer optimized performance for specific types of neural network operations. TPUs excel in performing dense matrix multiplications, which are core components of many deep learning models. They can significantly boost the speed of model training and are particularly effective when dealing with large-scale deployments. TPUs boast high computational throughput, thanks to their unique architecture where they perform operations on low-precision data types such as FP16 (half-precision floating-point), leading to faster computations and reduced memory requirements (Introduction to Cloud TPU, n.d.).

One critical strategy that leverages both GPUs and TPUs is mixed-precision training, which involves using lower-precision arithmetic (like FP16) during the forward and backward passes while maintaining higher-precision (FP32) for certain operations like weight updates. This method allows models to train faster due to less memory usage and increased throughput on supported hardware. Mixed-precision training is a software optimization technique facilitated by hardware accelerators, yielding faster training times without compromising model accuracy (Ntakouris, 2020).

In industry, multiple organizations have successfully implemented hardware optimization strategies to improve their AI workflows. For example, NVIDIA, a leader in GPU manufacturing, has shown how its GPUs can be used to enhance various AI applications. DeepMind's AlphaGo, which defeated human champions in the game of Go, leveraged massive GPU clusters for training its deep reinforcement learning models. Similarly, OpenAI's GPT-3 model, one of the largest language models to date, was trained using a combination of GPU and TPU resources, highlighting how important hardware optimization is for achieving breakthrough AI capabilities.

Another notable example is the use of TPUs in Google's own operations. Google Search, Gmail, and other services utilize TPUs to process vast amounts of data efficiently. These hardware accelerators allow Google to deliver fast and responsive experiences to billions of users every day while handling complex machine learning tasks in the background.

Beyond individual case studies, entire industries are shifting towards GPU and TPU adoption to stay competitive. In healthcare, for instance, GPUs have been employed to accelerate image recognition models used in medical imaging, leading to faster diagnosis and treatment planning. Financial institutions also use GPUs to speed up risk analysis and algorithmic trading models, enabling real-time decision-making based on complex data sets.

Hardware optimization doesn't only benefit large corporations; smaller startups and research groups can also achieve significant gains. By utilizing cloud-based GPU and TPU services, they can access cutting-edge hardware without upfront investment costs, democratizing access to powerful computational resources and fostering innovation across the field.

When applying these hardware-based strategies, it is crucial to align them with specific workload requirements. For instance, GPUs are generally preferred for workloads involving custom TensorFlow operations or medium-sized models with moderate batch sizes. Conversely, TPUs are more suited for workloads dominated by matrix computations and larger models that require extensive training over prolonged periods (Introduction to Cloud TPU, n.d.). By understanding the strengths and limitations of each hardware type, practitioners can make informed decisions that optimize their model performance and resource utilization.

Distributed Training Techniques

Investigating various distributed training methodologies is crucial for optimizing machine learning models using generative AI techniques. Distributed training divides the computational workload across multiple processors to accelerate model development and enhance performance. Two primary approaches to parallelism in distributed training are data parallelism and model parallelism, each with its unique operational mechanisms, benefits, and challenges.

Data parallelism involves dividing the dataset into several partitions, where each partition is processed independently by different worker nodes in a compute cluster. Every worker has a copy of the model and performs training on its subset of the data. The training process can be synchronous or asynchronous. In synchronous training, all workers start their forward pass simultaneously and compute gradients based on their data subsets. They then wait for other workers to finish before aggregating and updating the gradients using an all-reduce algorithm. This ensures that all workers have consistent weights before moving to the next iteration. While synchronous training maintains consistency, it is often slower due to the waiting periods.

On the other hand, asynchronous training allows each worker to proceed without waiting for others, updating weights independently. This reduces idle times but introduces inconsistency as some workers might use outdated weights. Asynchronous training also faces the challenge of potential communication bottlenecks, especially when dealing with large clusters. Nonetheless, data parallelism generally provides significant speed-ups and is relatively straightforward to implement.

Model parallelism, also known as network parallelism, addresses situations where the model is too large to fit into a single worker's memory. Instead of dividing the data, model parallelism splits the model itself either horizontally or vertically across multiple workers. Horizontal partitioning divides the model layers among workers, while vertical partitioning splits each layer into smaller segments. Each worker processes the same data but handles different parts of the model, synchronizing shared parameters after each forward or backward pass.

For example, in an encoder-decoder architecture, the encoder and decoder can be trained separately on different workers. Model parallelism is particularly useful for complex natural language processing models such as Transformers, GPT-3, and BERT. However, it necessitates frequent synchronization, making it more communication-intensive than data parallelism. Also, the complexity of dividing the model and coordinating the training increases with the number of layers and connections within the model.

Combining data and model parallelism results in hybrid parallelism, which leverages the strengths of both approaches. Hybrid parallelism is employed to efficiently utilize computational resources and manage large-scale models that would otherwise be challenging to train. For instance, in a scenario involving large language models like GPT-3, part of the model could be handled using model parallelism, while data parallelism manages the training data across multiple nodes. This combination helps balance the memory load and computation time, ensuring faster and more efficient training.

Examples of distributed training practices can be observed in significant AI research projects, such as OpenAI's GPT-3. GPT-3, one of the largest language models to date, was trained using a combination of advanced distributed training methodologies. The project utilized thousands of GPUs to handle different parts of the model and vast amounts of data, demonstrating the practical implementation and success of hybrid parallelism. This approach allowed OpenAI to scale training effectively, resulting in a powerful and capable generative model.

Through these methods, distributed training addresses the scalability issues inherent in deep learning, enabling more extensive and complex models to be developed. Utilizing parallelism not only speeds up the training process but also opens possibilities for innovations and breakthroughs in AI research. Future advancements in computing power and algorithms will likely further enhance these methodologies, paving the way for even more sophisticated AI systems.

Frameworks for Distributed Training

Distributed training is a critical component in the efficient optimization of machine learning models, particularly as datasets grow increasingly large and complex. Several frameworks facilitate this process, each offering unique benefits and challenges. This section explores some of the key frameworks including TensorFlow, PyTorch, and Horovod, examining their features, advantages, and practical applications in industry.

Overview of Key Frameworks

1. **TensorFlow**: Developed by Google, TensorFlow is one of the most widely-used frameworks for machine learning and deep learning tasks. TensorFlow supports both data parallelism and model parallelism, making it highly versatile for different types of distributed training scenarios. Through its high-level API, TensorFlow makes it easier to configure multiple GPUs and distribute workloads effectively.

1. **PyTorch**: PyTorch, developed by Facebook, has gained popularity due to its simplicity and flexibility. It is known for its intuitive interface and dynamic computational graph, which allows users to modify network behavior on the fly. PyTorch supports various forms of distributed training, including DataParallel, DistributedDataParallel, and torch.distributed.rpc, providing robust tools for both data-parallel and model-parallel strategies.

1. **Horovod**: Created by Uber, Horovod aims to make distributed deep learning fast and easy to use. It integrates seamlessly with TensorFlow, Keras, and PyTorch, leveraging the Message Passing Interface (MPI) library to enable efficient multi-node training. Horovod simplifies the migration of workloads from a single GPU to multiple GPUs or nodes, making it an attractive option for expanding existing projects.

Benefits Each Framework Provides for Distributed Training

- **TensorFlow**: One of the standout features of TensorFlow is its ability to manage large-scale distributed training efficiently. TensorFlow's Ecosystem, which includes TensorBoard for visualization and TensorFlow Serving for deployment, provides comprehensive support throughout the model development lifecycle. Additionally, TensorFlow's support for mixed-precision training helps optimize computational efficiency and memory usage, making it suitable for training extensive models like BigGAN (Barla, 2022).

- **PyTorch**: PyTorch is renowned for its straightforward implementation and user-friendliness. Its nn.DataParallel and nn.DistributedDataParallel modules offer out-of-the-box solutions for parallelizing tasks across multiple GPUs. PyTorch's adaptive dynamic graph construction allows for more flexible experimentation and debugging processes, enhancing the overall development experience. Moreover, cloud platform support ensures that PyTorch can be used seamlessly across different environments, both on-premise and in the cloud.

- **Horovod**: The primary benefit of Horovod is its focus on performance and ease of use. By employing MPI for communication, Horovod minimizes the overhead associated with synchronizing parameters across different nodes. This leads to faster training times, particularly when dealing with massive datasets that require distributed processing. Horovod's simple API enables rapid scaling of existing models without significant code refactoring, making it ideal for quick transitions to distributed training setups.

Comparative Analysis of the Frameworks

When comparing TensorFlow, PyTorch, and Horovod, several factors come into play, primarily in terms of functionality, efficiency, and ease of use.

- **Functionality**: TensorFlow stands out in terms of its comprehensive ecosystem, which integrates tools for every stage of model development, from training to deployment. PyTorch excels with its dynamic graph construction and flexibility, making it preferable for research and innovation. Horovod, while not a standalone framework, enhances TensorFlow and PyTorch by simplifying their distributed training capabilities.

- **Efficiency**: In terms of raw efficiency, Horovod often takes the lead due to its use of MPI for reducing synchronization overhead. TensorFlow's mixed-precision training also contributes to improved efficiency by optimizing GPU utilization. PyTorch maintains competitive performance, especially with its recent improvements in distributed data parallelism.

- **Ease of Use**: PyTorch is frequently praised for its intuitive syntax and user-friendly design, making it an excellent choice for beginners and researchers. TensorFlow, although more complex, offers extensive documentation and community support, which can ease the learning curve. Horovod simplifies distributed training but requires a foundational understanding of the underlying frameworks it extends.

Case Studies for Frameworks Application in Industry

To better understand the practicality of these frameworks, let's look at some real-world case studies:

1. **TensorFlow at LinkedIn**: LinkedIn uses TensorFlow to train its recommendation algorithms on large-scale datasets. The platform's ability to handle extensive computations and model complexities has significantly improved LinkedIn's personalized user experiences. Utilizing TensorFlow's data parallelism capabilities, LinkedIn manages to balance loads across multiple GPUs, reducing training time and enhancing model performance.

1. **PyTorch at Facebook AI Research (FAIR)**: PyTorch's dynamic nature has been a game-changer for Facebook's AI research initiatives. By allowing real-time modifications to neural networks, researchers at FAIR can rapidly iterate and experiment with new ideas. This flexibility has led to advancements in natural language processing (NLP) and computer vision, pushing the boundaries of what AI can achieve.

1. **Horovod at Uber**: Uber originally developed Horovod to expedite its machine learning models' training processes. By implementing Horovod, Uber has achieved substantial reductions in training times for its self-driving car models. The ease with which Horovod scales from single-node to multi-node configurations has enabled Uber to leverage its vast computational resources more effectively, driving faster iterations and innovations.

Wrapping Up

In this chapter, we have examined various techniques and methodologies for optimizing machine learning models through generative AI. We delved into hyperparameter tuning methods such as Grid Search and Random Search, discussing their efficiencies and limitations. Advanced tools like Hyperopt and Optuna were highlighted for their ability to automate and refine the tuning process, leading to better model performance with reduced computational costs. Additionally, we explored essential model compression techniques like quantization, pruning, and knowledge distillation, which are critical for deploying efficient models on resource-constrained devices. Real-world applications underscore the importance of these methods in enhancing performance while maintaining practicality.

Furthermore, we discussed hardware optimization strategies using GPUs and TPUs, showcasing their roles in accelerating model training and inference. Techniques like mixed-precision training were presented as ways to optimize computational efficiency without sacrificing accuracy. Distributed training techniques, including data parallelism, model parallelism, and hybrid approaches, were investigated for their capacity to handle large-scale models and datasets effectively. Finally, we reviewed key frameworks such as TensorFlow, PyTorch, and Horovod, emphasizing their unique features and benefits for distributed training. These insights provide a comprehensive understanding of how to leverage generative AI for optimizing machine learning models, driving advancements across various applications.

Reference List

4 Popular Model Compression Techniques Explained. (n.d.). Xailient.com. https://xailient.com/blog/4-popular-model-compression-techniques-explained/

Barla, N. (2022, July 22). *Distributed Training: Frameworks and Tools.* Neptune.ai. https://neptune.ai/blog/distributed-training-frameworks-and-tools

Distributed Training: Guide for Data Scientists. (2022, January 19). Neptune.ai. https://neptune.ai/blog/distributed-training

Distributed Training. (n.d.). Www.run.ai. https://www.run.ai/guides/gpu-deep-learning/distributed-training

Gülsüm Budakoğlu. (2023, March 26). *Hyper-parameter Tuning Through Grid Search and Optuna.* Medium; Medium. https://medium.com/@gulsum.budakoglu/hyper-parameter-tuning-through-grid-search-and-optuna-2bd89a2ece06

Hyperparameter Tuning in Python: a Complete Guide. (2020, August 24). Neptune.ai. https://neptune.ai/blog/hyperparameter-tuning-in-python-complete-guide

Introduction to Cloud TPU. (n.d.). Google Cloud. https://cloud.google.com/tpu/docs/intro-to-tpu

Model Parallelism on Distributed Infrastructure: A Literature Review from Theory to LLM Case-Studies. (n.d.). Arxiv.org. Retrieved July 30, 2024, from https://arxiv.org/html/2403.03699v1

Ntakouris, T. (2020, July 10). *Understanding ML In Production: Efficiently Training Models With GPUs and TPUs.* The Startup. https://medium.com/swlh/understanding-ml-in-production-efficiently-training-models-with-gpus-and-tpus-6607f211090

Rishi. (2024, January 30). *The Power of Model Compression: Guide to Pruning, Quantization, and Distillation in Machine Learning.* Medium; Medium. https://medium.com/@thisisrishi/the-power-of-model-compression-guide-to-pruning-quantization-and-distillation-in-machine-dbc6d28bd3a3

CHAPTER 17

Techniques for Stability and Robustness in Generative Models

Enhancing the stability and robustness of generative models is a key challenge in the field of artificial intelligence. These models, which are designed to generate new data instances similar to a given dataset, often struggle with issues such as instability during training and sensitivity to noise or adversarial attacks. Addressing these challenges is crucial for improving the reliability and performance of generative models. This chapter delves into various techniques aimed at fortifying these models, providing a comprehensive understanding of how to achieve greater stability and robustness.

The chapter explores multiple strategies, beginning with regularization techniques that help prevent overfitting by introducing constraints to model parameters. It then moves on to advanced methods like data augmentation, mixup, and cutout, which increase the diversity of training data to enhance model generalization. Adversarial training is also discussed, highlighting its role in making models more resilient against deceptive inputs. Furthermore, the chapter examines specific approaches for stabilizing Generative Adversarial Networks (GANs), such as feature matching, minibatch discrimination, and the use of Wasserstein distance. By the end, readers will have a solid grasp of the practical tools and methodologies available to ensure their generative models are both stable and robust.

Introduction to Regularization Techniques

Regularization is a critical technique in machine learning that helps improve model performance by preventing overfitting. Overfitting occurs when a model captures noise or random fluctuations in the training data instead of identifying the underlying patterns. This results in a model that performs well on training data but poorly on unseen data. Regularization techniques introduce additional constraints to the model, helping it generalize better to new data.

One common form of regularization is L1 and L2 regularization. Both techniques modify the cost function to include a penalty term that discourages large weights, but they do so in different ways. L1 regularization, also known as LASSO (Least Absolute Shrinkage and Selection Operator), adds the absolute values of the weights to the loss function. This penalty term forces some weights to become exactly zero, effectively performing feature selection by removing irrelevant features, which leads to sparser models. Sparse models are beneficial in many applications because they are simpler and easier to interpret.

L2 regularization, or Ridge regularization, penalizes the sum of the squared values of the weights. Unlike L1, L2 does not drive weights to zero but rather shrinks them to small values, maintaining all features but reducing their impact. This helps to distribute the weight more evenly across all features, thus preventing any single feature from dominating the prediction. By doing so, L2 regularization can improve the robustness of the model in the presence of noisy data.

Another powerful regularization technique is dropout. Dropout works by randomly "dropping out" a proportion of neurons during each iteration of training. Specifically, this means setting the output of these neurons to zero with a certain probability. By doing this, dropout prevents neurons from co-adapting too much, thus promoting independence between neurons. The randomness introduced by dropout forces the model to learn redundant representations of the data, which improves its ability to generalize. During testing, dropout is turned off, and all neurons contribute to the output, but their outputs are scaled down by the dropout rate to account for the reduced capacity during training.

Batch normalization is another technique that aids in improving both the stability and speed of training deep neural networks. It normalizes the input layer by adjusting and scaling the activations. By normalizing inputs of each mini-batch such that they have a mean of zero and a unit variance, batch normalization reduces internal covariate shift—the change in the distribution of network activations due to the update of parameters. This helps stabilize the learning process and allows for higher learning rates. Higher learning rates lead to faster convergence and potentially better performance. Additionally, batch normalization acts as a form of regularization by adding noise to the activations through mini-batch statistics, making the network less likely to overfit.

To implement L1 and L2 regularization, one typically adds an extra term to the loss function. For L1 regularization, the modified cost function *J* would be:

$$J(\theta) = J(\theta) + \lambda i = 1\sum n \mid \theta i \mid$$

For L2 regularization, the modified cost function would be:

$$J(\theta) = J(\theta) + 2\lambda \sum i = 1n\theta i2$$

Here, θ represents the model parameters, n is the number of parameters, and λ is the regularization strength. A larger λ will result in greater regularization effects, while a smaller λ will make the model behave more like an unregularized model.

In terms of dropout, assume that we have a fully connected network layer with n neurons. During training, each neuron is kept with a probability p and dropped with a probability $1 - p$. If a neuron's output is dropped, it means it does not contribute to the forward pass or backpropagation for that iteration. The output of a neuron i during training can thus be expressed as:

$$yi(drop) = zi(train) \cdot Bernoulli(p)$$

where $zi(train)$ is the output without dropout, and $Bernoulli(p)$ is a Bernoulli random variable with probability p.

Batch normalization involves computing the mean and variance of activations in the current mini-batch and using these statistics to normalize the activations. Mathematically, for a given activation p in a mini-batch, batch normalization transforms it into $\hat{X}$ as follows:

$$\hat{x} = \frac{x - \mu_B}{\sqrt{\sigma_B^2 + \epsilon}}$$

Here, μ_B and $\sigma_B 2$ are the mean and variance of the mini-batch, and ϵ is a small constant added for numerical stability. Subsequently, the normalized value is scaled and shifted using learnable parameters γ (scale) and β (shift):

$$Output = \gamma \hat{X} + \beta$$

This ensures that the model retains the capacity to represent complex functions while benefiting from the stabilization provided by normalization.

Advanced Regularization Techniques

One of the most promising methods for enhancing the robustness and stability of generative models lies in advanced regularization approaches, particularly data augmentation techniques. Data augmentation addresses limitations regarding the volume and quality of training data by artificially increasing the dataset's size and diversity using various transformations. These methods are crucial in scenarios where obtaining sufficient training data is challenging due to time, cost, or feasibility constraints (Mumuni & Mumuni, 2022). By leveraging such techniques, practitioners can improve model performance, reduce overfitting, and enhance generalization across multiple tasks.

Data Augmentation Methods and Applications

Data augmentation involves creating additional samples from existing data through transformations like rotation, scaling, flipping, and cropping. These operations yield new instances that preserve the original dataset's characteristics while introducing variability, which helps generative models generalize better to unseen data. In computer vision, methods such as random rotations, horizontal flips, color jittering, and zooms are common. More advanced techniques include feature-level augmentations and neural rendering, which generate more realistic synthetic data (Bendechache et al., 2023). By augmenting the training data, models become less prone to overfitting, resulting in improved robustness and performance.

Mixup and Cutout Techniques

Beyond basic augmentations, mixup and cutout techniques offer unique advantages. Mixup involves combining two or more images linearly, where the resultant image and its label are weighted averages of the originals. This technique encourages the model to create smoother decision boundaries, thus reducing memorization of noise and improving general robustness. For instance, an image of a cat could be mixed with one of a dog, and the resultant image would exhibit characteristics of both, along with a hybrid label. Mixup has been shown to significantly enhance the model's ability to handle variations in the input data and reduce classification errors.

Cutout, on the other hand, enhances robustness by randomly masking out sections of an image during training. This forces the model to focus on the unmasked parts and develop a more holistic understanding of the object being represented. By effectively preventing the model from relying too heavily on any specific features, cutout reduces overfitting and enhances generalization. For example, segmenting out a portion of a car's image encourages the model to recognize it even when part of the vehicle is occluded.

Case Studies of Successful Implementation

Several case studies validate the efficacy of these advanced regularization techniques in improving generative models. One notable example involves applying mixup to train a Generative Adversarial Network (GAN) for generating high-resolution images. Researchers found that the model trained with mixup-generated data exhibited less mode collapse—a common issue in GANs where the generator produces limited variety in outputs. The enhanced variety in training data allowed the GAN to produce a wider range of high-quality images, showing the practical benefits of mixup for generative tasks.

Another study applied cutout to improve the performance of a Variational Autoencoder (VAE) designed to generate synthetic medical images. By using cutout during training, the VAE learned to reconstruct images even when parts were missing, leading to more robust representations. This approach proved particularly beneficial for augmenting datasets in medical imaging, where obtaining large volumes of labeled data is often difficult.

Real-World Examples of Enhanced Model Performance

In real-world applications, these techniques have shown substantial improvements in generative model performance. One significant example is in autonomous driving, where augmenting datasets with mixup and cutout has led to more resilient models capable of handling diverse driving conditions. Autonomous vehicles must operate reliably under various scenarios, including different weather conditions, times of day, and unexpected obstacles. By training models with augmented data, developers create systems that better understand and navigate complex environments, leading to safer and more efficient autonomous driving solutions.

In the realm of natural language processing (NLP), data augmentation techniques have also proven valuable. Text data augmentation, such as synonym replacement, random insertion, and sentence shuffling, has been employed to enhance the robustness of language models. The application of mixup in NLP involves blending text sentences to create novel combinations, thereby enriching the training corpus. This method has been particularly effective in tasks requiring nuanced language understanding, such as sentiment analysis and machine translation.

Furthermore, advanced data augmentation has been pivotal in developing AI systems for healthcare diagnostics. Medical diagnostic algorithms often suffer from limited labeled data due to privacy concerns and the complexity of medical annotations. By using augmentation techniques like cutout and mixup, researchers have improved the sensitivity and specificity of diagnostic models. For instance, in diagnosing retinal diseases from eye scans, augmented data helped the models become more accurate and reliable, aiding early disease detection and intervention.

Understanding Adversarial Training

Adversarial training has emerged as a crucial technique in the quest for robust generative models. By integrating adversarial samples into the training process, this approach aims to fortify models against potential attacks, thereby enhancing their resilience and reliability.

Adversarial training fundamentally involves exposing a model to adversarial examples—inputs crafted to deceive the model into making errors. This exposure helps the model learn to recognize and correctly classify such deceptive inputs, ultimately bolstering its robustness. The significance of adversarial training lies in its ability to mitigate the vulnerabilities that generative models often exhibit when faced with adversarial attacks.

One common method for generating adversarial examples is the Fast Gradient Sign Method (FGSM). FGSM works by perturbing the original input image along the direction of the gradient of the loss function with respect to the input. Given the input image x, perturbation size ϵ, loss function $J(x, y)$, and target label y, the adversarial image $xadv$ can be computed as:

$$Xadv = x + \epsilon \cdot sign(\nabla xJ(x, y))$$

This single-step approach adjusts the pixel values in a manner aimed at maximizing the loss, thereby creating an adversarial example.

Another widely-used technique is Projected Gradient Descent (PGD), which is considered more effective for generating robust adversarial examples. PGD iteratively perturbs the input with smaller steps and projects the updated adversarial example back onto the ϵ-ball around the original input. This iterative process continues until the adversarial example effectively misleads the model. The PGD method can be mathematically represented as:

$$xt = \Pi\epsilon(xt - 1 + \alpha \cdot sign(\nabla xJ(xt, y)))$$

where $\Pi\epsilon$ denotes the projection onto the ϵ-ball around the original input. PGD's iterative nature makes it a potent tool for generating stronger adversarial examples compared to FGSM.

To successfully incorporate adversarial training into model development, several strategies and best practices should be followed. One key strategy is balancing the proportion of adversarial and clean examples in each training batch. Typically, a 50-50 split ensures that the model learns to handle both types of inputs effectively. It's also important to carefully tune the hyperparameters such as perturbation size ϵ and step size α during training. Too small perturbations may not provide significant robustness improvements, while excessively large perturbations can degrade the model's performance on clean data (Joel et al., 2022).

Another essential practice is employing diverse adversarial attack methods during training. Using only one type of attack might make the model robust to that specific attack but vulnerable to others. Incorporating a variety of methods like FGSM, PGD, and other advanced techniques ensures comprehensive robustness. Additionally, periodically evaluating the model's performance on both clean and adversarial test sets helps in monitoring and fine-tuning the training process.

Real-world case studies have demonstrated the effectiveness of adversarial training in various applications. For example, in medical imaging, adversarial training has been employed to improve the robustness of deep learning models used for classifying lung CTs, mammograms, and brain MRIs. Researchers used iterative adversarial training approaches, showing substantial improvements in model robustness across these different imaging modalities (Joel et al., 2022). Although adversarial training helped enhance accuracy on adversarial samples, it was observed that increasing perturbation sizes beyond a certain threshold could hinder model performance, highlighting the need for careful hyperparameter tuning.

Another notable application is in autonomous driving systems, where robustness is critical for safety. Adversarial training has been used to protect models against perturbations that could lead to incorrect decisions in vehicle control. By incorporating adversarial examples during training, these models become more resilient to visual distortions and noise in real-world environments, thus improving the reliability of autonomous vehicles.

Despite its advantages, adversarial training is not without challenges. It requires significant computational resources due to the iterative nature of generating adversarial examples, especially when using methods like PGD. Moreover, adversarial training alone might not suffice against highly sophisticated attacks, necessitating complementary defense mechanisms.

Challenges and Techniques in Stabilizing GAN Training

Generative Adversarial Networks (GANs) have revolutionized the field of machine learning by enabling the generation of new, synthetic data from input noise. However, training GANs presents several challenges that can hinder stability and robustness. Addressing these issues is critical for students, aspiring AI practitioners, professionals looking to upskill, and tech enthusiasts.

First, it's essential to identify common challenges in GAN training such as mode collapse and vanishing gradients. Mode collapse occurs when the generator produces limited types of outputs, reducing the diversity of generated samples. This issue arises because the generator learns to focus on a few modes of the data rather than the entire distribution. Vanishing gradients, on the other hand, occur when gradients become too small for meaningful updates during backpropagation, which slows down or entirely halts learning progress. These problems are detrimental to model performance and require robust techniques to address them.

One effective technique to stabilize GANs is feature matching. Feature matching aims to ensure that the statistics of features extracted from generated samples are similar to those from real samples. Specifically, instead of directly minimizing the distance between real and generated samples in pixel space, the generator tries to match the intermediate features from a pre-trained network or the discriminator. By doing so, it ensures the generated data captures the high-level structure and semantics of the real data, which helps mitigate mode collapse.

Minibatch discrimination is another powerful method for stabilizing GAN training. This technique involves comparing batches of generated samples to one another to encourage diversity among them. During training, small batches of data are processed together, allowing the discriminator to evaluate the similarity between generated samples within the same batch. Minibatch discrimination introduces a penalty for generating similar samples within a batch, promoting variability and helping to avoid mode collapse. It essentially forces the generator to produce a broader range of outputs, making the training process more stable.

Next, we introduce Wasserstein GAN (WGAN), an innovative approach that addresses instability in GAN training through the use of Wasserstein distance. Traditional GANs rely on the Jensen-Shannon divergence to measure the difference between real and generated data distributions, which can lead to unstable gradients. WGAN replaces this with the Wasserstein distance, also known as Earth Mover's distance, which provides a more meaningful measure even when distributions do not overlap. Using this distance helps ensure more stable and consistent updates during training, leading to better convergence properties and improved overall performance.

To understand the benefits of these techniques, consider the practical applications and improvements they bring. For instance, feature matching has shown significant success in tasks where capturing intricate details and variations in data is crucial, such as image generation. Similarly, minibatch discrimination enhances diversity, a key quality for applications like data augmentation where variety in generated samples enhances model robustness. Meanwhile, WGAN's stable training dynamics make it suitable for scenarios demanding high reliability, such as medical imaging or other critical fields.

Case Studies in Stabilized GANs

Generative Adversarial Networks (GANs) have shown remarkable potential in various fields by overcoming significant training challenges through innovative stabilization techniques. This section provides practical examples of stabilized GAN implementations, offering insights into how these methods enhance stability and robustness in generative models.

To start, the Deep Convolutional Generative Adversarial Networks (DCGAN) represents one of the most influential examples of stable GAN implementation. DCGAN addresses common issues like mode collapse and vanishing gradients by integrating convolutional layers, replacing deterministic pooling functions with strided convolutions, and using batch normalization extensively. These architectural adjustments contribute significantly to stabilizing the training process, leading to more reliable and high-quality image generation. The success of DCGAN has been demonstrated in applications such as unsupervised representation learning and image manipulation tasks (Radford et al., 2015).

Another notable example is the DiscoGAN, which excels in discovering cross-domain relationships without paired data. DiscoGAN implements a novel approach by learning to transfer styles between different domains while preserving essential attributes. This model effectively mitigates instability during training by employing cycle-consistency loss, ensuring that an image transformed from domain A to B and back to A remains similar to its original form. Applications of DiscoGAN include tasks like translating sketches to photographs and vice versa, showcasing its versatility and robustness (Kim et al., 2017).

In more specialized contexts, the DRAGAN (Deep Regret Analytic GAN) demonstrates significant improvements in training dynamics by introducing gradient penalty schemes. The main idea behind DRAGAN is to prevent sharp gradient regions around real data points, thus avoiding undesirable local equilibria that cause mode collapse. By maintaining smoother gradients, DRAGAN ensures faster convergence and enhanced stability across different architectures. Its application spans various fields, including medical imaging and realistic scene synthesis, where stable and accurate generation of complex images is crucial (Kodali et al., 2017).

Boundary-Seeking GAN (BGAN) presents another breakthrough in stabilizing GAN training, especially for discrete data. Traditional GANs struggle with non-differentiable data, but BGAN overcomes this by using importance weights derived from the discriminator's decision boundary. These weights guide the generator updates, improving the stability and performance of the entire network. BGAN's effectiveness has been demonstrated in tasks like character-based natural language generation and discrete image generation, expanding the applicability of GANs to new data types (Hjelm et al., 2018).

A critical aspect of these stable GAN implementations is their impact on real-world applications. For instance, DCGAN's architecture has been instrumental in enhancing the quality of synthesized images in creative industries, such as generating artwork and designing fashion items. Similarly, the robust performance of DiscoGAN has enabled practical applications in style transfer, aiding graphic designers and digital artists in innovative projects.

Analyzing the metrics and outcomes of these stabilizations reveals significant improvements in model performance. DCGAN, for example, exhibits lower Inception Scores (IS) and Fréchet Inception Distances (FID), indicating better image quality and diversity. DiscoGAN's cycle-consistency loss metric ensures the preservation of key attributes during cross-domain translations, highlighting the model's robustness. DRAGAN's gradient penalty terms result in reduced mode collapse frequency and faster convergence rates, as evidenced by smoother training curves and consistently high-quality output images. BGAN showcases improved accuracy in discrete data tasks, validated by higher BLEU scores in language generation and better visual coherence in image outputs.

Insights and Implications

This chapter has delved into various techniques to enhance the stability and robustness of generative models, emphasizing the importance of regularization methods. We explored fundamental techniques like L1 and L2 regularization, dropout, and batch normalization, all aimed at preventing overfitting and improving model generalization. Additionally, advanced regularization approaches such as data augmentation, mixup, and cutout were discussed, highlighting their effectiveness in creating diverse and robust training datasets. These methods are crucial for ensuring that generative models perform well on unseen data, thereby increasing their practical applicability in real-world scenarios.

Moreover, the chapter touched on adversarial training and stabilization techniques for GANs, presenting strategies to mitigate challenges like mode collapse and vanishing gradients. Methods such as feature matching, minibatch discrimination, and the use of Wasserstein distance were shown to significantly improve GAN training stability. Practical examples, including DCGAN, DiscoGAN, DRAGAN, and BGAN, demonstrated the successful implementation of these techniques, showcasing their impact across various applications. By integrating these techniques, practitioners can foster more resilient and reliable generative models, advancing the field of AI and enabling innovative solutions in technology and beyond.

Reference List

Aggarwal, A., Mittal, M., & Battineni, G. (2021, January). *Generative adversarial network: An overview of theory and applications.* International Journal of Information Management Data Insights. https://doi.org/10.1016/j.jjimei.2020.100004

Joel, M. Z., Umrao, S., Chang, E., Choi, R., Yang, D. X., Duncan, J. S., Omuro, A., Herbst, R., Krumholz, H. M., & Aneja, S. (2022, March 10). *Using Adversarial Images to Assess the Robustness of Deep Learning Models Trained on Diagnostic Images in Oncology.* JCO Clinical Cancer Informatics. https://doi.org/10.1200/CCI.21.00170

Kumar, T., Turab, M., Raj, K., Mileo, A., & Bendechache, M. (2023). *Advanced data augmentation approaches: A comprehensive survey and future directions.* ResearchGate. https://doi.org/10.48550/arXiv.2301.02830

Linder-Norén, E. (2023, April 10). *eriklindernoren/PyTorch-GAN.* GitHub. https://github.com/eriklindernoren/PyTorch-GAN

Mumuni, A., & Mumuni, F. (2022, November). *Data augmentation: A comprehensive survey of modern approaches.* Array. https://doi.org/10.1016/j.array.2022.100258

Regularization in Machine Learning. (n.d.). AlmaBetter. Retrieved July 30, 2024, from https://www.almabetter.com/bytes/tutorials/data-science/regularization-in-machine-learning

Zhao, W., Alwidian, S., & Mahmoud, Q. H. (2022, August 12). *Adversarial Training Methods for Deep Learning: A Systematic Review.* Algorithms. https://doi.org/10.3390/a15080283

kothiya, aditi. (2020, July 29). *Regularization: Batch-normalization and Drop out.* Analytics Vidhya. https://medium.com/analytics-vidhya/everything-you-need-to-know-about-regularizer-eb477b0c82ba

CHAPTER 18

Evaluation Metrics and Benchmarking in Generative AI

Evaluation metrics and benchmarking are vital components in the assessment of generative AI models. These elements help ensure that models meet specified standards of performance, allowing for consistent and reliable comparisons. Evaluation metrics provide a structured approach to quantify aspects such as image quality, diversity, and fidelity, while benchmarking facilitates the objective comparison of different models under controlled conditions.

In this chapter, we will delve into both quantitative and qualitative methods used to evaluate generative AI models. We will explore specific metrics like the Inception Score (IS), Fréchet Inception Distance (FID), and Perceptual Path Length (PPL), explaining how they measure various aspects of model performance. Furthermore, we will examine case studies that apply these metrics in real-world scenarios to illustrate their practical implications. Additionally, the chapter will cover qualitative assessments involving human judgment and user studies, discussing their significance in evaluating the creative and contextual relevance of generated content. Finally, we will look at the role of standardized benchmarks in ensuring fair and comprehensive evaluations across diverse applications and datasets. This multifaceted approach aims to provide a thorough understanding of how to effectively evaluate and benchmark generative AI models.

Quantitative Metrics

Evaluation metrics play a fundamental role in the development and assessment of generative AI models. These metrics are essential to quantify the performance of generative models in a consistent manner and ensure that they meet the desired standards. Without robust evaluation metrics, it would be challenging to measure improvements, compare different models, or understand their limitations.

Objective Assessment of Generative Models

An objective assessment is vital for evaluating the performance of generative AI models. Objective metrics provide a standardized way to evaluate models, ensuring consistency and repeatability across various experiments and studies. This is especially important in academia and industry, where models need to be benchmarked reliably to validate their effectiveness.

Inception Score (IS)

The Inception Score (IS) is one of the most widely used quantitative metrics for evaluating the performance of generative adversarial networks (GANs). It measures the classification accuracy of generated images using a pre-trained neural network, typically the Inception v3 model. The IS metric is based on two key principles: diversity and fidelity.

Diversity refers to the variety of samples generated by the model. A good generative model should produce a wide range of distinct samples that cover the entire distribution of real data. Fidelity, on the other hand, measures the quality of the generated samples. High-fidelity images are those that are indistinguishable from real images.

To calculate the IS, each generated image is passed through the pre-trained Inception v3 model, which outputs a probability distribution over various classes. The conditional probability distribution (the label distribution given the generated image) is then compared with the marginal probability distribution (the overall label distribution for all generated images) using Kullback-Leibler (KL) divergence. A higher IS indicates both high fidelity and diversity in the generated images, suggesting that the model is performing well.

However, the IS has several limitations. It only evaluates the generated images without comparing them to real images. Additionally, its reliance on the Inception v3 model means that the score can be biased toward the dataset on which the Inception model was trained. Finally, the IS assumes that the classifier's predictions are highly confident, which may not always be accurate.

Fréchet Inception Distance (FID)

The Fréchet Inception Distance (FID) offers several advantages over the IS by incorporating a direct comparison between the distributions of real and generated images. The FID calculates the Wasserstein-2 distance (also known as the Fréchet distance) between the multivariate Gaussian distributions fitted to the feature representations of the real and generated images. These feature representations are obtained from an intermediate layer of the Inception v3 network.

The FID captures both the mean and covariance of the features, providing a more comprehensive assessment of the similarity between real and generated images. A lower FID indicates a smaller distance between the distributions, implying that the generated images are closer to the real images in terms of visual quality and diversity.

One of the main advantages of the FID is its consistency with human judgment. Studies have shown that the FID metric correlates well with human evaluations of image quality, making it a reliable metric for assessing generative models. Moreover, the FID can detect intra-class mode collapse, a common issue in GANs where the model generates limited variations of certain classes while ignoring others.

However, the FID also has some drawbacks. It requires a large number of samples to produce reliable estimates, typically around 50,000 images. Smaller sample sizes can lead to an overestimation of the FID score. Additionally, the assumption that the feature representations follow a Gaussian distribution may not hold in practice, potentially limiting the accuracy of the FID.

Perceptual Path Length (PPL)

Perceptual Path Length (PPL) is another important metric used to evaluate generative models, particularly in terms of the smoothness of the latent space. The latent space is the mathematical space in which the generative model operates to produce new samples. PPL assesses how smoothly the transitions occur within this space, which is crucial for understanding the robustness and generalizability of the model.

A low PPL indicates that small changes in the latent space result in correspondingly small and smooth changes in the generated images. This suggests that the model has learned a well-behaved and coherent representation of the data. On the other hand, a high PPL signifies abrupt changes, which can indicate issues such as poor generalization or mode collapse.

To calculate PPL, pairs of points are sampled in the latent space, and the perceptual distance between the corresponding generated images is measured. The average perceptual distance is then normalized by the Euclidean distance between the latent points. This normalization accounts for the scale of the latent space, ensuring that the PPL metric is invariant to the specific parameterization of the generative model.

Example of Metric Application: Inception Score (IS)

In utilizing the Inception Score for evaluating generative models, it's important to apply the metric appropriately to gain meaningful insights. Here's a guideline for employing the IS effectively:

1. **Sample Generation**: Collect a large and diverse set of samples from the generative model. Ensure the sample size is sufficient to capture the variability in the generated data.

1. **Model Selection**: Use a pre-trained Inception v3 model, which is commonly accepted for calculating the IS. Ensure that the model is correctly implemented and tested for consistency.

1. **Probability Distribution Calculation**: Pass each generated image through the Inception v3 model to obtain the conditional probability distribution over classes. Ensure that the model is calibrated correctly to provide reliable probabilities.

1. **KL Divergence Computation**: Compare the conditional probability distribution with the marginal probability distribution using KL divergence. Calculate the IS by averaging these values over all samples.

1. **Result Interpretation**: Analyze the IS considering both diversity and fidelity. A high IS indicates good performance, but it's important to recognize the limitations and potential biases involved.

By following this guideline, researchers and practitioners can leverage the IS effectively to evaluate and improve their generative models.

Case Studies on Quantitative Metrics

In this section, we will delve into the application of quantitative metrics used in evaluating generative AI models through various case studies. By examining specific instances involving Generative Adversarial Networks (GANs) and Variational Autoencoders (VAEs), we aim to provide an in-depth understanding of how these metrics function in real-world scenarios.

First, let's explore a case study involving a comparison of several GAN models evaluated using Inception Score (IS) and Fréchet Inception Distance (FID) metrics. These two metrics are widely recognized for their effectiveness in assessing the quality of generated images. The IS metric measures the diversity and quality of the generated images by evaluating the classification accuracy of a pre-trained Inception network on the generated samples. A higher Inception Score indicates that the generated images are both diverse and high-quality. Conversely, FID evaluates the similarity between the distribution of real and generated images by calculating the Fréchet distance between feature vectors extracted from a pre-trained Inception network. Lower FID values indicate greater similarity and higher quality of the generated images (Parakatta, 2023).

To illustrate, consider a comparative analysis conducted on multiple GAN architectures, including DCGAN, WGAN, and StyleGAN, trained on the CIFAR-10 dataset. The study found that while DCGAN achieved a decent Inception Score, it lagged behind in terms of FID. On the other hand, StyleGAN not only had a high IS but also significantly lower FID scores, indicating superior performance in generating realistic images. This instance underscores the importance of using both IS and FID together to gain a comprehensive assessment of a model's output. While IS focuses on diversity and recognizability, FID provides insight into the actual visual fidelity of the images.

Next, we move to the analysis of VAE models using the Perceptual Path Length (PPL) metric. PPL is particularly useful in assessing the smoothness of the latent space of generative models, which is crucial for tasks that require interpolation or traversal within the latent space. To put it simply, PPL measures how smoothly changes in the latent space result in changes in the generated output. Lower PPL values indicate smoother transitions and higher consistency in the generated images.

An example of this can be seen in a study examining VAEs trained on the FashionMNIST dataset. Researchers assessed the effectiveness of these models by calculating their PPL. They discovered that models with lower PPL produced images with more consistent features and less noticeable artifacts during interpolation. This finding highlights the utility of PPL in identifying models that generate visually coherent outputs, especially when transitioning between different points in the latent space.

Additionally, we can look at a real-world example where IS and FID metrics were employed to benchmark improvements in image generation techniques. In a research project aimed at enhancing the resolution and quality of synthetic images for medical imaging applications, researchers developed an upgraded GAN variant designed to produce high-resolution images from low-resolution inputs. Using IS and FID metrics, they quantified the improvements achieved by their new model compared to traditional GAN architectures.

The results showed that their advanced model outperformed baseline GANs with a higher Inception Score and significantly lower FID scores. This real-world application demonstrates how quantitative metrics like IS and FID can effectively measure advancements and validate improvements in generative modeling techniques, providing clear evidence of progress in developing higher-quality generative models.

Finally, we reflect on the lessons learned from these evaluations, emphasizing the strengths and limitations of each metric. One key strength of the Inception Score is its ability to provide a straightforward measure of image quality and diversity. However, it has limitations, such as its reliance on the classifier's pre-trained data, which might not generalize well to all types of images.

Conversely, FID addresses some of these limitations by comparing the statistical properties of real and generated images, offering a more nuanced evaluation. Yet, it too has drawbacks, including its sensitivity to the pre-trained Inception network it uses for feature extraction, potentially leading to biases if applied across vastly different datasets or domains.

PPL, while invaluable for assessing the interpolation capabilities and latent space smoothness of models, does not provide a direct measure of image quality or diversity. It serves a specialized role, making it most beneficial when used in conjunction with other metrics to offer a rounded evaluation of generative models.

In conclusion, the case studies discussed underscore the multifaceted nature of evaluating generative AI models. By applying metrics like IS, FID, and PPL in real-world scenarios, we can obtain a holistic view of a model's strengths and weaknesses. These evaluations not only help in benchmarking and comparing different models but also drive improvements in generative technology, paving the way for more sophisticated and reliable AI-generated content. Understanding these metrics' application and limitations is crucial for aspiring practitioners and professionals seeking to master generative AI.

Qualitative Assessment

Discussing the need and methods for qualitative evaluation of generative AI models highlights how human judgment and various qualitative techniques play an essential role in assessing these models. Quantitative metrics might provide numerical insights, but understanding the nuanced quality and applicability of generated content often requires a human touch.

Human judgment is indispensable in evaluating the creativity and relevance of content produced by generative AI models. Unlike traditional algorithms that operate based on predefined rules, generative AI models create outputs that can vary significantly in style, context, and cultural relevance. This variability means automated metrics alone cannot capture the full spectrum of performance. Human evaluators bring their subjective experience and insight into the review process, enabling them to assess aspects like originality, humor, emotional resonance, and contextual appropriateness which are difficult to quantify.

One primary method of qualitative assessment is visual inspection. This involves experts manually reviewing generated samples to identify visual quality and coherence. For instance, when evaluating AI-generated artwork or images, visual inspection helps detect artifacts, inconsistencies, and overall aesthetic appeal. Experts can pinpoint flaws such as unnatural textures, disproportionate features, or elements that clash visually. They can also appreciate creative choices that enhance the piece's uniqueness. The process demands a keen eye for detail and an understanding of artistic principles, ensuring that only high-quality outputs pass the scrutiny.

Moreover, user studies are instrumental in collecting feedback from a broader audience to evaluate user satisfaction and practical impact. These studies can take multiple forms, ranging from surveys and questionnaires to more immersive experiences where participants interact with the generative AI outputs. For example, in evaluating a text generation model, users might rate the fluency, coherence, and engagement level of AI-produced stories or articles. Broader user participation provides diverse perspectives, capturing various demographics' tastes, preferences, and sensitivities. Consequently, developers better understand how different groups perceive and engage with the content, informing improvements and tailoring models to meet real-world expectations.

The Turing Test is another significant method employed to gauge the indistinguishability between human-created and AI-generated content. Named after Alan Turing, this test assesses whether a human evaluator can differentiate between responses generated by a human and those created by an AI system. Passing the Turing Test implies a high level of naturalness and realism in AI outputs, marking a significant milestone in AI development. While the test was initially designed for conversational agents, its principles apply broadly across various generative tasks, including text, music, and even visual art. Achieving success in the Turing Test demonstrates a generative AI model's capability to produce content that seamlessly integrates into human-centric contexts without betraying its artificial origins.

However, qualitative evaluation methods also face challenges. The subjective nature of human judgment can introduce biases, leading to inconsistent assessments. Individual preferences, cultural backgrounds, and personal experiences significantly influence qualitative evaluations. To mitigate these biases, a diverse panel of evaluators is recommended. This diversity ensures a more balanced perspective, reducing the impact of any single evaluator's biases. Moreover, structured evaluation frameworks and guidelines can standardize the review process, enhancing consistency and reliability.

Including both expert reviews and widespread user studies provides a well-rounded evaluation. Experts offer deep, specialized knowledge crucial for identifying subtle details that general users may overlook. Their insights guide the initial stages of model development and refinement. On the other hand, user studies reveal the broader societal impact and acceptance of AI-generated content. Combining these approaches allows developers to address both technical excellence and user-centric design, fostering the creation of more robust and appealing generative models.

Furthermore, integrating quantitative metrics with qualitative methods creates a comprehensive evaluation framework. For example, while statistical measures can indicate the overall performance trends, qualitative assessments delve into specific strengths and weaknesses. This dual approach ensures models undergo rigorous scrutiny from multiple angles, enhancing their robustness and suitability for deployment in varied applications.

Benchmarking Generative Models

Standardizing model evaluation is crucial in ensuring fair comparisons across different approaches and datasets in generative AI. As the field continues to evolve, a multitude of models with diverse architectures and training methodologies emerge, making it imperative to have a standardized framework for evaluation. This standardization allows for consistent measurement of performance, fostering an environment where improvements can be accurately tracked and understood.

Popular benchmarks serve as reference points in this landscape. For instance, CIFAR-10 is frequently used for image synthesis tasks due to its well-defined structure and wide acceptance in the academic community. Similarly, CelebA has gained prominence for face generation models, providing a large dataset of celebrity faces that enables robust testing and comparison. LSUN (Large-scale Scene Understanding) serves as another critical benchmark for scene generation tasks, offering extensive labeled data for training and evaluation.

Tasks utilized for benchmarking span various domains, reflecting the versatility and broad applicability of generative models. Image synthesis remains a cornerstone, where models are evaluated based on their ability to produce realistic images that are indistinguishable from real photographs. Text generation is another vital domain, with benchmarks designed to assess how well models can produce coherent and contextually appropriate sentences and paragraphs. Video creation represents a more complex challenge, requiring models to understand and generate temporal sequences that maintain consistency and continuity over time.

Despite these structured benchmarks, challenges persist in ensuring fair comparisons. One significant issue is the inherent variability in generative tasks and datasets. Different datasets come with varying levels of difficulty, and models may perform well on one but poorly on another due to differences in data distribution, complexity, and annotation quality. This variability complicates the task of drawing definitive conclusions about a model's overall effectiveness.

Moreover, the diversity in evaluation metrics further adds to the challenge. Quantitative metrics like Inception Score (IS) and Fréchet Inception Distance (FID) are commonly used, yet they each have limitations and may not fully capture the nuanced performance of generative models. Additionally, qualitative assessments involving human judgment introduce subjectivity, making it harder to achieve a standardized comparison.

Ensuring fair comparisons also involves addressing potential biases in the evaluation process. For example, choosing models trained under different conditions or using distinct hyperparameters can skew results. It becomes vital to ensure that experiments are conducted under comparable circumstances, adjusting for variables that could introduce unfair advantages or disadvantages.

The role of public repositories and shared datasets cannot be overstated in this context. By providing access to standardized datasets and benchmark results, these repositories enable researchers to validate their findings against established baselines. This transparency helps in building trust within the community, validating claims of superiority or innovation made by new models.

One notable initiative in this regard is ArtBench-10, introduced to benchmark artwork generation models. ArtBench-10 offers a class-balanced, high-quality dataset that addresses some common pitfalls observed in previous datasets, such as imbalanced class distributions and low-quality annotations. This dataset facilitates extensive benchmarking experiments, allowing for rigorous testing of representative image synthesis models. The standardization applied in creating ArtBench-10 exemplifies best practices that can be replicated in other domains to ensure comprehensive and fair evaluations (Keutzer et al., 2022).

Additionally, maintaining up-to-date benchmarks is essential due to the rapid advancements in generative AI. New techniques and models continuously push the boundaries, necessitating regular updates to benchmarks to reflect the current state-of-the-art. This dynamic aspect of benchmarking ensures that evaluation frameworks remain relevant and capable of capturing the true capabilities of contemporary models.

Another layer of complexity arises from the interdisciplinary applications of generative AI. Models are now being applied to fields ranging from healthcare to entertainment, each with unique requirements and challenges. Benchmarking in these varied domains requires tailored approaches to evaluation, considering industry-specific metrics and standards. For example, generative models in healthcare may need to adhere to stringent accuracy and reliability criteria due to the critical nature of the applications.

Furthermore, developing comprehensive user studies is paramount to understanding the practical impact of generative models. These studies provide valuable insights into user satisfaction, usability, and the perceived value of generated content. By gathering feedback from diverse user groups, researchers can identify strengths and weaknesses that may not be evident through quantitative metrics alone. This holistic approach to evaluation contributes to the design of more effective and user-friendly generative models (Arxiv-Sanity, n.d.).

Case Studies on Benchmarking

The chapter on "Evaluation Metrics and Benchmarking in Generative AI" can greatly benefit from real-world examples that illustrate the benchmarking of generative models in both research and industry settings. This subpoint aims to provide such examples and showcase the practical application of benchmarking techniques.

One prominent case study involves comparing various GAN architectures using the CIFAR-10 dataset. GANs, or Generative Adversarial Networks, have revolutionized image generation by pitting a generator against a discriminator in a minimax game. In this case study, researchers benchmarked different GAN variants—such as DCGAN, WGAN, and StyleGAN—by evaluating their performance on the CIFAR-10 dataset, which consists of 60,000 32x32 color images in 10 classes. The main metrics used for evaluation included the Inception Score (IS) and Fréchet Inception Distance (FID), which measure the quality and diversity of generated images, respectively. This comparative analysis revealed that while all three GAN variants produced high-quality images, StyleGAN particularly excelled in generating more realistic and diverse samples, reflecting significant advancements in the underlying architecture (brylevkirill, 2024).

Another example of benchmarking can be found in text generation models evaluated using the GLUE benchmark, which stands for General Language Understanding Evaluation. GLUE is a collection of various natural language understanding tasks designed to assess the generality and robustness of NLP models. In this context, models like GPT-3 and BERT were subjected to rigorous testing across multiple datasets within GLUE, including tasks such as sentiment analysis, linguistic acceptability, and textual entailment. By standardizing the evaluation process, GLUE enables researchers to compare different models effectively and provides insights into their strengths and weaknesses. For instance, GPT-3 demonstrated superior performance in narrative comprehension tasks, while BERT showed strong results in sentence-level predictions, underlining how benchmarking helps identify specific capabilities of each model (<i>Generative Adversarial Networks</i>, 2022).

In the realm of facial image generation, Variational Autoencoders (VAEs) have been extensively studied using the CelebA dataset, which comprises over 200,000 celebrity images annotated with 40 attribute labels. Researchers benchmarked multiple VAE models, including Vanilla VAE, β-VAE, and Conditional VAE, to assess their performance in generating high-quality facial images. Key metrics such as reconstruction error and latent space representation were used to evaluate these models. The findings indicated that Conditional VAE outperformed others in generating images with more accurate attribute control, providing valuable insights into how altering the architecture and training paradigms can impact model performance.

In an industry setting, video synthesis models are often benchmarked on custom datasets to enhance content creation processes. For instance, companies specializing in entertainment and media production utilize these benchmarks to improve automated video editing and generation tools. A notable use case involved benchmarking models like MoCoGAN and TGAN on custom video datasets tailored to specific genres, such as action sequences or animated clips. These benchmarks consider metrics like frame consistency, visual coherence, and temporal resolution. Through iterative benchmarking, developers were able to refine their models, leading to significant improvements in generating seamless and visually appealing video content. This practical application showcases how industry-specific benchmarks can drive innovation and optimize generative models for real-world applications.

By examining these examples, it becomes clear that benchmarking is an essential practice in advancing generative AI. In research, benchmarks like CIFAR-10 and CelebA help standardize evaluations, making it easier to compare and contrast different models. In industry, bespoke benchmarks tailored to specific needs accelerate the development of technology tailored to particular use cases, such as video synthesis.

Summary and Reflections

The chapter has provided an in-depth look at the various evaluation metrics used in generative AI, both quantitative and qualitative. It detailed how Inception Score (IS), Fréchet Inception Distance (FID), and Perceptual Path Length (PPL) are employed to measure the performance of models, highlighting each metric's strengths and limitations. Additionally, the importance of human judgment in qualitative assessments was discussed, emphasizing the role of visual inspections and user studies in capturing elements that automated metrics might miss.

Through case studies and examples, the chapter illustrated real-world applications of these metrics and their significance in benchmarking generative models. The need for standardized benchmarks was also underscored, highlighting their role in enabling fair comparisons across different models and datasets. By integrating both quantitative and qualitative methods, we can achieve a comprehensive evaluation framework, essential for advancing and refining generative AI technologies.

Reference List

Borji, A. (2022, January). *Pros and cons of GAN evaluation measures: New developments.* Computer Vision and Image Understanding. https://doi.org/10.1016/j.cviu.2021.103329

Carrasco, S. (2022, April 7). *On the evaluation of Generative Adversarial Networks.* Medium. https://towardsdatascience.com/on-the-evaluation-of-generative-adversarial-networks-b056ddcdfd3a

Generative adversarial networks. (2022, February 12). SlideShare. https://www.slideshare.net/slideshow/generative-adversarial-networks-251160988/251160988

Gupta, P., Ding, B., Guan, C., & Ding, D. (2024, February 15). *Generative AI: A systematic review using topic modelling techniques.* Data and Information Management. https://doi.org/10.1016/j.dim.2024.100066

Liao, P., Li, X., Liu, X., & Keutzer, K. (2022). *The ArtBench dataset: Benchmarking generative models with artworks.* Retrieved from https://www.researchgate.net/publication/361502844 The ArtBench Dataset Bench marking Generative Models with Artworks

Navar, C., Lucila, A., & Javier, L. (2023, September 24). *Exploration of Metrics and Datasets to Assess the Fidelity of Images Generated by Generative Adversarial Networks.* Applied Sciences; Multidisciplinary Digital Publishing Institute. https://doi.org/10.3390/app131910637

Parakatta, A. (2023, June 15). *VAE v/s GAN — A case study.* Medium. https://medium.com/@parakatta/vae-v-s-gan-a-case-study-b09c7169ac02

arxiv-sanity. (n.d.). Www.arxiv-Sanity-Lite.com. Retrieved July 30, 2024, from https://www.arxiv-sanity-lite.com/?rank=pid&pid=2407.12069

arxiv-sanity. (n.d.). Arxiv-Sanity-Lite.com. Retrieved July 30, 2024, from https://arxiv-sanity-lite.com/?rank=pid&pid=2311.02049

brylevkirill. (2024). *notes/Deep Learning.md at master · brylevkirill/notes*. GitHub. https://github.com/brylevkirill/notes/blob/master/Deep%20Learning.md

CHAPTER 19

Advanced Topics in Generative AI

Exploring advanced techniques in Generative AI reveals a frontier of innovation that pushes the boundaries of what artificial intelligence can achieve. Diving into this realm involves understanding complex algorithms and methodologies that enable machines to create, enhance, and optimize new content with unprecedented capability. These generative models are not just limited to producing realistic images or coherent text but extend their functionality across various domains, including healthcare, finance, entertainment, and more. The sophistication of these models lies in their ability to learn from minimal data and adapt to new tasks, demonstrating a level of versatility and efficiency that is crucial for modern AI applications.

This chapter delves into the intricate world of Generative AI by examining advanced topics such as reinforcement learning and its integration with generative models. First, the concept of reinforcement learning will be explored, elucidating how agents interact with environments to maximize cumulative rewards. Next, the chapter will cover how combining reinforcement learning with generative models can lead to significant performance enhancements. Practical applications, ranging from drug discovery to personalized content generation, will illustrate the transformative impact of these techniques. Furthermore, strategies for effective implementation and optimization of these integrated systems will be discussed. By the end of this chapter, readers will gain a comprehensive understanding of the advanced methods driving Generative AI forward and their real-world implications.

Introduction to Reinforcement Learning for Gen AI

Understanding Reinforcement Learning (RL) and its Role in Generative Models

Reinforcement Learning (RL) is a type of machine learning concerned with how agents ought to take actions in an environment to maximize cumulative reward. Unlike supervised learning, where the model learns from labeled data, RL involves learning from the consequences of actions, similar to how humans learn by interacting with their surroundings.

At its core, RL consists of several key elements:

- The agent: This is the learner or decision-maker.

- The environment: Everything the agent interacts with.

- Actions: All possible moves the agent can make.

- States: Situations returned by the environment on taking actions.

- Rewards: Feedback from the environment based on the agent's actions.

The agent aims to optimize its policy, which is a strategy that defines the action the agent should take in any given state to maximize cumulative rewards over time.

Reinforcement Learning has several real-world applications across diverse fields. In robotics, RL helps robots learn tasks through trial and error, such as grasping objects or navigating spaces. In gaming, RL has been used to create intelligent agents capable of playing and mastering complex games, exemplified by AlphaGo, which defeated human champions in the game of Go. In finance, RL assists in developing trading strategies that adapt to changing market conditions.

Combining RL with generative models enhances their performance significantly. Generative models like GANs (Generative Adversarial Networks) and VAEs (Variational Autoencoders) generate new data samples that mimic a given distribution. When integrated with RL, these models can be fine-tuned to produce more optimal outcomes based on specific objectives.

One common approach is to use RL to guide generative models in creating content that meets particular criteria. For example, in drug discovery, generative models can propose novel molecules, while RL optimizes these proposals for desirable properties, such as high binding affinity to a target protein. This combination allows scientists to navigate vast molecular spaces efficiently and discover promising drug candidates.

Key case studies highlight the benefits of integrating RL with generative models. One notable example is in the field of drug discovery, where traditional methods can be time-consuming and costly. Researchers have combined RL with generative models to optimize molecules for specific properties, addressing challenges like reward sparsity, where only a fraction of generated molecules possess the desired traits.

In a study by Korshunova et al. (2022), the team utilized RL to shift the distribution of predicted active class probability for generated molecules. By treating the generative model as a policy network, they could predict the next action in designing molecules, optimizing for bioactivity. Their work demonstrated how RL could effectively handle the sparse rewards problem in molecular design, significantly accelerating the drug discovery process.

Another compelling case is in the domain of personalized content generation. Companies are leveraging RL-enhanced generative models to tailor recommendations and generate content that aligns closely with user preferences. Netflix, for example, employs such systems to personalize movie recommendations, enhancing user satisfaction and engagement.

Integrating RL with generative models also shows promise in creative fields such as art and music. Artists and musicians can use these enhanced models to explore novel styles and compositions, pushing the boundaries of creativity. The application of RL ensures that generated outputs are continuously refined based on feedback, leading to increasingly sophisticated and innovative creations.

Moreover, in autonomous vehicles, RL-driven generative models play a crucial role in scenario simulation. These models can generate a myriad of driving scenarios, while RL optimizes the vehicle's responses to ensure safety and efficiency. This synergy is pivotal in training autonomous systems to handle real-world complexities better.

Transfer Learning in Generative Models

Transfer learning plays a pivotal role in advancing generative AI, offering an efficient way to develop models with limited data and resources. This technique allows existing models trained on large datasets to be adapted for new, often related tasks, thus leveraging prior knowledge and minimizing the need for extensive retraining.

What is Transfer Learning and Why it Matters

Transfer learning involves taking a pre-trained model and applying it to a new but similar problem. This approach is significant because it mitigates one of the primary challenges in AI: the scarcity of labeled data. By reusing models trained on vast datasets, transfer learning accelerates development timelines, reduces computational costs, and improves performance, especially in contexts where collecting labeled data is challenging. For example, if a model has been trained to recognize general objects in images, its learned features can be adapted to identify specific items like medical instruments or retail products (Sharma, 2021).

Techniques for Implementing Transfer Learning in Gen AI

Implementing transfer learning in generative models involves several techniques. One common method is fine-tuning, which involves adjusting the weights of a pre-trained model to perform a new task effectively. This is typically done by training the final layers of the network on the new dataset while keeping the earlier layers fixed. Another approach is feature extraction, where the pre-trained model's layers serve as a fixed feature extractor, and only the newly added layers are trained on the new data. These techniques enable the reuse of previously learned representation patterns, expediting the training process and improving model accuracy (Team, 2023).

In generative AI, transfer learning can also be applied using domain adaptation and multitask learning. Domain adaptation adjusts a model trained on one domain to work well in another by minimizing the differences between the two domains. Multitask learning trains models on multiple tasks simultaneously, allowing the shared layers to learn generalized features beneficial across tasks.

Benefits and Challenges Associated with Transfer Learning

The benefits of transfer learning are manifold. First, it significantly reduces the time and computational power required to train models from scratch. Second, transfer learning enhances model performance, particularly when the target task has limited data. Third, it democratizes access to advanced AI technologies, enabling smaller organizations with fewer resources to build powerful models by leveraging existing ones.

However, transfer learning is not without challenges. One primary challenge is domain shift, where the source and target domains have substantial differences. If the pre-trained model's knowledge does not align well with the new task, the transferred model may underperform. Another challenge is overfitting, especially if the new dataset is small; the model may become too specialized to the noisy or limited data. To mitigate this, techniques like data augmentation and regularization are employed. Additionally, careful consideration is needed to choose the appropriate pre-trained model that closely matches the target task requirements.

Concrete Examples of Successful Applications

Transfer learning has seen successful applications across various domains in generative AI. In natural language processing, models like GPT-3 have been pre-trained on massive text corpora and fine-tuned for specific tasks such as summarization or translation. This approach allows for high-quality performance even in niche areas with less available data. In computer vision, pre-trained convolutional neural networks (CNNs) are commonly used for image generation tasks. For instance, a CNN trained on the ImageNet dataset can be repurposed to generate artistic styles or enhance low-resolution images (Sharma, 2021).

Another notable example is in the healthcare sector, where generative models pre-trained on general medical imaging databases are adapted for specific diagnostic purposes, such as detecting anomalies in MRI scans. This application not only improves diagnostic accuracy but also enables quicker deployment of AI solutions in clinical settings.

Explainability and Interpretability of Generative Models

Making Generative Models Explainable and Interpretable

In the rapidly evolving field of Artificial Intelligence (AI), generative models are gaining significant traction due to their ability to create new, original data. However, for these models to be effectively integrated and trusted across various sectors, their explainability and interpretability become critical. This subpoint delves into why transparency and accountability in AI models are essential and explores notable techniques like SHAP and LIME that contribute to making these models more understandable.

Need for Transparency and Accountability in AI Models

Transparency and accountability in AI models serve as cornerstones for building trust and ensuring ethical use. As generative AI techniques become more advanced, so does their complexity, which often leads to the "black box" problem where the decision-making process is opaque. Without sufficient transparency, stakeholders—including developers, users, and regulators—may find it challenging to trust or validate the model's outcomes.

For instance, in sensitive fields like healthcare and finance, lack of transparency can have severe consequences. If a generative model incorrectly generates medical diagnoses or financial predictions, the implications could be life-threatening or economically devastating. Thus, ensuring these systems are interpretable helps mitigate risks by making their operations transparent and allowing for better accountability.

Overview of SHAP and Its Use in AI

SHAP (**SH**apley **A**dditive ex**P**lanations) is a game-theoretic approach to explain the output of machine learning models. It provides a unified measure of feature importance that applies to any model. The core idea is derived from Shapley values, a concept in cooperative game theory that distributes payoffs fairly among players based on their contributions.

In an AI context, SHAP attributes the prediction of an instance among input features, shedding light on how each feature impacts the final output. For example, when predicting whether customers will buy vehicle insurance, SHAP can show how factors like age, previously insured status, and vehicle damage influence individual predictions (Nasirudeen, 2020).

This technique proves valuable in interpreting complex generative models. For instance, when a generative model creates text or images, SHAP values can help explain why particular elements were chosen, thus demystifying the generation process.

Overview of LIME and Its Use in AI

LIME (**L**ocal **I**nterpretable **M**odel-agnostic **E**xplanations) is another robust technique aimed at providing local explanations for individual predictions. Unlike SHAP, which offers global insights, LIME focuses on explaining specific instances, making it particularly useful for local interpretability.

The method works by perturbing the input data around the instance being explained, generating synthetic data points. A simpler, interpretable model is then trained on this perturbed dataset to approximate the behavior of the complex model near the specific instance. This allows us to understand what aspects of the input most influenced the prediction.

For example, LIME can be employed to explain why a generative model created a particular piece of text or imagery by highlighting the key features influencing the output (Nasirudeen, 2020). This localized understanding is invaluable in debugging and improving model performance.

Practical Cases With Explainability Techniques

Several real-world applications illustrate the effectiveness of explainability techniques like SHAP and LIME in making generative models more transparent.

One prominent case involves the use of SHAP in natural language processing (NLP). Here, SHAP values have been used to interpret predictions made by generative text models. By attributing importance to different words or phrases, SHAP helps researchers understand how linguistic features influence the generated content. This insight is crucial for refining model accuracy and ensuring the outputs align with user expectations and ethical standards.

Another practical application pertains to image generation in the art domain. Artists and designers often use generative models to create new visual pieces. By integrating LIME, developers can offer explanations about why certain visual elements were included, enhancing the artist's creative process and providing a deeper understanding of the underlying algorithms.

Explainability also plays a pivotal role in regulatory compliance. In the financial sector, generative models are increasingly used for algorithmic trading, risk assessment, and fraud detection. Techniques like SHAP and LIME facilitate the auditing process by providing clear explanations of model decisions, aiding in meeting stringent regulatory requirements.

Moreover, in recommendation systems used by e-commerce platforms like Amazon or Netflix, explainable AI can shed light on why particular products or content are suggested to users. This not only builds user trust but also enables developers to fine-tune the models for better personalization.

Techniques for Combining Reinforcement Learning with Generative Models

Integrating Reinforcement Learning (RL) with generative models is an advanced technique in Generative AI that holds tremendous potential. This section aims to provide a detailed exploration of methods to achieve this integration, outline the benefits and limitations, and present real-world applications showcasing its effectiveness.

Step-by-Step Guide on Combining RL with Generative Models

1. **Define Objectives and Setup**: Begin by clearly defining the objectives for integrating RL with generative models. These could range from optimizing content generation based on user feedback to enhancing decision-making processes within autonomous systems. Set up the environment in which both the generative model and RL agent will operate. This typically involves selecting

appropriate datasets, defining reward functions, and establishing policies for the RL agent.

1. **Choose the Right Generative Model**: Depending on the application, select a suitable generative model such as Variational Autoencoders (VAEs), Generative Adversarial Networks (GANs), or Transformer-based models like GPT-3. Ensure that the chosen model can effectively generate quality data that aligns with your project goals.

1. **Train the Generative Model**: Train your generative model using the selected dataset. This involves feeding the model large amounts of data so it learns to produce high-quality outputs. Use techniques such as backpropagation and gradient descent to minimize loss and improve accuracy.

1. **Integrate the RL Agent**: Introduce the RL agent to the trained generative model. The RL agent will interact with the generative model's output, taking actions based on predefined policies and receiving rewards based on performance metrics. For instance, if the goal is to create engaging content, the reward function might be based on user engagement metrics like click-through rates or time spent on content.

1. **Simulate and Optimize**: Run simulations where the RL agent takes actions, receives rewards, and updates its policy iteratively. Use these simulations to fine-tune both the generative model and the RL agent. Techniques like Q-learning, policy gradients, and Actor-Critic methods are commonly employed during this phase.

1. **Validate and Deploy**: Once optimized, validate the integrated system through extensive testing. Assess its performance using metrics relevant to your objectives. Upon satisfactory validation, deploy the system in a real-world environment, monitoring its performance and making adjustments as needed.

Benefits Derived from Integrating the Two Methodologies

The integration of RL and generative models offers numerous benefits:

- **Enhanced Creativity and Adaptability**: The combination allows for the generation of creative and novel content that can adapt in real-time based on user interactions and feedback. This dynamic adaptability leads to more personalized and engaging user experiences.

- **Improved Decision-Making**: By leveraging RL's ability to learn from trial and error, the generative model can make better decisions autonomously. This is particularly beneficial in fields like finance and healthcare, where decision-making is critical.

- **Efficiency in Training**: Integrating RL with generative models can reduce the amount of manual oversight required during training. The RL agent constantly optimizes the generative model, leading to quicker convergence and improved efficiency.

- **Scalability**: These integrated systems can easily be scaled to handle larger datasets and more complex tasks. This scalability makes them suitable for a wide range of applications, from personalized marketing to autonomous driving.

Potential Limitations and How to Address Them

Despite their advantages, integrating RL and generative models comes with certain limitations:

- **Complexity and Computational Cost**: The combined approach can be computationally intensive and complex to implement. Addressing this involves using efficient algorithms and leveraging cloud-based resources to manage computational demands cost-effectively.

- **Data Requirements**: Both RL and generative models require large amounts of high-quality data for effective training. Ensuring that your data is clean, well-structured, and relevant can mitigate this issue. Additionally, employing data augmentation techniques can help in generating more diverse datasets.

- **Stability Issues**: Integrating RL with generative models can sometimes lead to instability during training, especially if the reward function is not well-defined. To tackle this, carefully design reward functions and use techniques such as reward shaping to guide the learning process more effectively.

- **Ethical and Bias Concerns**: As with any AI system, there are ethical considerations and risks of inherent biases. Continuous monitoring and incorporating fairness algorithms can help address these concerns, ensuring that the system operates ethically and transparently.

Real-World Applications Showing the Effectiveness of This Integration

1. **Healthcare Diagnosis and Treatment Optimization**: In healthcare, combining RL with generative models can assist in generating patient-specific

treatment plans. For example, IBM's Watson leverages these technologies to analyze vast medical datasets and recommend personalized treatments, improving both the speed and accuracy of medical diagnosis and treatment.

1. **Personalized Marketing Strategies**: E-commerce giants like Amazon use generative models for creating dynamic product recommendations, enhanced by RL to optimize these recommendations based on user behavior. This leads to more personalized shopping experiences, increasing customer satisfaction and boosting sales.

1. **Autonomous Vehicles**: Self-driving cars benefit immensely from the integration of RL and generative models. Generative models simulate various driving scenarios, while RL agents learn optimal driving strategies through continuous interaction with these simulations. Companies like Waymo employ these integrated systems for safer and more efficient autonomous driving solutions.

1. **Content Creation in Social Media**: Platforms like Facebook and Instagram use this integration to generate and optimize content for users. Generative models create engaging posts, which RL agents then refine based on user engagement metrics. This results in more relevant and appealing content, significantly enhancing user interaction and satisfaction.

1. **Financial Trading Systems**: In the financial sector, RL combined with generative models can predict market trends and automate trading strategies. Firms like Goldman Sachs utilize these systems to analyze historical trading data, generate potential market scenarios, and optimize trading decisions, thereby maximizing profits and minimizing risks.

Successful Use Cases of Explainable and Transfer Learning in Generative AI

Exploring the advanced techniques of Generative AI, particularly explainable and transfer learning, reveals significant progress and application in real-world scenarios. The aim here is to elucidate successful implementations and illustrate their practical benefits through detailed case studies.

Firstly, let's delve into the importance of explainability in generative AI, particularly through a case study on lunar operations by NASA. Researchers at Mosaic developed Explainable AI (XAI) to aid in the autonomous navigation of lunar rovers. This technology uses imagery data to help rovers assess traversability, enhancing operations' autonomy while ensuring safety. Traditionally, interplanetary missions depend heavily on human teleoperation, but communication delays and resource limitations pose challenges. By integrating XAI, NASA could calibrate trust in automated systems, providing transparency in machine learning (ML) model outputs. Such explainability allows human operators to understand and trust the decision-making processes of these models, leading to safer and more effective autonomous operations (Gerosa, 2023).

In industry, transfer learning has shown remarkable success, particularly in natural language processing (NLP) applications. OpenAI's GPT-3 is a prime example. Transfer learning involves pre-training a model on large datasets and fine-tuning it for specific tasks. This approach significantly reduces the data required for training and speeds up development. Industries have leveraged this technique to create sophisticated AI models that can perform a range of tasks, from chatbots to content generation. Pre-trained models like GPT-3 are used as a foundation, with minor adjustments needed to tailor them to specific needs, demonstrating the efficiency and practicality of transfer learning.

A comparative analysis of pre- and post-transfer learning outcomes further underscores its advantages. Before transfer learning, developing high-performance models from scratch was time-consuming and resource-intensive. Models often required vast amounts of labeled data and extensive computational resources. Post-adoption, companies observed a drastic reduction in development time and costs. For instance, Google's BERT model revolutionized NLP by using transfer learning, enabling state-of-the-art results with relatively modest additional training. The success rates and accuracy of tasks such as text classification and sentiment analysis improved significantly, showcasing the transformative impact of this technique.

The lessons learned from these implementations are invaluable. Firstly, explainability fosters trust and acceptance among users. In critical applications like healthcare and aerospace, understanding AI decisions is paramount. For example, diagnostic tools powered by XAI provide clinicians with transparent insights into AI-generated suggestions, which enhances their confidence in integrating these tools into clinical practice. Secondly, transfer learning democratizes access to advanced AI capabilities. Smaller companies and startups can leverage pre-trained models to develop competitive AI solutions without needing enormous datasets or extensive computational power.

Moreover, adopting these techniques reveals broader insights into AI deployment strategies. Companies must prioritize model interpretability and user trust when implementing AI solutions. Integrating XAI methods like SHapley Additive exPlanations (SHAP) or Local Interpretable Model-Agnostic Explanations (LIME) helps clarify model predictions, aiding stakeholders in making informed decisions. These methods frame complex AI outputs in understandable terms, bridging the gap between technical intricacies and practical applications.

Transfer learning also emphasizes the reuse of knowledge across different domains, promoting efficient resource utilization. For instance, models trained on general language datasets can be fine-tuned for specialized areas such as legal document analysis or medical report summarization. This adaptability not only saves time and resources but also accelerates innovation across various fields. Companies should consider building modular and flexible AI architectures that support seamless integration of transfer learning techniques.

Furthermore, the journey from research to implementation highlights the significance of collaboration between academia and industry. Academic research provides the foundational theories and methodologies, while industry applications validate and refine these concepts through real-world challenges. This synergy ensures that cutting-edge advancements are practically viable and beneficial. Encouraging open-source contributions and shared benchmarks can foster a collaborative ecosystem where both researchers and practitioners contribute to the collective progress of AI technologies.

Another critical aspect is continuous monitoring and evaluation. Implementing explainable and transfer learning techniques is not a one-time task. Regular assessments ensure that models remain accurate, reliable, and aligned with evolving goals. For instance, periodic audits of AI systems in financial services can identify biases or inaccuracies early, preventing potential risks and maintaining trust. Establishing robust evaluation frameworks that incorporate both technical performance metrics and user feedback is essential for sustained success.

Implementing explainable and transfer learning techniques also necessitates a shift in organizational culture. Companies need to cultivate a mindset that values transparency, accountability, and ethical considerations in AI development. Training programs and workshops can educate teams about the importance of these aspects, fostering a culture of responsible AI usage. Additionally, involving diverse teams in the development process enhances the inclusivity and fairness of AI solutions, addressing potential biases from multiple perspectives.

As AI continues to evolve, the integration of explainable and transfer learning techniques will likely become even more widespread. Future advancements may include more sophisticated methods for quantifying uncertainty and improving model robustness. Organizations should stay abreast of these developments, adapting their strategies to leverage emerging opportunities.

Insights and Implications

The chapter's exploration into advanced techniques and applications in Generative AI has provided a comprehensive look at both Reinforcement Learning (RL) and Transfer Learning. By understanding how RL can guide generative models to create optimized content based on specific criteria, readers can appreciate its real-world benefits in fields like drug discovery, personalized content generation, and autonomous vehicles. Similarly, Transfer Learning offers an efficient way to develop high-performing generative models with limited data by leveraging pre-trained models, which significantly reduces training time and computational costs.

Integrating these techniques into generative AI not only enhances model performance but also addresses practical challenges such as data scarcity and computational demands. The use of explainability tools like SHAP and LIME further ensures transparency and trustworthiness in these models, making them more acceptable and reliable for critical applications. Through successful case studies and practical examples, the chapter underscores the transformative potential of combining RL and Transfer Learning in advancing generative AI capabilities, paving the way for innovative solutions across various industries.

Reference List

Bhutanadhu, K. (2023, October 20). *Integrating Generative AI and Reinforcement Learning for Self-Improvement.* Analytics Vidhya. https://www.analyticsvidhya.com/blog/2023/10/generative-ai-and-reinforcement-learning/

Gerosa, S. (2023, July 27). *Explanations in Lunar Surface Exploration for ML Models.* Mosaic Data Science. https://mosaicdatascience.com/2023/07/27/explainable-ai-for-lunar-operations/

Korshunova, M., Huang, N., Capuzzi, S., Radchenko, D. S., Savych, O., Moroz, Y. S., Wells, C. I., Willson, T. M., Tropsha, A., & Isayev, O. (2022, October 18). *Generative and reinforcement learning approaches for the automated de novo design of bioactive compounds.* Communications Chemistry. https://doi.org/10.1038/s42004-022-00733-0

Nasirudeen, R. (2020, October 24). *Unveiling the Black Box model using Explainable AI(Lime, Shap) Industry use case.* Analytics Vidhya. https://www.analyticsvidhya.com/blog/2020/10/unveiling-the-black-box-model-using-explainable-ai-lime-shap-industry-use-case/

Sharma, P. (2021, October 30). *Transfer Learning | Understanding Transfer Learning for Deep Learning.* Analytics Vidhya. https://www.analyticsvidhya.com/blog/2021/10/understanding-transfer-learning-for-deep-learning/

Smith, A. (2023, December 19). *2024's Comprehensive Guide to Generative AI: Techniques, Tools & Trends.* HatchWorks. https://hatchworks.com/blog/software-development/generative-ai/

Team, T. Q. (2023, June 30). *What Is Transfer Learning? - The Role of Transfer Learning in Building Powerful Generative AI Models.* Quiq. https://quiq.com/blog/what-is-transfer-learning/

What is Explainable AI? - Part II. (2023, November 1). RAD. https://www.rad.com/blog/what-explainable-ai-part-ii

Zhang, Y., Weng, Y., Lund, J., Faust, O., Su, L., & Acharya, R. (2022). *Citation.* Applications of Explainable Artificial Intelligence in Diagnosis and Surgery. https://doi.org/10.3390/diagnostics12020237

CONCLUSION

Generative AI stands as a transformative force, undoubtedly reshaping the landscape of technology and beyond. The significance of generative AI lies in its capacity to create new data from existing patterns, an ability that sets it apart from other forms of artificial intelligence. This capability has bridged the gap between human-like creativity and machine efficiency, making it an invaluable tool across various sectors. From crafting realistic images to composing symphonies, generative AI has showcased its versatility and importance in today's digital era.

Historically, the journey of generative AI has been marked by significant milestones. Beginning with simple algorithms, it has evolved through advancements like neural networks and deep learning. Key breakthroughs, such as the development of Generative Adversarial Networks (GANs) and transformers, have propelled this field forward, enabling machines to generate high-quality content that was previously unimaginable. This progress underscores not only the rapid evolution of technology but also the increasing potential for AI to integrate seamlessly into our daily lives.

Unlike traditional AI, which primarily focuses on analysis and prediction, generative AI is characterized by its ability to produce novel outputs. This distinction is crucial as it opens doors to applications that require a blend of creativity and computational power. While predictive models can foresee trends and outcomes, generative AI can design, innovate, and bring abstract ideas to life, thus offering a fresh perspective and expanding the horizons of what technology can achieve.

The applications of generative AI are vast and varied, touching upon numerous fields. In the realm of art and design, it has enabled artists to experiment with new styles and techniques, creating pieces that push the boundaries of creativity. The entertainment industry benefits from AI-generated music, movies, and video game content that enhances user experiences. In healthcare, generative AI aids in drug discovery and personalized medicine, paving the way for more effective treatments. Marketing professionals leverage AI to create personalized advertisements that resonate more deeply with audiences. Educators use AI-driven tools to develop customized learning materials, while scientific researchers employ it to simulate complex phenomena and generate hypotheses. These diverse applications highlight just how integral generative AI has become across multiple domains.

The impact of generative AI on innovation and creativity cannot be overstated. By automating mundane tasks and providing new ways to approach problems, it frees up human intellect to focus on higher-order creative processes. This automation boosts efficiency, allowing for quicker iteration and development cycles in various creative fields. For instance, designers can use generative AI to rapidly prototype multiple versions of a product, while artists can explore unconventional methods without the constraints of traditional tools. This synergy between human ingenuity and machine capability is driving a new wave of innovation that transcends conventional limits.

Despite its myriad benefits, generative AI also presents ethical and social challenges that must be addressed. The creation of convincing fake media, such as deepfakes, raises concerns about misinformation and privacy breaches. It's imperative to develop robust frameworks that mitigate these risks while promoting responsible use of generative AI technologies. Ongoing research is essential to establish guidelines and best practices, ensuring that AI advancements do not compromise ethical standards or societal values.

Looking ahead, the future of generative AI appears promising yet complex. Emerging trends suggest continued improvements in model accuracy and efficiency, enabling even more sophisticated and realistic outputs. However, these advancements come with potential challenges, including the need for greater computational resources and the risk of widening the digital divide. Addressing these issues will require collaborative efforts from technologists, policymakers, and society at large to harness the full potential of generative AI while mitigating its downsides.

As we conclude our exploration of generative AI, it's important to stay informed about ongoing developments in this rapidly evolving field. The pace of innovation in AI is accelerating, and keeping abreast of new trends and technologies will be crucial for anyone looking to make a meaningful impact in their respective domains. Whether you are a student, a professional seeking to upskill, or a tech enthusiast, continuous learning and adaptation will be key to navigating the changes brought about by generative AI.

Furthermore, we encourage you to take the insights gained from this book and apply them in your endeavors. The tools and knowledge presented here are not just theoretical constructs but practical instruments for innovation. Experiment with generative AI in your projects, explore its capabilities, and push the boundaries of what is possible. By doing so, you not only contribute to the growing body of knowledge in this field but also position yourself at the forefront of technological advancement.

In conclusion, generative AI represents a significant leap forward in artificial intelligence, offering unprecedented opportunities for creativity, efficiency, and innovation. Its unique ability to generate new data and solutions positions it as a critical asset in various industries. However, with great power comes great responsibility. Ethical considerations and the need for ongoing research are paramount to ensure that generative AI is used responsibly and for the greater good. As we look to the future, embracing the potential of generative AI while remaining vigilant about its challenges will be essential. Let us embark on this exciting journey, armed with knowledge and driven by curiosity, to explore the limitless possibilities that generative AI holds.

BONUS

Dear Reader,

We are excited to offer you an exclusive BONUS to enrich your journey with *Generative AI for Beginners*! To support your understanding of this fascinating field, we have prepared a special set of resources designed to enhance your learning experience.

As part of this BONUS, you will receive:

- **350+ Prompts for ChatGPT**: A comprehensive collection of prompts to help you experiment and practice with generative AI models, making your learning more interactive and insightful.
- **5 Exams on Easy Chapters**: Test your understanding of the fundamental concepts with five exams focusing on the easier chapters of the book. These exams are designed to reinforce your knowledge and ensure you have a solid grasp of the basics.
- **2 Exams on Hard Chapters**: Challenge yourself with two exams covering the more advanced chapters. These are meant to push your understanding further and test your grasp of more complex topics.

To access these BONUS resources, simply click on the provided link or scan the QR code displayed on this page. These additional materials are crafted to complement your learning and provide you with valuable tools to master generative AI.

We invite you to download these resources and use them alongside the chapters to deepen your knowledge and skills. Thank you for choosing *Generative AI for Beginners*, and we hope these extras help you on your journey to becoming proficient in generative AI.

Download your BONUS resources now!

https://drive.google.com/drive/folders/1vtLX_ozNBogKaVwd2RgwV8_gn28vOqSo?usp=sharing

Printed in Great Britain
by Amazon